The *Pokémon Go*
Phenomenon

Studies in Gaming

The *Pokémon Go* Phenomenon

Essays on Public Play in Contested Spaces

Edited *by* Jamie Henthorn, Andrew Kulak,
Kristopher Purzycki *and* Stephanie Vie

STUDIES IN GAMING,
Series Editor Matthew Wilhelm Kapell

McFarland & Company, Inc., Publishers
Jefferson, North Carolina

LIBRARY OF CONGRESS CATALOGUING-IN-PUBLICATION DATA

Names: Henthorn, Jamie, 1983– editor. | Kulak, Andrew, editor. |
  Purzycki, Kristopher, 1973– editor. | Vie, Stephanie, editor.
Title: The Pokemon Go phenomenon : essays on public play in
  contested spaces / edited by Jamie Henthorn, Andrew Kulak,
  Kristopher Purzycki and Stephanie Vie.
Description: Jefferson, North Carolina : McFarland & Company, Inc.,
  2019 | Series: Studies in gaming | Includes bibliographical refer-
  ences and index.
Identifiers: LCCN 2019012610 | ISBN 9781476674131 (paperback. :
  acid free paper) ∞
Subjects: LCSH: Pokemon Go (Game)—Social aspects. | Pokemon Go
  (Game)—Psychological aspects.
Classification: LCC GV1469.35.P634 A84 2019 | DDC 794.8—dc23
LC record available at https://lccn.loc.gov/2019012610

ISBN (print) 978-1-4766-7413-1
ISBN (ebook) 978-1-4766-3651-1

BRITISH LIBRARY CATALOGUING DATA ARE AVAILABLE

Front cover images © 2019 Shutterstock

Printed in the United States of America

McFarland & Company, Inc., Publishers
  Box 611, Jefferson, North Carolina 28640
    www.mcfarlandpub.com

Table of Contents

Part Three. The Impact of Play

Acknowledgments

General thanks:

The audacity to pursue *The* Pokémon Go *Phenomenon* came about through the Computers & Writing Conference and the numerous occasions when the editors would cross paths. Without the invigorating and innovative spirit of the C&W community, we may never have thought an edited collection about an augmented reality game would have merit. The editors heartily thank the organizers, volunteers, and participants of this annual event for fostering scholarship in the field.

We would also like to thank the contributors to this collection—it is your work that validates the title of this project. Finally, thanks go out to Layla Milholen at McFarland for working with us through the process of publishing this collection.

Jamie Henthorn:

I'd like to thank Chris Turner for introducing me to Pokémon in the late '90s (even though I, your older sister, was too cool to geek out on the franchise at the time). Joyce Turner is my go-to for questions about the mechanics of the game. Thank you to the other editors of this collection. When Kristopher and I started thinking through this project, he recommended we invite Andrew and Stephanie and that was the best idea because they are amazing and talented scholars. My son, Dorian, has been my most dedicated teammate. In addition to playing *Pokémon Go* with you, I got to experience the Pokémon franchise through your young eyes. In deck building, battling, and collecting across media, we experienced the franchise's core belief that the world always has more to give the dedicated and curious.

Andrew Kulak:

I first encountered Pokémon on the playground outside my middle school. I still remember waiting in line to use the one link cable we all shared to finally evolve a Gengar. I'm not sure I would have rediscovered the games as an adult, however, were it not for my friend Erik, and so I should thank him for starting me on a new Pokémon adventure that has led to my work on this book. I am fortunate to have support from great colleagues at Virginia Tech in the Department of English, the Human-Centered Design interdisciplinary graduate education program, and the THIRD Lab in the Department of Computer Science. My cat Mango has always kept me company during late nights working on academic projects. Lastly, I would be remiss were I not to thank my coeditors for this collection. We first discussed this idea together after a panel at Computers & Writing in 2017, and it has been quite the journey from that first meeting to realizing this collection. I couldn't have found better collaborators with whom to share that journey.

Kristopher Purzycki:
   I might never have played *Pokémon Go* if not for my wife Sarah, who was required to walk many miles as part of her post-surgery recuperation in the summer of 2016. Apologies go out to our boys Noah and Elijah who hung up their trainer hats in disgust after they were forced to watch in horror as we infiltrated their childhood. Many thanks go out to the player communities here in Milwaukee and abroad, as well as the legislators and citizens who shared their perspectives. Finally, I confess that *The* Pokémon Go *Phenomenon* was simply an excuse to work with Jamie, Andrew, and Stephanie. It's been a gift.

Stephanie Vie:
   I'd like to thank Jeff Stockberger, who always patiently supports all of the academic writing I do; as well, in the case of this particular edited collection, thank you for raiding with me, trading with me, and patiently waiting while I reached level 40. Now let's wait for the level cap to be raised. Thanks also to the University of Central Florida College of Arts and Humanities for supporting my research and writing activities. Finding time to write and edit as a department chair can be difficult, and the understanding and support of the CAH Dean's office, and Dean Jeffrey Moore in particular, were central to the creation of this collection. UCF Texts & Technology Ph.D. students Emily Hensley, Leah Corinne Jones, and Rachel Winter were wonderful early copy editors and readers for the collection. My coeditors Jamie, Kristopher, and Andrew were wonderful to work with—but why aren't we all Best Friends yet in *Pokémon Go*? Finally, thanks to George and Cheri Vie, who have always been supportive of my academic work and output. I know neither of you play *Pokémon Go*, but I know you will be pleased to see this collection come to fruition, nevertheless.

Introduction

Not Just Play: Spaces of Contention

Jamie Henthorn, Andrew Kulak, Kristopher Purzycki *and* Stephanie Vie

Many of us who work in some way in media and game studies recall July 2016 as a month full of trepidation, tension, and exhilaration. Terrorist attacks seemed to be increasing in number, with the most devastating taking place in Baghdad, where nearly three hundred were killed. In Nice, France, a cargo truck driven by Islamic State of Iraq and the Levant (ISIL) agent Mohamed Lahouaiej-Bouhlel careened through a Bastille Day crowd, killing 86 and injuring hundreds more. High-profile political sea changes seemed to have left the world reeling with ideological questions and burgeoning polarization. An attempted coup in Turkey ravaged the nation, while nationalist sentiments culminated in the British election of conservative Theresa May.

Meanwhile, the American presidential election, which would prove to embroil the nation for years to come, was becoming increasingly contentious. One of the many issues that would exacerbate the nation's already hostile division would be gun violence, particularly between police and African Americans. After a year that witnessed nearly thirty deaths of African American men at the hands of police, smoldering tensions ignited: a sniper attack on police in Dallas; three more police homicides in Baton Rouge. In July alone, 72 people, an inordinate number of them black, were killed by non-pursuant officers (Tate, Jenkins, Rich, & Muyskens, 2018). In response, the #BlackLivesMatter movement held over a hundred protests during those first two weeks of July (Lee, Mykhyalyshyn, Omri, & Singhvi, 2016).

Then the monsters appeared.

Released in this tumultuous context, *Pokémon Go* seemed to be an excuse for the media to avert its gaze from the killings and protests. Seemingly overnight, the augmented reality (AR) game quickly piqued our collective curiosities with reports of parks being overrun by Eevees, Pidgeys, and their scrambling captors. Children, for whom the outdoors had increasingly become foreign terrain, took to the streets, plazas, and public spaces. The adults were not far behind. Playful curiosity turned to concern for urban planners as long-forgotten public spaces teemed with a previously absentee population. Shopkeepers fortunate enough to have their shops designated as Poké Stops quickly seized on the financial opportunity, offering Pokémon-themed discounts to capture the transient players before they were lured elsewhere.

Almost as quickly as it emerged, *Pokémon Go* dissipated into the haze of pop culture memory. A series of setbacks and circumstances (many of which are detailed in this collection) frustrated and eventually repelled many players. The inaugural *Pokémon Go* Fest, which attracted 20,000 players to downtown Chicago, was devastated by networking issues. The sold-out event, which was to celebrate the anniversary of the game's release, ended up being a costly fiasco for Niantic, Inc. (creators of *Pokémon Go*), who refunded admission costs to players.

As of this writing, *Pokémon Go* has largely been forgotten. American news coverage, which had profiled players in hues of sarcasm and pity, have lately found far more lucrative fodder in our public figures and politicians. The dense swarms of players that seemed to erupt from the earth have long dispersed. Stalwart player communities nevertheless persist on social media, eventually descending to nearby gyms for coordinated raids. Individual players occasionally pass by, their phones tethered to warming portable power packs.

The Pokémon Go *Phenomenon: Essays on Public Play in Contested Spaces* is a collection that hopes to articulate the player experience of *Pokémon Go* and the phenomenon of AR play. Although tensions exist within this collection—especially when considering the climate within which the game is played—they are typically framed as opportunities.

How We Play: A History of Pokémon Go

Before proceeding, it is worth reviewing the history of *Pokémon Go* and its predecessor, *Ingress*, also produced by Niantic. The two games demonstrate how visualization and geolocation not only open the world up to the public, but also invite *Pokémon Go*'s user base to participate in the platform itself. In summer 2016, *Pokémon Go* became a global phenomenon and created a new landscape for AR games. A subtler effect was how it promoted the use of geolocational data by the public: No longer was Google Maps being used to simply direct drivers to their destinations; it was now used to direct *Pokémon Go* players to various areas of their cities and towns in order to catch

Pokémon. In addition to providing data brokers like Google with information about individual trends in vehicular traffic, *Ingress* and *Pokémon Go* delivered insights into individual tastes and trends. Finally, these and other AR games invoked a new sense of trust in these service providers, ushering in a new era built upon a crowd-sourced economy. At the same time, the initial levels of access to consumer data in the *Pokémon Go* app by Google and Niantic prompted concerns about consumer data safety, damaging this newly emerging sense of trust.

But before one can even explore *Pokémon Go*, one must understand both Keyhole and *Ingress*, two crucial elements that made *Pokémon Go* possible. Cresting the dot-com boom, a little-known start-up promised to radically transform the way we would view the world. Keyhole's bold claim to "deliver a 3D model of the entire earth via the Internet" ("About Keyhole," 2004) went largely unnoticed among the innumerable other start-ups boasting claims of similar magnitude at the turn of the twentieth century. The savviness of Keyhole founder and CEO John Hanke, a graduate of the University of California Berkeley's Haas School of Business, anticipated an increasingly accessible and potentially lucrative convergence of 3D graphics, geospatial computation, and broadband networking. This proved to be the foundation for one of the most significant and wide-reaching foundations for twenty-first-century mobile technology.

Keyhole became part of Google's growing enterprise in 2004, with Hanke transforming his spatial rendering project into Google Earth (Markowitz, 2012). Until 2010, Hanke's Google Geo team directed the institution of Google Maps and Google Street View into the company's ecology. At that point, Hanke and some of his original Keyhole colleagues formed Niantic, Inc., within Google. In 2012, Niantic released *Field Trip,* a mobile application where users could discover strange and unique places around them. Later that same year, they also published *Ingress*, an AR game that pits the "Resistance" against the "Enlightened" in control over portals, stores of exotic matter (XM). To extract the XM and potentially claim the portal, a player needed to physically move to the immediate vicinity of that portal. Once nearby, a player would use their mobile device to claim the XM or attack the portal if it was owned by the enemy faction.

Released exclusively to Android devices in December 2013, *Ingress* used player-contributed data to crowdsource the expansion of Google Maps' geolocational services. Players used their mobile devices to view a digitally rendered map of their real-world surroundings, establishing or taking control of portals and creating connections between them. One of the more significant qualities of *Ingress* was that it allowed players to submit portals to Niantic for consideration. To submit a portal, users submitted a photo of a storefront, monument, or an otherwise static, unique landmark to Niantic for review.

Other criteria listed on the *Ingress* website included "a location with a cool story, a place in history or educational value," "a cool piece of art or unique architecture," and "a hidden gem or hyper-local spot" ("Candidate Portal Criteria," n.d.). Players were asked to avoid areas unfriendly to pedestrians, private property, natural landscapes, and seasonal or temporary displays. After a lengthy waiting period (one of the authors of this introduction waited nearly eight months), a submitter would receive a verdict on whether their portal candidate was accepted or not.

In this fashion, the AR map of *Ingress* rapidly filled up with portals that included everything from familiar, recognizable monuments (such as Big Ben in London, a portal owned by a player named cichy98z) to places that only locals would find interesting. Through *Ingress*, Google became privy to an unrivaled network of places and spaces that were important to area residents and visiting tourists alike. By the time Niantic departed Google in 2015, *Ingress* had been downloaded over 12 million times (Ingress, 2015). In 2016, *Ingress*'s more than one million players were conquering portals in 4,000 global regions (Goel, 2016). But this was not the only thing Niantic had to brag about. In September of that year, Hanke announced that they were partnering with the Pokémon Company to develop *Pokémon Go,* a new AR game based on a 21-year-old iconic game (Hanke, 2015).

Until this point, AR games had been a niche form of play. In the handheld console market, only a few games had been popular. Nintendo's *Pokédex 3D Pro* (2012), playable on the Nintendo 3DS gaming system, was the first foray in placing Pokémon in the real world. For PlayStation's Vita system, *Table Ice Hockey* (2012) and the puzzle game *PulzAR* (2014) used tabletop cards as markers to superimpose a game area where two players could compete. For smartphones, *Ingress* accumulated a dedicated but niche player base. But there was still a dearth of notable additions to the location-based, AR game library. One of the more successful games, Six to Start's running trainer *Zombies, Run!* (2012), used a serial zombie apocalypse narrative to add interest (and zombie chases) to one's jogging routine. Other popular titles included the mafia simulator *Turf Wars* (MeanFreePath, 2009), ghost hunter *SpecTrek* (Games4All, 2010), and first-person shooter *Paintball* (Mambo Studios, 2011).

The cozy marriage of AR and games had been anticipated nearly a decade prior. Experiments out of the Georgia Institute of Technology demonstrated how using games to interface with AR systems promoted experimentation and unforeseen forms of interaction (Starner et al., 2000). The following year, the game *Can You See Me Now?* sent three chasers after twenty participants over a weekend throughout the streets of Sheffield in the United Kingdom (Flintham et al., 2003). This capacity for emergent interaction within real-world arenas enabled those forms of scholarship that had traditionally been constrained by spatial demands to connect participants beyond both the laboratory and the classroom. Schrier's (2006) early work advocated for the use of AR games to impart much-needed data management, media fluency, critical thinking, and collaboration skills to millennial students. By the end of the decade, medical (Burke et al., 2010), pedagogical (Dunleavy, Dede, & Mitchell, 2009; Klopfer & Sheldon, 2010; Squire, 2010), and environmental (Klopfer & Squire, 2008) applications for AR had been embraced by academics.

The popular press responded with as much anticipation as players. Eager to explore the impacts of the game, journalists immediately postulated on *Pokémon Go*'s significance to AR marketing (Hobbs, 2016), technological access (Tassi, 2016), and physical activity. Niantic's new project was expected to deliver an expansive interest in geolocational technology. On July 6, 2016, *Pokémon Go* was released in 37 countries to much enthusiasm.

Why We Play: The Pokémon Phenomenon and Socialized Play

This anticipation was fostered, in no small part, by the inheritance of a two-decade-old brand. Briefly exploring the history of Pokémon offers some perspective as to why *Pokémon Go,* as a socio-cultural phenomenon, is a lucrative area for study. The first *Pokémon* (short for Pocket Monsters) games were released by Satoshi Tajiri and Nintendo in 1996. Tajiri saw the Game Boy, particularly the Game Link Cable, as a way to create games that allowed players to collect and trade creatures, much like he had collected small creatures in nature as a child living in a less-industrialized Tokyo suburb of Kantō. In the *Pokémon* games, the first generation of Pokémon are found in a 1960s version of Kantō, a less industrial, nostalgic version of Japan where children spend much of their time doing what Tajiri did as a child: exploring, observing, and collecting small creatures in the wild. This portrayal of real places in virtual spaces was thereafter a common trait of future *Pokémon* games.

In creating *Pokémon Red* (1996) and *Pokémon Green* (1996), released later in North America as *Pokémon Red* (1998) and *Pokémon Blue* (1998), Tajiri worked with Shigeru Miyamoto, creator of *Super Mario Bros.* and *The Legend of Zelda*, among others. The *Pokémon* franchise has always relied on creatures that were equal parts cute and consumable as a design choice to spread a distinct (though some argue softened) Japanese style of cuteness for global consumption (Surman, 2009). Players are supposed to want to collect them all, or as McCrea (2017) noted,

> From the outset, the rarity and collecting dynamics of *Pokémon* signal to players that they'll be invited to grow obsessive about their process—not just towards the norma-

tive and surface-level goal of completing the Pokédex by collecting everything you can, but towards inhabiting the in-narrative moral goal of "loving" and "respecting" *Pokémon* [pp. 43–44].

The rapid expansion of the franchise to other forms of media spurred this obsessive collecting. In 1996, Pokémon trading cards were published in Japan (coming to North America in 1999), and they have grown in popularity over their currently 20-plus-year lifespan. In 2017, when the news was still focused on *Pokémon Go*, the trading card game was finding even wider markets, particularly in Europe (Dring, 2018). A *Pokémon* anime series was launched in 1997; it has been in near-continuous production since and has contributed to the popularization of anime globally. With the additions of movies, manga, toys, and a wealth of other paratexts, consumers can now consume Pokémon in almost any medium they wish.

Pokémon games tend to attract a younger demographic who may stay interested in the franchise for decades. As such, the games are intentionally made to be simple to execute but require a certain level of community knowledge to master (McCrea, 2017). Games share enough similarities between play and lore that skills developed playing one *Pokémon* game can easily transfer to the next. *Pokémon* games were distinct when released in that players were meant to level up the creatures collected, meaning "players learned to shift their focus onto the entire set of creatures as sites of attention, care, and focus" (McCrea, 2017, p. 43).

To promote exploration and collection, *Pokémon* has always had a strong relationship with public and community participation. Both *Pokémon Red* and *Green/Blue* encouraged players to trade and battle together using a Game Boy Game Link Cable. With the launch of the Nintendo 3DS, this trading was done wirelessly. Games and paratexts have only further encouraged this community involvement. For example, the Pokémon Pikachu 2 GS (1999) was a virtual pet toy with a built-in pedometer where one used steps to interact with the beloved Pokémon character Pikachu. *Pokémon HeartGold* (2010) and *Pokémon SoulSilver* (2010) included a Pokéwalker, a pedometer that allowed players to gain experience points and catch wild Pokémon while walking around. These earlier innovations set the stage for many of the technologies connected to *Pokémon Go* that are explored in this edited collection, such as *Pokémon Go* wrist-based technologies like the Go-tcha or *Pokémon Go* Plus.

Similarly, many of the game mechanics found in *Ingress* could be recognized beneath the cartoon sheen of *Pokémon* (and later *Pokémon Go*). In both *Pokémon Go* and *Ingress*, players navigated the landscapes of a physical world overlaid with a digital surface accessed through their smartphones and tablets. With *Pokémon Go,* the conspiratorial narrative of its predecessor was replaced with the colorful patina of a global pop culture phenomenon. Several distinctions stand out, however, in how players can engage with either game and with one another. First, *Ingress* players possess the ability to contribute to the game space (and Google's database). *Pokémon Go* players, however, are not able to contribute Poké Stops and are limited to those culled by Niantic from *Ingress*. Second, *Ingress* players were infrequent and ignorable, while *Pokémon Go* players, especially in the early months of the game, were often seen en masse. Someone looking at their phone near the Auschwitz Museum in order to play *Ingress* might not draw attention, but when a horde of people show up to play *Pokémon Go*, it's understandable why there might be concerns.

Third, players of *Pokémon Go* are unable to communicate through in-game channels as of the time of this writing while *Ingress* players can communicate through chat. This requires *Pokémon Go* players to communicate in the physical world, facilitating small cohorts that share information and coordinate tactics to maximize the effects of lures or more effectively complete raids. In contrast, *Ingress* players could coordinate sudden reclamations of territory across the in-game channel. Due to the smaller base of people playing *Ingress*, this capability enabled immediate response to infractions on territory that could—like the tactics of Electronic Disturbance Theater's SWARM (in 2006, South West Action to Resist the Minutemen, or, in 1998, Stop the War in Mexico) project—immediately disperse after successfully capturing enemy nodes (Lecher, 2017, para. 3; Raley, 2009, p. 40).

Finally, portals were replaced with Poké Stops that could be spun to receive various items once the player moved within range. Some of these portals were selected to be Pokémon gyms. Similar to *Ingress* portals, these sporadically placed gyms are controllable by players. Also attracted to these Poké Stops are the Pokémon themselves, digital creatures who appear on the map overlay that serves as the primary interface of the game. Once a player taps on a Pokémon on the map, the application shifts to a capture screen. The player can then opt to view the game in the default AR mode or in a static mode, where the creature appears on a digitally rendered grassy field. In the default AR mode, Pokémon and the game's interface are overlaid atop the device camera's input.

Despite some initial technological setbacks due to the enormous burdens on Niantic's servers, *Pokémon Go* quickly became the most downloaded application in history (Mac, 2016) with an estimated daily income of $1.6 million from in-game purchases (Hobbs, 2016). Fueled by a mix of nostalgia, curiosity, and simply having something to do while enjoying the summer months, players took to the outdoors in hopes of finding their favorite Pokémon. And they did so in unprecedented numbers. Once players were able to get the game working, they took to the spaces—mostly public, sometimes private— of their respective cities. Those in rural areas or less popular urban spaces (such as more impoverished areas) where there were a dearth of Poké Stops ventured to those spaces more densely populated with Pokémon.

Scholarly Attention

Even during the turmoil of July 2016, Niantic's *Pokémon Go* somehow left indelible marks on the public landscape. Perhaps it was due to the public's desire for release. Or nostalgia. Maybe it was just another pop culture phenomenon that would (and did) come and go. Whatever the cause, *Pokémon Go* seemed to confound and baffle the public. Until this point, few digital games had impacted non-players in the world outside of the game. Geolocational technology, which undergirds the game's core mechanic, was familiar, but only when providing directions.

For those of us in media and game studies, however, the release of this game seemed poignant and timely. Not that it seemed ludicrous to be paying attention to a game during such volatile acts on the global stage, but because it seemed to fit right in. Now a durable but somewhat stagnant discipline, game studies needed an excuse to shake loose the dust of tired debates about narrative, play, and disciplinary value. #Gamergate had given credence to those who had been prophesying the seriousness of games and player communities. Unlike the sludge of misogyny that had been dredged up during this scandal, *Pokémon Go* offered something different. While sub- and popcultural toxicity was to be found, it was difficult to look past the enthusiasm of players and the energy that emerged within the protests and violence of that summer.

So, with giddy steps, we recalled the proselytizing at conferences and in academic journals about the potentials for games and AR. Earlier that year, in their introduction to *Social, Casual and Mobile Games*, Willson and Leaver (2017) hinted at a geolocationally networked media landscape where privacy was going to be a considerable issue (p. 2). The conspiratorial theme of *Ingress* provided an excellent springboard for other investigations into these concerns (Hulsey & Reeves, 2014; Majorek & du Vall, 2016). Stakes had been claimed in anticipation of a work that publicly demonstrated *just how serious games are*. And here it was: a geolocationally connected laboratory realized in the (digital) flesh. In the years since *Pokémon Go* was released, hundreds of papers have been published focusing on the game from within various fields and disciplines.

Anticipating an inevitable decline in popularity, medical researchers immediately took notice. These earliest studies focused on assessing the perceived health benefits and viewed the game with optimism. Later studies provided a soft confirmation, acknowledging that players demonstrated increased physical activity (Althoff, White, & Horvitz, 2016; LeBlanc & Chaput, 2017) and lower emotional distress (Hussain, 2018). Most pointed out that these benefits were short-lived, and this activity was useful only so long as play was complemented with other forms of exercise such as dog-walking (Kogan, Hellyer, Duncan, & Schoenfeld-Tacher, 2017). More cautionary arguments about injury stemming from driving (Joseph & Armstrong, 2016), walking (Barbieri et al., 2017), and mosquito exposure (Oidtman et al., 2016) while playing emerged as the game's popularity waned and new research rolled in.

Interdisciplinary studies also pounced on this data-rich opportunity. Clark and Clark (2016) echoed the medical field's sense of immediacy in offering a methodology for identifying interventions within "supercomplex platforms" like *Pokémon Go* (p. 2). Instructional designers and pedagogically focused scholars similarly advocated for the more positive qualities of the game and its impact on the classroom (Bruno, 2018; Euteneuer, 2018; Walker, McMahon, Rosenblatt, & Arner, 2017; Wohlwend, 2017). *Pokémon Go* and similar supercomplex platforms, however, were hotbeds for researchers looking at the potentials and pitfalls for geolocational media. The game's reliance on free labor, for instance, was ripe for warnings about the game's contribution to multinational neoliberalism (Jin, 2017), while privacy in AR space was central to de Souza e Silva's (2017) work on digitally hybridized spaces where social mobility and surveillance were intertwined in *Pokémon Go*.

Published at a time when racial boundaries were already being violently contested, other scholars interested in the spaces invested in the game were keen to use *Pokémon Go* as a tool for evaluating social trends and issues. Many of these studies were reported with tempered enthusiasm. Conservationists applauded the game's penchant for getting people outdoors but worried that the collection mechanic promoted wanton consumption of the environment and its inhabitants (Dorward, Mittermeier, Sandbrook, & Spooner, 2017). Colley et al. (2017), for example, led a study on location-based gaming across five countries, arguing that the game promoted group mobility but "follows and reinforces existing geographic contours of advantage and disadvantage" (p. 1184).

While *Pokémon Go*'s popularity has waned, investigations into the game's significance have not. As the game is further refined and developed by Niantic, so too are the theoretical and empirical perspectives that scholars have applied to it. Collected here are several essays that further articulate various facets of *Pokémon Go* from interdisciplinary perspectives. The collection is divided into three parts. The first, "How We Play," interrogates how *Pokémon Go* has impacted interpersonal relationships as well as one's own relationship with health and fitness. Beginning with Wendi Sierra and Ginger Burgoon, the authors consider the intergenerational possibilities of augmented reality gaming in "Gaming Across the Years: Gotta Catch 'Em All Together." In particular, the authors explore how *Pokémon Go* builds on existing family dynamics to offer new and unexpected modes of interaction. Sierra and Burgoon take an autoethnographic approach to studying how the game has impacted multiple generations in one family. For the participants in this case study, *Pokémon Go* became a site of meaningful connection between family members of different ages due to the different prior knowledge about the game that older and younger players possessed. The authors argue that the unique exigence created by the game's combination of a familiar video game franchise and physical location "can change the way families experience their local environment, creating new opportunities for shared contexts and interaction." In other words, asymmetries in knowledge of Pokémon history and local geography between younger and older players—rather than serving as an impediment to playing—created moments of shared meaning making across generations.

Next, Ryan S. Eanes and Claire Y. van den Broek explore the game's "interpersonal privacy shield" in their essay, "Playing Alone, Together: *Pokémon Go*, Public Mobility and Locational Privacy." Anyone who walked down a street in early 2016 where *Pokémon Go* players were gathered recognized the phenomenon of multiple people standing together playing a game without seemingly talking or interacting with each other at all. This phenomenon, which Eanes and van den Broek dub "playing alone, together," is necessarily complicated by players' desires for privacy. At the same time, however, the game presses players to seek out others in order to progress further in the game. Through a survey of *Pokémon Go* players, the authors address team dynamics, group kinship, and other interpersonal gameplay factors to hypothesize why players might play alone together with "a strange opacity between physically co-present players who might literally be sitting next to each other, particularly in urban settings, where interaction with other individuals is essentially inevitable."

Jamie Henthorn next discusses "The World's Most Popular Fitness App," historicizing the rise of leisure and fitness over time and tying this rise to socioeconomic markers as well as gender roles. Leisure, fitness, and health are connected, too, to civic duties and capitalist practices. *Pokémon Go*, Henthorn argues, "works within this long history of fitness and public spaces, connecting these green spaces with contemporary understandings of individualism." By exploring how gender, race, and socioeconomic status map on to the seemingly innocuous game of *Pokémon Go*, Henthorn shows that class mobility, the color of one's skin, and one's experiences with gender-based street harassment all impact how *Pokémon Go* might be played (or if it is played at all). Ultimately, Henthorn focuses on the game's privileging of a kind of "ambulatory fitness" that seems less about motivating players to become faster runners, but instead encourages daily leisure activities, meandering, and playing along with others.

In the final essay of Part One, Jill Anne Morris considers pedagogical implications of *Pokémon Go* in "Augmented Reality Design Through Experience Architecture." Where other augmented reality platforms failed to engage students in her classroom, "*Pokémon Go* created a needed point of entry where all students could understand why AR was something that could be useful" both as a storytelling platform and as a technical communication tool relevant to employers. After having students play *Pokémon Go* and share their own experiences with the game, Morris asked students to design their own augmented reality projects. The experience with *Pokémon Go* offered students insight into how, why, and where people engage with augmented reality. In combination with an experience architecture approach, students designed multimodal interactions targeted at audiences, such as students on campus tours, that took advantage of the affordances of augmented reality to engage users in specific sited contexts.

In Part Two, "Why We Play," authors explore some of the psychosocial motivators that have kept *Pokémon Go* popular despite the years since its inception. What keeps us coming back for more? And what persuades us to consume via in-app purchases, leading us to the possibility of *Pokémon Go* addiction? Throughout "Rhetorical Argumentation: Public Play, Place and Persuasion in *Pokémon Go*," Jason Chew Kit Tham and Deondre Smiles "seek to build a theory of user experience that considers the marriage between physical and digital representations of location" by studying the rhetorics of augmentation technology. The authors build from an examination of the interface of the *Pokémon Go* and its rhetorical qualities to further consider email marketing materials and interviews with players in order to better understand how the game motivates players and encourages them to engage with its augmented reality features. As a result of their analysis, the authors reimagine augmented reality as a layered social phenomenon encompassing interfaces, locations, players, and communities. Drawing from Rieder's work on transductive rhetoric, Tham and Smiles describe how a user's experience spans these distinct yet interacting layers and discuss implications for the design and analysis of augmented systems from a rhetorical perspective.

Next, in "To Be the Very Best … You Gotta Pay: Motivation, Resources and Monetizing Frustration," Eric Murnane offers an analysis of the economics of *Pokémon Go* in terms of walking, time, and money. Murnane uses Burke's method of cluster criticism to examine how these three currencies intersect in moments of gameplay and the experiences of users. Contrasting the high exchange value of money in the game with marketing material that promotes health and community interaction, Murnane argues that "money as a substitute for frustration undermines the positive potential of *Pokémon*

Go." This analysis suggests that the game negates its own claims concerning the value of exercise and community engagement by reproducing them as tedium in terms of its internal system of incentives and economic logic.

Kristen L. Cole and Alexis Pulos take on one of the more popular metaphors for video gaming and *Pokémon Go* in their essay, "Addiction and the Apocalypse: The Pathology of *Pokémon Go*," which explores the tropes of addiction and the zombie apocalypse through metaphoric criticism. By "unraveling the basic assumptions upon which [these metaphors] rely," the authors articulate which ones "reproduce and bolster dominant views of technology and social interaction." Technological anxieties are reflected in the use of the zombie metaphor, seen in images of *Pokémon Go* players shuffling along, staring intently at their phones and not at anything else around them. Shifts in social relationships that move us away from only privileging human-to-human (rather than human-to-device) relationships are reflected in the metaphor of addiction, resulting in numerous articles and even comedy sketches expressing concern about the number of hours a given player might be putting in to *Pokémon Go* gameplay.

Finally, in his essay "PokéStories: On Narrative and the Construction of Augmented Reality," Cody Mejeur builds a model of narrative, long explored in game studies, to help us "grasp narrative as a living and playful process that structures our experiences and realities." The game's narrative is built from determined narrative (structured by Niantic, Inc., and unchangeable by the player) as well as personal narrative (the individual player's actions and story arc) and collective narrative (the stories built from team interactions and shared experiences over time). The confluence of these three narrative approaches reflect culture as well as provide moments of potential resistance to dominant cultural values or approaches. Narrative, as Mejeur reminds us, "can be a place to start, and it can contribute, even if slowly and incrementally, to changing our realities."

Leading from Mejeur's articulation of the potential power for games like *Pokémon Go* to shape culture and thus reality, Part Three of the collection organizes essays around "The Impact of Play." How has our world been shaped by *Pokémon Go*? The authors in this section take on diverse examples drawn from popular culture as well as academia to hypothesize how our world has changed and will continue to change as a result of augmented reality games and *Pokémon Go* in particular. The first essay in this section, from Peter Schaefer and Margaret Schwartz, takes on the relationship between augmented reality and historical and material conditions in "Raid Pass: Constitutive Capital Flows for Augmented Reality." The authors offer a history of a September 9, 2017, field test of the *Pokémon Go* EX Raid Pass system, a test which happened to share the same physical space as a protest against the rescinding of the Deferred Action of Childhood Arrivals (DACA) immigration policy by the Trump administration. Through an analysis of the context of the event as well as narratives from raid participants, the authors contrast *Pokémon Go* players and protestors in terms of their relationship to capital. While police limited the movement of protestors, the EX Raid Pass granted raid participants agency in space because it connected *Pokémon Go* players with a commercial event, which legitimized their presence as consumers. In this case, the augmented reality of the game world thus functioned to transect "the real world/physical world binary with the result that these two worlds are linked by a single flow, that of capital."

Next, Kristopher Purzcyki spends time with a 2017 court case pitting game designer Candy Lab against Milwaukee County, the Milwaukee County Board of Supervisors, and the Milwaukee County Department of Parks, Recreation, and Culture in his essay, "For Anatopistic Places: *Pokémon Go* vs. Milwaukee County." In his essay, he argues that this particular court case is a moment in which we can examine "conflict that ensued between … communities that convened in an already politicized public space" while playing *Pokémon Go* in the early days of 2016 after its release. Backing up from a specific discussion of the conflict between these groups, Purzycki addresses the role of place and space in game studies thus far, using data from his 2018 player survey to argue that "place is a concept crucial to recognizing the phenomenon of play." Dwelling on the example of *Pokemon Go* players as situated in anatopistic, or out-of-place, spaces, Purzycki traces flows of power in such spaces and questions the power of such spaces for different kinds of mobilization.

Luiz Adolfo Andrade's "A Tale of Two Screens: Space, Ubiquitous Computing and Locative Gaming" spends time with optional devices associated with *Pokémon Go* gameplay—such as the Go-tcha wristband, *Pokémon Go* Plus wrist device, or Apple Watch—to articulate a theory of "two screens," showing how designers can develop locative games meant for multiple devices or screens. Exploring multiple waves of locative gaming and the shifts in communications processes that followed, Andrade provides personal examples of playing the game using wrist devices in locations such as Copenhagen's Royal Library courtyard; he draws on Latour's actor-network theory to showcase the different actors in such a network, such as the urban space of Copenhagen; the game design process, including the designers and programmers; the game scripts, codes, and rules; and the players themselves. Ultimately, he argues, *Pokémon Go* "highlights a place-based communication process among the players, the game, and everyday life that uses the space as support for the agencies among them."

The final essay of the collection, William Heili, Chen Xu and Nicholas Jon Crane's "Placemaking Across the Digital-Physical Divide: Location-Based Mobile Gameplay as a Relay in the Emergence of Singularities" frames a discussion of *Pokémon Go* through scholarship on the physical-digital divide. Instead, the authors assert, "*Pokémon Go* should be understood as a mode of computation by which physical reality is produced." That is, drawing on Deleuze and Guattari's work, the authors note that interactions in the game itself impact physical space in the offline world, allowing game players to see familiar sights in the offline world anew through the game's use of "constellations of meaning." Highlighting commentary from focus groups with students at the University of Wyoming, the authors show how these players interacted with campus features differently as a result of their gameplay, and these "player-cyborgs" reflected on how *Pokémon Go* offered them new horizons "in which the known is supplemented and the unknown is playfully made available."

As we reflect on the impact of *Pokémon Go* over two years since the game's initial release, we see great potential for continued discussions regarding significant cultural and social issues. Games themselves may come and go, but the augmented reality gaming environment that *Pokémon Go* made wildly popular will continue to influence a variety of arenas, including medical, pedagogical, and cultural environments. Our relationships with technologies and with each other will continue to evolve, and as mobile devices and gameplay evolve along with us, we will see further development as well as critique. Even as the game itself continues to change, we foresee space to gradually develop existing scholarship on augmented reality gaming, privacy and data mining in networked game environments, free-to-play and freemium gaming models, and transmedia gaming narratives across multiple devices, consoles, and media—among others. As we type this introduction, another generation of Pokémon (Gen 4) is just days from release in *Pokémon Go*, and we prepare to head out of our houses to hit the streets in search of new Pokédex entries. Crossover gameplay activity between *Pokémon Go* and Nintendo's newest games for the Switch device, *Pokémon: Let's Go, Pikachu!* and *Pokémon: Let's Go, Eevee!*, show that Nintendo and Niantic, Inc., have no plans to slow down development of Pokémon franchise material any time soon. And, given all of the exciting conversations we've managed to capture here in this collection, we're all for it.

References

About Keyhole. (2004). Internet Archive Wayback Machine. Retrieved from https://web. archive.org/web/20031203131432/http://www.keyhole.com:80/body.php?h=about.

Althoff, T., White, R.W., & Horvitz, E. (2016). Influence of *Pokémon Go* on physical activity: Study and implications. *Journal of Medical Internet Research, 18*(12). doi:10.2196/jmir. 675.

Barbieri, S., Vettore, G., Pietrantonio, V., Snenghi, R., Tredese, A., Bergamini, M., … Feltracco, P. (2017). Pedestrian inattention blindness while playing *Pokémon Go* as an emerging health-risk behavior: A case report. *Journal of Medical Internet Research, 19*(4). doi: 10.2196/jmir.6596.

Bruno, L.E. (2018). Embracing technology and pop culture trends in physical education: Ready, set, (Pokémon) go! *Journal of Physical Education, Recreation & Dance, 89*(4), 45–51.

Burke, J.W., McNeill, M.D.J., Charles, D.K., Morrow, P.J., Crosbie, J.H., & McDonough, S.M. (2010, March). Augmented reality games for upper-limb stroke rehabilitation. *2010 Second International Conference on Games and Virtual Worlds for Serious Applications,* USA, 75–78. doi: 10.1109/VS-GAMES.2010.21.

Candidate portal criteria. (n.d.) *Ingress Help Center.* Retrieved from https://support.ingress.com/hc/en-us/articles/207343987-Candidate-Portal-criteria.

Clark, A.M., & Clark, M.T.G. (2016). *Pokémon Go* and research: Qualitative, mixed methods research, and the supercomplexity of interventions. *International Journal of Qualitative Methods, 15*(1), 1–3. https://doi.org/10.1177/1609406916667765.

Colley, A., Thebault-Spieker, J., Lin, A.Y., Degraen, D., Fischman, B., Häkkilä, J., ... & Schöning, J. (2017, May). The geography of *Pokémon GO*: Beneficial and problematic effects on places and movement. In *Proceedings of the 2017 CHI Conference on Human Factors in Computing Systems* (pp. 1179–1192). New York: ACM.

de Souza e Silva, A. (2017). *Pokémon Go* as an HRG: Mobility, sociability, and surveillance in hybrid spaces. *Mobile Media & Communication, 5*(1), 20–23.

Dorward, L.J., Mittermeier, J.C., Sandbrook, C., & Spooner, F. (2017). *Pokémon Go*: Benefits, costs, and lessons for the conservation movement. *Conservation Letters, 10*(1), 160–165.

Dring, C. (2018, March 1). Pokémon toys and trading card sales spike in Europe. *Gamesindustry.biz.* Retrieved from https://www.gamesindustry.biz/articles/2018-03-01-pok-mon-toys-and-trading-card-sales-spike-in-europe.

Dunleavy, M., Dede, C., & Mitchell, R. (2009). Affordances and limitations of immersive participatory augmented reality simulations for teaching and learning. *Journal of Science Education and Technology, 18*(1), 7–22.

Euteneuer, J. (2018). *Conspicuous computing: Gamified bodies, playful composition, and the monsters in your pocket. Computers and Composition.* Advance online publication. doi://doi.org/10.1016/j.compcom.2018.07.001.

Flintham, M., Benford, S., Anastasi, R., Hemmings, T., Crabtree, A., Greenhalgh, C., ... & Row-Farr, J. (2003). Where on-line meets on-the-streets: Experiences with mobile mixed reality games. In *Proceedings of the SIGCHI Conference on Human Factors in Computing Systems: Vol. 5, Issue 1. People at leisure: Social mixed reality* (pp. 569–576). New York: ACM.

Goel, V. (2016, June 8). *Ingress* has the world as its game board. *The New York Times.* Retrieved from https://www.nytimes.com/2016/06/09/technology/ingress-has-the-world-as-its-game-board.html.

Hanke, J. (2015, October 15). Niantic Inc. raises $20 million in financing from The Pokémon Company, Google and Nintendo. Nianticlabs.com. Retrieved from https://www.nianticlabs.com/es/blog/niantic-tpc-nintendo/.

Hobbs, T. (2016, July 18). Why *Pokémon Go* is a game changer for augmented reality and marketers. *Marketing Week.* Retrieved from https://www.marketingweek.com/2016/07/18/why-pokemon-go-is-a-game-changer-for-augmented-reality-and-marketers/.

Hulsey, N., & Reeves, J. (2014). The gift that keeps on giving: Google, *Ingress*, and the gift of surveillance. *Surveillance & Society, 12*(3), 389–400.

Hussain, W.M.H.W. (2018). Augmented reality games (ARG) and *Pokémon Go*: Preventing hikikomori in Malaysia. *International Journal of Civil Engineering and Technology, 9*(5), 1128–1135.

Ingress. (2015, August 12). Important account information. Retrieved September 17, 2018, from https://plus.google.com/+Ingress/posts/GVvbYZzWyTT.

Jin, D.Y. (2017). Critical interpretation of the *Pokémon GO* phenomenon: The intensification of new capitalism and free labor. *Mobile Media & Communication, 5*(1), 55–58.

Joseph, B., & Armstrong, D.G. (2016). Potential perils of peri-Pokémon perambulation: The dark reality of augmented reality? *Oxford Medical Case Reports, 2016*(10), 265–266. doi:10.1093/omcr/omw080.

Klopfer, E., & Sheldon, J. (2010). Augmenting your own reality: Student authoring of science-based augmented reality games. *New Directions for Youth Development, 2010*(128), 85–94.

Klopfer, E., & Squire, K. (2008). *Environmental Detectives*—The development of an augmented reality platform for environmental simulations. *Educational Technology Research and Development, 56*(2), 203–228.

Kogan, L., Hellyer, P., Duncan, C., & Schoenfeld-Tacher, R. (2017). A pilot investigation of the physical and psychological benefits of playing *Pokémon GO* for dog owners. *Computers in Human Behavior, 76,* 431–437.

LeBlanc, A.G., & Chaput, J.-P. (2017). *Pokémon Go*: A game changer for the physical inactivity crisis? *Preventive Medicine, 101,* 235–237.

Lecher, C. (2017, Apr. 14). Massive attack: How a weapon against war became a weapon against the web. *The Verge.* Retrieved from https://www.theverge.com/2017/4/14/15293538/electronic-disturbance-theater-zapatista-tactical-floodnet-sit-in.

Lee, J.C., Mykhyalyshyn, I., Omri, R., & Singhvi, A. (2016, July 16). At least 88 cities have had protests in the past 13 days over police killings of blacks. *New York Times.* Retrieved from https://www.nytimes.com/interactive/2016/07/16/us/protesting-police-shootings-of-blacks.html.

Mac, R. (2016, July 26). The inside story of "Pokémon GO's" evolution from Google castoff to global phenomenon. *Forbes.* Retrieved from https://www.forbes.com/sites/ryanmac/2016/07/26/monster-game/.

Majorek, M., & du Vall, M. (2016). *Ingress*: An example of a new dimension in entertainment. *Games and Culture, 11*(7–8), 667–689.

Markowitz, E. (2012, December 20). Exclusive: Inside the mind of Google's greatest idea man, John Hanke. *Inc.* Retrieved from https://www.inc.com/eric-markowitz/inside-the-mind-of-googles-greatest-idea-man.html.

McCrea, C. (2017). *Pokémon's* progressive revelation: Notes on 20 years of game design. *Mobile Media & Communication, 5*(1), 42–46.

Oidtman, R.J., Christofferson, R.C., ten Bosch, Q.A., Espana, G., Kraemer, M.U.G., Tatem, A., ... Perkins, T.A. (2016). *Pokémon Go* and exposure to mosquito-borne diseases: How not to catch 'em all. *PLoS Currents, 8.* doi:10.1371/currents.outbreaks.2d885b05c7e06a9f72e4656d56b043cd.

Raley, R. (2009). *Tactical media.* Minneapolis: University of Minnesota Press.

Schrier, K. (2006, July). Using augmented reality games to teach 21st century skills. In *Proceedings of SIGGRAPH '06: ACM SIGGRAPH 2006 educators program* (article 15). New York: ACM.

Squire, K. (2010). From information to experience: Place-based augmented reality games as a model for learning in a globally networked society. *Teachers College Record, 112*(10), 2565–2602.

Starner, T., Leibe, B., Singletary, B., Lyons, K., Gandy, M., & Pair, J. (2000). Towards augmented reality gaming. *College of Computing, Georgia Tech.* Retrieved from http://wearables.cc.gatech.edu/publications/imagina2000/.

Surman, D. (2009). *Pokémon 151*: Complicating *kawaii*. In L. Hjorth & D. Chan (Eds.), *Gaming cultures and place in Asia-Pacific* (pp. 158–178). New York: Routledge.

Tassi, P. (2016, July 6). "*Pokémon Go*" finally just went live on iOS and Android in the United States. *Forbes.* Retrieved from https://www.forbes.com/sites/insertcoin/2016/07/06/pokemon-go-finally-just-went-live-on-ios-and-android-in-the-united-states/#1591bd523afe.

Tate, J., Jenkins, J. Rich, S., & Muyskens, J. (2018). Fatal force: 2018 police shootings database. *The Washington Post.* Retrieved from https://www.washingtonpost.com/graphics/2018/national/police-shootings-2018/.

Walker, Z., McMahon, D.D., Rosenblatt, K., & Arner, T. (2017). Beyond Pokémon: Augmented reality is a universal design for learning tool. *SAGE Open, 7*(4), 1–8. https://doi.org/10.1177/2158244017737815.

Willson, M., & Leaver, T. (Eds.). (2017). *Social, casual and mobile games: The changing gaming landscape.* New York: Bloomsbury.

Wohlwend, K. (2017). Chasing literacies across action texts and augmented realities: E-books, animated apps, and *Pokémon Go*. In C. Burnett, G. Merchant, A. Simpson & M. Walsh (Eds.), *The case of the iPad: Mobile literacies in education* (pp. 49–66). Singapore: Springer Singapore.

PART ONE

How We Play

Gaming Across the Years

Gotta Catch 'Em All Together

WENDI SIERRA *and* GINGER BURGOON

Like many young children, Ethan loves dinosaurs. He wears dinosaur clothes, plays with dinosaur toys, and even carries a dinosaur wallet. He thinks Cheri, his grandmother, is the coolest because she has "dinosaurs" in her phone. In reality, the dinosaurs are Cheri's Pokémon in *Pokémon Go*. Ethan lives roughly five hours from his grandmother, but one of his favorite parts of visiting her is seeing what new dinosaurs she has captured and hearing stories from her about the dinosaurs she keeps on her phone.

One night at a restaurant, when faced with a long wait between ordering and receiving their meals, Cheri pulled out her phone to show Ethan some dinosaurs. The bright blue baby Pokémon Totodile immediately captured his attention with its big eyes and toothy grin. Ethan quickly discovered he could feed candies to the Totodile. When fed, Totodile would twirl while a fanfare played. So Ethan did it again. And again. And again. Of course, what Ethan didn't know was that Cheri had been hoarding those candies to evolve her Totodile. Nonetheless, while other people might have gotten upset or taken the game away to save their candies, Cheri was more than happy to let Ethan spend all of her candy making the dinosaur dance.

Because sometimes Totodiles evolve. And sometimes Totodiles eat candy and make little boys laugh.

Introduction

This essay uses case study research to explore the experiences of three generations in one family playing *Pokémon Go* as a shared hobby. Having played since launch, the adult members of the family have incorporated *Poké-mon Go* into many of their daily activities, and the game is an important way for the entire family to connect through a shared context. Implicit ageism has shaped much of the conversation about intergenerational gaming, which often results in a view of shared gaming activity as a way to ameliorate perceived problems for parents or older family members. In our essay, we hope to shift the focus toward exploring the potential for games to create a positive family space through knowledge-sharing and mentoring. The first section of this essay looks at previous research on intergenerational gaming and the challenges ageism creates for intergenerational connection in contemporary society. From there, we move to closely examine one family's successful use of *Pokémon Go*.

Acknowledging and Assessing Intergenerational Gaming

Intergenerational gaming, also known as co-gaming in some research, refers to parents and/or grandparents playing games with their children or grandchildren. While the phenomenon of intergenerational gaming may run counter to popular stereotypes about gamers, the children who played some of gaming's earliest hits have now grown up, likely with children or grandchildren of their own. Indeed, players who first encountered gaming through Minnesota Educational Computing Consortium's *The Oregon Trail* (1985) when it was released to elementary schools in the late seventies to early eighties would now be in their forties or fifties. Likewise, the kids who got hooked on gaming with their first Nintendo Game Boy (1989) or Sega Game Gear (1991) would now be in their thirties or forties. According to a recent Pew Research Center survey, 40 percent of Americans between the ages of 50 and 64 report playing games and 25 percent of Americans over 65 play (though, interestingly, only four percent of adults over 50 choose to identify as gamers) (Duggan, 2015). Further, it seems likely these numbers will only increase as more children and young adults find a passion for games and continue that passion throughout their lifetimes.

While intergenerational gaming is a growing phenomenon receiving increasing academic attention, the ways intergenerational gaming is studied often fall back on a deficit model of thinking, one focused either on mitigation of perceived deficiencies in the elderly or on assuaging various concerns over moral panics regarding children in gaming. In this essay, we seek to move beyond these approaches and instead follow the lead of Comunello and Mulargia (2017) in looking to games not as "a tool to solve problems," but instead as "an environment that can potentially host meaningful interactions" (p. 239).

Rather than focus on the potential corrective or mitigating possibilities of intergenerational gaming, we will examine how "video games can represent a shared context hosting social interaction, prioritizing physical mixed reality (i.e., the integration of physical objects and digital communication tools)" (Comunello & Mulargia, 2017, p. 230). However, prior to doing this, it will be useful to explore the corrective perspectives on gaming, as they are currently foundational to much of the existing research on intergenerational gaming.

De Schutter and Abeele (2015), in their gerontoludic manifesto, identified two main themes pervasive in academic research and industry publications dealing with elders either as players or as subject matter in games: "the theme of usefulness and the theme of accessibility" (p. 112). At the core of either theme is the implication that games must fix something in order to be relevant to older audiences. Games such as Nintendo's *Brain Age* (2006) or *Wii Fit* (2007) attempt to remedy deficiencies or declines associated with aging through gaming. Indeed, a fair number of studies in the field of health and human services focus particularly on this angle, including Jung, Li, Janissa, Gladys, and Lee (2009), who advocated for the use of Wii games in nursing homes, and Brauner, Valdez, Schroeder, and Ziefle (2013), who explored exergames and gamification for fitness and pain mitigation. While not explicitly designed to be geared toward elderly gamers, *Pokémon Go* has even been explored from a corrective perspective, as Althoff, White, and Horvitz (2016) considered the motivating impact of mixed-reality games like *Pokémon Go* on physical activity.

As both De Schutter and Abeele (2015) as well as Comunello and Mulargia (2017) identified, this prescriptive approach of using games to correct faults falls back on the traditional divide between work and play. This perspective would seem to imply that games only become appropriate or acceptable for the elderly if they serve some function above and beyond the play experience (highlighting the usefulness criterion), in this case improving health outcomes (addressing perceived deficiencies). De Schutter and Abeele (2015) stressed that "an exclusive emphasis on the external purpose of 'games for older adults' is detrimental to the very nature of play" (p. 115). Indeed, the games mentioned in Costa and Veloso's (2016) meta-analysis of research on intergenerational gaming finds that the most commonly cited games are ones whose marketing materials highlight the corrective nature. These games promise to foster "intergenerational interaction by facilitating the communication ... [allow] the elderly to play harmoniously together with children ... [and encourage] physical and tangible interaction" (pp. 50–53). These descriptions tell us little about the games grandparents play with their grandchildren and everything about the problems these games are meant to solve. *Pokémon Go* is not a game designed to play into this rhetoric of usefulness.

Though certainly players found many purposes and functional ways to change their interactions with their local environments based on *Pokémon Go* (taking more frequent walks with the game as motivation, for example), its primary purpose is not corrective. Rather, *Pokémon Go* has the potential to change the way families experience their local environment, creating new opportunities for shared contexts and interaction. By carefully considering how the game does this, we might think more broadly about the role non-educational games play in family environments.

While research on gaming and the elderly often prioritizes the idea of usefulness, research on parents gaming with children often focuses on mitigating moral panics, concerns about inappropriate material, or behavioral problems resulting from gaming. Again, these studies take a deficit model, exploring what might be wrong with gaming and proposing intergenerational gaming as a solution to mitigate some of these perceived dangers. Coyne, Padilla-Walker, Stockdale, and Day (2011) noted that the American Academy of Pediatrics Council on Communication and Media themselves take this approach, suggesting that co-watching all media types may decrease potential negative effects for children. Coyne et al. underscored the differences between co-playing and co-viewing: Co-playing is substantially more involved than co-viewing and requires active engagement (through skill development and demonstration) on the part of parents. Interestingly, Conye et al. found substantial benefits for girls whose parents co-played games with them. Girls whose parents co-played reported lower levels of depression, anxiety, and aggressive behavior, and higher levels of prosocial connection with family members. As with the research on aging, however, we find this angle of study begins from a deficit model, suggesting something inadequate in either the player or the game, and seeking to mitigate this inadequacy through intergenerational gaming.

Though we wish to avoid implying physical or moral deficits in either players or in games, it is worth highlighting the very real social and cultural forces that often segregate contemporary society by age. As Hagestad and Ublenberg (2005) demonstrated, age segregation is embedded at a foundational level in many of our cultural institutions. They identified three particular areas of codified separation: institutional segregation, which relegates children to school, parents to work, and grandparents to retirement; spatial segregation, the geographic grouping of people by age brackets into physical locations; and cultural segregation, which distinguishes people through the consumption of popular media, manner of dress, and vocabulary, among other things. The pervasiveness of these various segregations make identifying a shared context—a "communal activity" that invites the sharing of knowledge and mixes skills and challenges in ways in which multiple generations can participate—difficult for many families (Costa & Velso, 2016, p. 49). While

Hagestad and Ublenberg (2005) focused specifically on the elderly and factors contributing to a culture of ageism, this tripartite model of separation is useful when thinking about how this separation occurs across all generations: places catering to families often have separate areas for adults and children, there is clearly a marked difference between children's media and media for adults, and institutional barriers separate children of different age groups into homogenous groups.

Intergenerational gaming challenges this separation by creating shared moments of connection, particularly at the cultural and spatial level. Successfully navigating the game system and local environment requires a variety of different knowledges and skill sets. Playing *Pokémon Go* together invites grandparents, parents, and children to draw on and share these skills with each other, creating a co-mentoring space that allows each participant to contribute in different ways.

Pokémon Go: *Ideally Suited for Intergenerational Gaming*

Among non-educational games, there are a number of cultural and structural features that make *Pokémon Go* ideally suited to intergenerational gaming. Structurally, the technical features of *Pokémon Go* lend themselves nicely to this style of play. First, *Pokémon Go* is readily accessible to most Americans. According to a 2017 Entertainment Software Association survey, 81 percent of households in America and 77 percent of all adults owned smartphones. Dedicated gaming consoles, however, were only present in 48 percent of households, while dedicated gaming handhelds were in 22 percent of households. Thus, it's highly likely multiple members of a family will have access to and familiarity with the technology required to play the game even if they are not familiar with gaming as a pastime, something not true of many other commercial games. *Pokémon Go* can also be downloaded for free from the Apple App Store or Google Play, meaning there is no cost barrier to play the game (and thus no monetary reason to be hesitant to at least try it out). Being digital, there's also no cartridge or disc to keep track of. Finally, and perhaps most importantly, *Pokémon Go* is easy to play for only a few minutes at a time. Unlike other games, which may have long battles, timed levels, or intricate puzzles, it's fairly quick to open the app and spin a Poké Stop or capture a wild Pokémon while in line at Starbucks. This means families can easily integrate the game into their daily life.

Culturally, the Pokémon franchise is one that has the potential to resonate with a wide variety of age groups, addressing in some part the cultural segregation that Hagestad and Ublenberg highlighted above. People who were kids when the first versions of Pokémon were released are now adults, many with children of their own. The initial wave of Pokémon appeared in the United States in the late nineties. The first generation of Pokémon games (*Red/Blue*) was released in 1997; an anime television series debuted a year later in 1998 (*Pokémon: Indigo League*) and was quickly followed by an anime movie in theaters (*Pokémon: The First Movie: Mewtwo Strikes Back*, 1999). A new generation of Pokémon is released about every three years, with a corresponding set of games, television episodes, and movies. The latest generation of games (*Ultra Sun/Ultra Moon, Gen 7*) came out in 2017. This has been matched with both a new anime series, *Sun and Moon*, and a new movie, *I Choose You!*, which is a nostalgic remake of the anime series' first episode. Thus, given the longevity and popularity of the Pokémon franchise across multiple media and generations, it is entirely possible either generation or even both may possess knowledge about the Pokémon franchise and Pokémon-specific mechanics. As Keogh (2017) noted, the franchise thus appeals both to older gamers and to new audiences, possessing "nostalgia for those who grew up playing the Pokémon games, even as the brand remains a contemporary franchise for new generations of gamers, with regular releases of new games with new creatures to collect and new systems to master" (p. 39).

A Note on Autoethnographic Methods in Gaming

Prior to exploring our take on intergenerational gaming as transformative rather than corrective, it will be useful to briefly touch on method. As Nardi (2010) explained in her foundational text on *World of Warcraft*, *My Life as a Night Elf Priest*, doing any sort of ethnographic work in gaming requires that researchers take on the role of participant much more strongly than in other environments. Reflecting on her time playing *World of Warcraft* and researching social organizations within the game, Nardi wrote that "in a game world, the overwhelming need to *play* dominates interaction much of the time" (p. 35, emphasis in original). Further, large game franchises often have their own history and culture. Thus, researchers must be able to engage with the game as well as its players within the context of the game: that is, through the play experience.

Studying intergenerational gaming adds an additional layer of challenge to research. As Shaw (2013) has previously explored, attempts to understand issues related to concepts like identity and interaction often include developing a more complete picture of a player's media experience. Similarly, because examining intergenerational gaming involves exploring family structures and nuances, it seemed most appropriate to conduct this research from the perspective of autoethnography. Thus, while there exist a substantial number of large-scale and quantitative studies on gaming (Williams et al.'s 2006 study of guilds in *World of Warcraft* and Williams et al.'s 2009 study of gender in *EverQuest II* are both exemplary examples of this model of research), for our purposes we feel autoethnography to be an appropriate choice.

In this essay, we follow the model of Takayoshi (2007), whose "Gender Matters: Literacy, Learning, and Gaming in One American Family" used autoethnographic methods (close analysis and reflection on one's own experiences and communities) and case study research to explore intergenerational gaming with an eye toward how female role models impact girls' approaches to gaming. Takayoshi interviewed four female gamers in her family: her sister, her two step-daughters, and her niece. Takayoshi explained both the use of a single family in her study and her relationship with these gamers as an essential element in her research, as she was able to "contextualize their answers against the ecology of our shared experiences as a family" (p. 232).

Like Takayoshi and Shaw, our data collection for this project was highly recursive. We first interviewed our family members (described in detail below) about their experiences with *Pokémon Go*. These methods were followed up with numerous emails, phone calls, and text messages as we sought further clarification and more of our participants' own language. Drafts of this essay were circulated among the family members to ensure that we were capturing their perspectives and not misquoting or misinterpreting important moments and ideas. As Takayoshi and Shaw acknowledged, small-scale ethnographic case studies cannot make claims about generalizability the way larger quantitative studies might. However, what they can do is offer us a detailed, nuanced picture of how people actually use the technologies we theorize about, and how these technologies can become incorporated into everyday life in new and interesting ways.

A Family of Gamers

Gaming has always been a family pastime for Cheri and her children. She and her husband Ken were early adopters of some of the first gaming technologies, purchasing an Atari 2600 in the early eighties. As their children Wendi, Ginger, Kim, and Tessa grew up, they purchased each new Nintendo system and eagerly played these games as a family. Some of Wendi's earliest memories are playing *The Legend of Zelda* (1986) with her father and *Bubble Bobble* (1986) with her mother. Likewise, Ginger frequently played *Super Smash Bros.* (1999) cooperatively with her youngest sister Tessa, the two sisters working collaboratively to defeat the AI rather than fighting against each other. When Wendi and Ginger left home for a college a few hundred miles away, the whole family began to play *World of Warcraft* (2004), keeping in touch with each other and hanging out regularly in the virtual environment. Now Cheri is a grandmother of three, and this passion for games has been passed on from her and her husband through their children and into the grandchildren's generation. Ginger's daughter Anya and Kim's son Ethan are both under the age of ten. They partake in adventures and exploration led by their parents and grandparents as part of playing *Pokémon Go*, though given their ages, they do not play the game themselves. As is discussed below, the game presents a new opportunity for the entire family to play and interact with each other through the mixed-reality environment.

Before continuing, it is worth noting that there are several factors at work in this story that enabled intergenerational gaming to be so successful for this family. First, Cheri and Ken have held jobs involving computers and programming since the early eighties. Given their careers, they anticipated the importance of computers and technology and viewed it as a priority to expose their children to technology as early as possible, and they were financially able to do so. Indeed, Ken recalls buying the family's first home computer in 1984, a Zenith Z-160, and was one of the early users of AOL with Internet in their home in 1991. As mentioned above, their family has always held an early-adopter mindset, and thus they have been particularly receptive to new technologies and games. Moreover, Ken and Cheri made it a priority to purchase and give their children access to as many educational games and technologies as possible. *The Oregon Trail, Where in the World Is Carmen Sandiego?* (1985), and other various literacy, reading, and learning games were an important part of their children's early years.

Additionally, Ken and Cheri live in a fairly large and affluent suburb near a major metropolitan city. As is discussed in the introduction and elsewhere in this volume, *Pokémon Go* was built using data from Niantic's earlier game *Ingress* (2012). Relying heavily on user-created input from the player base of *Ingress* meant that areas like the ones where Cheri's family lived were extensively populated with Poké Stops, gyms, and other important features for successful gameplay. Thus, both in terms of their family culture and in relation to game mechanics, this family was ideally situated to have success with intergenerational gaming through *Pokémon Go*.

The Family That Plays Together

Pokémon Go, as a mixed-reality game based on a beloved franchise, requires many different streams of knowledge to successfully navigate. This provides fantastic opportunities for intergenerational gaming, as it invites children, parents, and grandparents to contribute their expertise and learn from each other in order to have a successful play experience. In doing so, the game achieves what many researchers see as the ideal for intergenerational gaming: creating a shared context across family members of different age groups and encouraging peer-to-peer mentoring between all family members. In this section, we explore how local knowledge, franchise knowledge, and technological expertise are all essential game elements that allow family players to act as mentors to each other in their gaming experience.

Pokémon Hunting in the Wilds of Suburbia

Knowledge of the local environment and means to successfully navigate it are essential to *Pokémon Go*. The game cannot be played from a static location, and Pokémon spawns are based on real-world geography in ways that matter to gameplay. Specific Pokémon can only be caught in certain areas (Water-type Pokémon near actual bodies of water, for example) and locations of interest in the game (for example, Poké Stops, which are needed to refill in-game supplies) are often based on real-world locations of interest: schools, churches, and places where groups of people generally congregate often show up in game as gyms, raids, and Poké Stops. Thus, to maintain a decent supply of Poké Balls and catch a variety of Pokémon, players will need to travel outside of their home.

Given the crucial nature of travel for the game, younger players will depend on their elders to help them travel to new places and to identify the locations of potential hubs of activity. In addition to the gyms and Poké Stops based on real-world places of interest, there are also sponsored Poké Stops at Starbucks coffee shops and Sprint stores. Families could certainly just leave their house and wander toward whatever Pokémon they happen to see, but the more a player knows about her local area, the more strategic she can be in her pursuit. For example, Tessa worked in downtown Dallas when the game launched and was familiar with Main Street Garden, a large park in downtown Dallas often used as a meeting place and local gathering spot during work days. The area is a hub of downtown life, filled with food trucks and people looking for a brief escape in the middle of their workday. When she began playing, she immediately decided to use this as a regular Pokémon hunting ground, suspecting its real-world prominence as a gathering spot for busy professionals would translate to some sort of in-game advantage. Sure enough, she found it was a great hunting ground and an easily accessible Poké Stop for her to maintain her supplies.

Cultural Knowledge and Sharing

While knowledge of the local area is most likely something grandparents and parents (rather than children) will possess, the culturally based knowledge of the Pokémon franchise is something any of the generations may draw on. Franchise knowledge can be incredibly helpful in navigating the game, either in predicting where to find specific Pokémon (as mentioned above based on type and geographic features) or in strategizing evolutions. The original 150 Pokémon continue to show up in multiple games/media and are heavily featured in *Pokémon Go*, meaning players with previous knowledge will have some advantage in their play experience. It may be easy to predict that Magikarp (a fish) is a Water-type Pokémon and will be found in creeks, lakes, and ponds, but Cheri recalled that she thought Slowpoke (a pink Water-type Pokémon) was a bear. While her daughter Ginger grew up watching the original series and playing many of the early games, Cheri had very little franchise knowledge at all. Without this knowledge, she had no idea either of Slowpoke's type or where to find it. Similarly, the basic mechanics of the game remain unchanged (weaken Pokémon, throw balls to capture, fight at gyms to progress, etc.). This existing franchise knowledge is incredibly helpful for new players, as *Pokémon Go* offers fairly minimal instruction through its interface. Likewise, as the story below demonstrates, there are a number of potentially unexpected evolutions of which players with cultural knowledge will have insight. It's important to note here that in the current version of the game (at the time of this writing), the Pokémon details screen displays an outline of what the Pokémon will evolve into, while at the time the story took place, that feature hadn't been implemented.

Cheri explained how she and her daughter Ginger combined their knowledge of the local area and Pokémon history to achieve one of the more time-consuming evolutions in the game, Magikarp into Gyarados:

> *Pokémon Go* was my first encounter with the world of Pokémon. As a newbie, I had no knowledge of the relationship between Pokémon and their environments nor of the various evolutions. One day, out of curiosity, I asked my daughter about the magnificent and extremely impressive Pokémon on the opening screen. Was it an evolved creature, or a rare find? I was surprised when she told me it was a Water Pokémon and it came from the lowly Magikarp. Once I knew what it came from and its environment, I tried to think of where could I find a Water Pokémon when I lived more than 200 miles from a large body of water. A nearby neighborhood contains a creek, and I wondered if it was large enough to be recognized by the game and house Magikarp. As I thought about the creek, I began to hope Magikarp were there. A portion of the creek was ringed by roadways; the roads were lightly traveled and there was plenty of room to pull over and park without impeding traffic. It would be a very easy and convenient trip if the Magikarp were there. Sure enough, after a quick drive over to the creek, the first Pokémon we encountered was a Magikarp!
>
> It now became a challenge to catch enough Magikarp to get to 400 candies! Our route along the creek became a daily trek for us; any simple outing or errand now involved a circuit around the creek—and we did indeed get our Gyarados!

As Cheri's story above demonstrates, without the cultural knowledge to know that Gyrados evolves from Magikarp, she might have had no idea how to ulti-

not launch with features supporting collaborative play. Cheri, Ginger, Tessa, and Ethan have found meaningful connections within the context of their family and local environment that have made this particular game such a useful interface for their family. For Ethan and Cheri, it has created a shared passion: Ethan's perception of the Pokémon as dinosaurs. For Cheri and her daughters, it added some enjoyment to the mundane business of running errands and gave them a new activity to do together.

For example, Cheri recalls the joy Ethan felt catching Pokémon with her:

When Ethan comes to visit, I always try to line up physical activities for him to do. One warm day, his mother and I decided to take him over to a large playground. He immediately ran off to explore and play on all the equipment. After a little while I thought I would open *Pokémon Go* to see if there were any interesting Pokémon nearby. A Totodile was in my nearby list, so I decided to see if I could find him as I was close to having enough Totodile candies to get the final evolution, the Feraligatr! I started walking down one of the paths to see which direction and how far it was. I hadn't gone very far when I heard Ethan calling me: "Grammi, Grammi! Where are you going?" I turned around and beckoned him. As he approached I showed him my phone and told him I was looking for a "baby dinosaur" (what he calls the Totodile). He excitedly asked if he could hold the phone and help me catch the dino. I said "of course," and we set off down the path.

We spent time slowly walking while Ethan explained the difference between dinosaurs and Godzilla to me, and that my Totodile would actually grow up to be a Godzilla. It was a very engaging conversation between just the two of us! I was so happy to share this time with him and listen to his ideas and opinions. We did find the "dinosaur," which he then captured. As we walked back to his mother, he excitedly ran to her, yelling, "Look what Grammi and I caught!" Ethan eagerly shared our adventure and the story of the Godzilla's capture with his mother. The rest of our time at the playground, Ethan kept asking if more Godzillas spawned, but none ever did.

I finally did get enough Totodile candies to evolve it, but I decided to wait. I wanted to let Ethan hit the evolve button and watch the transformation. He did so gleefully, and promptly had me rename my Feraligatr "Godzilla." Every time he comes to visit, he loves to check on his Godzilla. Eventually, I evolved a Croconaw and caught another Totodile. Ethan named them BigGodzilla and BabyGodzilla.

A year and a half after the game's launch, they still regularly head to Cheri's creek route to see what Pokémon have spawned and pull out their phones at any new location to look for potential additions to their collection. *Pokémon Go* did not fix anything that was wrong in their family, but it did provide new opportunities for interaction, connection, and sharing. In other words, the game was not corrective for these players, but it was transformative, and thus profoundly meaningful in shaping intergenerational relationships. While this family was perhaps more receptive to using this particular game as a tool for intergenerational gaming than others, they nonetheless demonstrate how games can create new opportunities for families to connect and interact.

REFERENCES

Althoff, T., White, R.W., & Horvitz, E. (2016). Influence of *Pokémon Go* on physical activity: Study and implications. *Journal of Medical Internet Research, 18*(12). DOI: 10.2196/jmir.6759.

Brauner, P., Valdez, A.C., Schroeder, U., & Ziefle, M. (2013). Increase physical fitness and create health awareness through exergames and gamification. In A. Holzinger, M. Ziefle, M. Hitz & M. Debevc (Eds.), *Human Factors in Computing and Informatics: Vol. 7946. SouthCHI 2013* (pp. 349–362). Berlin, Germany: Springer.

Chambers, D. (2012). "Wii play as a family": The rise in family-centred video gaming. *Leisure Studies, 31*(1), 69–82.

Comunello, F., & Mulargia, S. (2017). My grandpa and I "gotta catch 'em all." A research design on intergenerational gaming focusing on *Pokémon Go*. In J. Zhou & G. Salvendy (Eds.), *Human Aspects of IT for the Aged Population, Vol. 10298. Applications, Services and Contexts* (pp. 228–241). Cham, Switzerland: Springer.

Costa, L., & Veloso, A. (2016). Being (grand) players: Review of digital games and their potential to enhance intergenerational interactions. *Journal of Intergenerational Relationships, 14*(1), 43–59.

Coyne, S.M., Padilla-Walker, L.M., Stockdale, L., & Day, R.D. (2011). Game on ... girls: Associations between co-playing video games and adolescent behavioral and family outcomes. *Journal of Adolescent Health, 49*(2), 160–165.

De Schutter, B., & Abeele, V.V. (2015). Towards a gerontoludic manifesto. *Anthropology & Aging, 36*(2), 112–120.

Duggan, M. (2015, December 15). Gaming and gamers. *Pew Research Center*. Retrieved February 3, 2018, from http://www.pewinternet.org/2015/12/15/gaming-and-gamers/.

Entertainment Software Association. (2017). Essential facts about the computer and video game industry. *Entertainment Software Association*. Retrieved February 5, 2017 from http://www.theesa.com/wp-content/uploads/2017/09/EF2017_Design_FinalDigital.pdf.

Griffin, J. (2007). Relationship gaming and identity: Stephanie and Josh. In C.L. Selfe & G.E. Hawisher (Eds.), *Gaming lives in the twenty-first century: Literate connections* (pp. 133–142). New York: Palgrave MacMillan.

Hagestad, G.O., & Uhlenberg, P. (2005). The social separation of old and young: A root of ageism. *Journal of Social Issues, 61*(2), 343–360.

Jung, Y., Li, K.J., Janissa, N.S., Gladys, W.L.C., & Lee, K.M. (2009). Games for a better life: Effects of playing Wii games on the well-being of seniors in a long-term care facility. *Proceedings of the Sixth Australasian Conference on Interactive Entertainment, Australia* (article 5). doi: 10.1145/1746050.1746055.

Keogh, B. (2017). *Pokémon Go*, the novelty of nostalgia, and the ubiquity of the smartphone. *Mobile Media & Communication, 5*(1), 38–41.

Nardi, B.A. (2010). *My life as a night elf priest: An anthropological account of* World of Warcraft. Ann Arbor: University of Michigan Press.

Shaw, A. (2013). Rethinking game studies: A case study approach to video game play and identification. *Critical Studies in Media Communication, 30*(5), 347–361.

Sheffield, A., & Lin, L. (2013). Strengthening parent-child relationships through co-playing video games. In *IADIS International Conference on Cognition and Exploratory Learning in Digital Age (CELDA 2013), USA,* 429–431.

Takayoshi, P. (2007). Gender matters: Literacy, learning, and gaming in one American family. In C.L. Selfe & G.E. Hawisher (Eds.), *Gaming lives in the twenty-first century: Literate connections* (pp. 229–249). New York: Palgrave Macmillan.

Williams, D., Consalvo, M., Caplan, S., & Yee, N. (2009). Looking for gender: Gender roles and behaviors among online gamers. *Journal of Communication, 59*(4), 700–725.

Williams, D., Ducheneaut, N., Xiong, L., Zhang, Y., Yee, N., & Nickell, E. (2006). From tree house to barracks: The social life of guilds in *World of Warcraft*. *Games and Culture, 1*(4), 338–361.

Playing Alone, Together

Pokémon Go, *Public Mobility and Locational Privacy*

RYAN S. EANES *and*
CLAIRE Y. VAN DEN BROEK

In her 2011 book *Alone Together,* Sherry Turkle argued that technologies ranging from text messaging to anthropomorphic robots have fundamentally changed the ways in which we interact with each other on an intimate, interpersonal level. Turkle acknowledged that social media and other networking technologies were originally conceived as a means to stay tethered to other people, and she did not argue that technology is something bad that should be shunned or avoided entirely, given its ubiquity in modern life. Nevertheless, she did strongly caution that computer-mediated communication already appears to have left an indelible imprint on our interpersonal relationships. More specifically, Turkle argued that technologies, particularly those that are used as means "to control the intensity of our connections" (p. 13), can—and do—hinder, or even jeopardize, our abilities to develop and engage in deeply meaningful interactions with each other.

Pokémon Go, for better or worse, appears to fit into this category of technologies that exhibit the ability to connect disparate and unrelated individuals while simultaneously serving as a shielding mechanism between those very individuals. This fact, considered in conjunction with the sheer number of people that play the game—which, shortly after launch, boasted more peak daily active users than any other previous game (Allan, 2016)—make it an object worthy of scrutiny. This essay seeks to examine the paradoxical interpersonal effects generated by *Pokémon Go*: As the game ostensibly appears to remove or reduce communication barriers by encouraging more physical interaction with the real world, including other players, it also has the ability to generate a sort of interpersonal involvement shield that allows players to virtually isolate themselves, even when co-present others are in close proximity. Despite this seemingly problematic paradox, we also explore the ways in which Niantic has successfully moved players to explore the physical world while also employing strategies to generate a sense of loyalty and empathy among teammates.

Outside Together: Improving Quality of Life Through Gameplay

One of the most remarkable aspects of *Pokémon Go* has been its inarguable success in convincing its players to physically move—since, of course, this is a requirement for a gameworld that has been mapped to physically extant geographies. *Pokémon Go* cannot be played (at least in any particularly worthwhile way) while one is physically stationary; that is, locomotion is a requisite part of the game. Research has in fact confirmed significant increases in physical activity among players, not to mention hundreds of billions of steps taken by players as they track down their virtual quarries (Althoff, White, & Horvitz, 2016). Niantic has gone to significant lengths to discourage players from using vehicles; these have included setting speed limits that deactivate the ability to spin Poké Stops or hatch eggs while driving, and by adding an "I'm a passenger" dialog box, which ostensibly requires players to confirm that they are not driving. These limitations encourage players to physically walk, not just drive, though limited progress can be made in the game while standing still near a Poké Stop or driving slowly.

In the wake of *Pokémon Go*'s initial release, a wealth of tweets and articles appeared that praised *Pokémon Go* for its ability to get a range of people—young, old, sedentary, and active—outside and walking, and even more important, for its apparent positive effect on people who experience anxiety and depression, and for those looking specifically for an excuse or reason to get outside and make new connections (Grohol, 2016; MacDonald, 2016; Tateno et al., 2016; Yang & Liu, 2017). Various Twitter posts provide additional anecdotal evidence of the game's production of these types of effects:

- "#PokémonGO has changed me so much for the better in only a week. Dealing with BPD, depression & anxiety it has helped me get out of the house" [Lara, 2016]
- "#PokémonGO this is actually making me want to leave my room and interact with people finally after years of depression I love this so much" [Amy, 2016]
- "#PokémonGo has already been a better treatment for my depression than anything my doctor prescribed or therapist recommended" [Jesse, 2016]

These anecdotes skew overwhelmingly toward the positive regarding the quasi-therapeutic potential of *Pokémon Go*, yet no substantive evidence or research exists to prove that these effects are lasting, or that those who claimed to overcome their anxiety experienced any kind of clinically significant improvement. Nevertheless, interest in the potential of using augmented reality (AR) games like *Pokémon Go* as a social tool persists, with some researchers having suggested that such games could be "leveraged to create social opportunities for individuals who may struggle in this area" (Khalis & Mikami, 2018, p. 38). That is certainly a possibility, and anecdotal evidence supports this theory, yet this seems a bold assumption considering the fact that the study only showed a positive correlation between existing social competence and success in gameplay; it did not provide evidence that games like *Pokémon Go* can somehow teach or train one to *develop* greater social competence. Furthermore, the aforementioned study also found that those with social anxiety tend to feel self-conscious and may experience a fear of being negatively evaluated by those around them (Khalis & Mikami, 2018), suggesting that the game has limited use as an alternative form of treatment for anxiety. Since the game encourages but does not require social behavior, it is possible that those players who suffer from social anxiety may in fact *perceive* themselves as being more social thanks to their participation in the game, when in reality they are simply playing alone, in public.

Pokémon Go *as Sociopolitical Catalyst: The Challenge of Overcoming Apathy*

Whether or not *Pokémon Go* has any particular therapeutic value remains to be seen, but its perceived ability to catalyze physical movement through public spaces has been seized upon by a range of actors with varying degrees of success. During the 2016 presidential election, for example, candidate Hillary Clinton was widely mocked for her attempt to appeal to younger generations by saying she wanted her voters to "*Pokémon Go*-to-the-polls." Indeed, in a tongue-in-cheek article, *Business Insider* speculated whether Hillary was trying to get players to "help her take over the toughest gym of all: The White House" (Grebey, 2016, para. 1). In an even more bizarre twist of events, a story surfaced on CNN in late 2017 which placed *Pokémon Go* at the center of an election scandal that ultimately resulted in multiple indictments of Russian hackers for interfering in American politics (O'Sullivan & Byers, 2017). An investigation by CNN journalists uncovered how Russian agents posed as Black Lives Matter activists and launched a fake campaign titled "Don't Shoot Us" in an apparent attempt to stoke discord and inflame racial tensions. The campaign encouraged *Pokémon Go* players to seek out areas where incidents of police brutality had occurred, to catch and name Pokémon after victims of racial violence, and to then share images of these captures with the community through social media site Tumblr; Amazon gift cards were promised as incentives for these efforts. While it is unclear what the underlying aims of the campaign were, it was ultimately unsuccessful, suggesting that players are resistant to using the game to engage in (alleged) social or political movements, even when they could be paid for the effort. CNN's research indicated that very few *Pokémon Go* players attempted to enter this contest, and no violence seemed to have been stoked by the campaign.

Although this particular effort failed to mobilize young people to engage in an alleged social movement, *Pokémon Go* players have embraced the game's requirement that players go outside and explore, and perhaps even meet other players. It stands to reason that the dramatic increase in physical movement through public spaces by millions of concurrent users that *Pokémon Go* has generated should also create a concomitant increase in interpersonal interactions as a natural side effect. Indeed, Humphreys (2016) argued that *Pokémon Go* engenders a "sense of commonality among strangers" (p. 16). This "parochialization" process (Humphreys, 2010, para. 9) draws on the work of Lofland (1998), who argued that there exists a third parochial realm which is distinct from the public and private sphere. For example, consider

> a neighborhood, wherein those living have a sense of familiarity or commonality with others in the area. The sense of connection comes from the expectation of a shared experience having lived in the same area within the city or potentially knowing some of the same people [Humphreys & Llao, 2013, para. 6].

Pokémon Go overlays physical environments with a virtual dimension that is exclusively available to other players, which allows players to imagine themselves as part of a unique community within their neighborhood. Within this parochial sphere, trainers enjoy a sense of commonality and familiarity as they are jointly privy to a rich fauna of Pokémon and a collection of battlegrounds (gyms) that are only accessible to a select group of people with active *Pokémon Go* accounts who can mutually witness events. *Pokémon Go* functions almost as a subculture that pervades neighborhoods and creates a bond between players, yet is separate from the public sphere and only visible to those who are in the know.

The AR Revolution: Blending Real and Virtual Worlds

This social potential interestingly parallels the game's arguably revolutionary AR option, which seems to represent the largest mainstream exposure of smartphone users to this particular technological paradigm. For the unini-tiated, AR provides access to additional layers of information that are pegged to specific physical locations but that are otherwise invisible, such as virtual layers. (See also Tham and Smiles's essay in this book, in which they inves-tigated how *Pokémon Go* uses rhetorical transduction to create an experience that bridges digital and analog layers.) Information and items accessible via AR might be metaphorically likened to objects that were termed "out of phase" in the various *Star Trek* series; while the "thing" in question physically cohabitates in directional and dimensional terms with other "things," some unseen element prevents the physical overlap of these otherwise disparate and discrete entities. In other words, a fifth dimension (beyond length, width, depth, and time) is assumed, and AR provides access to this fifth dimension.

This dimension, which Heili, Xu and Crane identified as a form of the cognisphere in their essay of this book, has the power to mediate social inter-actions, yet they pointed out that "cognisphere-mediated human relationships may indeed be different from human relationships built on direct bodily inter-actions and can certainly disrupt intimacies among humans." These hybrid spaces offer new opportunities, yet they can simultaneously be limiting, espe-cially if we begin to think of them as real or allow them to replace more mean-ingful bodily interactions. In the case of *Pokémon Go*, we can see that the Pokémon are not real in the same way that a tree or a dog or a fence is real; you cannot touch a Pikachu, beyond tapping it on your phone's screen. Nev-ertheless, the AR interface provided by the smartphone allows one to see a Pikachu that has been programmed to appear at a specific time and place. It is overlaid onto the real world; the smartphone's otherwise accurate and straight-forward depiction of the individual's environment, drawn from the phone's camera, is augmented (hence the name) with this additional presence that can be interacted with via the game app. This encourages players to see the fifth dimension as real and significant, possibly to the exclusion of offline interac-tions if we overvalue that dimension, as Turkle (2011) warned in *Alone Together*.

The game's inclusion of AR tech is, again, arguably revolutionary. The *New York Times* noted, shortly following the release of the game, that its incorporation caught many off guard:

> Many technology companies thought A.R. might first take off through specialized business applications that, for example, allow architects to visualize finished building projects in situ. Instead, it took a game based on a beloved entertainment franchise from the mid–1990s in Japan to help the technology go mainstream [Wingfield & Isaac, 2016, para. 9].

Despite this initial enthusiasm, it would seem that an apparent minority of *Pokémon Go* users even use its AR functionality, according to an informal online survey of a convenience sample of players recruited via Reddit that we conducted in early 2018. The survey, which was posted to two Reddit communities relevant to *Pokémon Go* (/r/TheSilphRoad and /r/PokemonGO), was evaluated by the Washington College Institutional Review Board and found to be exempt from IRB review. 92 percent of the 1,657 respondents said that they rarely or never used the AR function, suggesting that this specific aspect of the game is not a significant driver of usage. Nevertheless, the game developers must be acknowledged for their efforts in nudging this relatively fledgling technology forward.

Why, though, might the majority of *Pokémon Go* players be inclined to disregard the game's relatively straightforward access to the AR world? The answer may in fact lie in the nature of the technology used to play the game. Assuming that the end user's device is a smartphone (though in some cases it may be a tablet), access is provided to the third realm offered by *Pokémon Go*; this realm also holds the potential to create a sense of community. Nevertheless, the device also holds the potential to serve as what might be called an *involvement shield* that enables or permits civil inattention, and that can be used as a means to exclude outsiders who coexist in the same public sphere but are nevertheless not part of the user's affinity group.

Locational Privacy: The Smartphone as Involvement Shield

To be more specific, the smartphone offers the ability to generate locational privacy, which requires a nuanced definition of privacy. Privacy is a problematic term simply because of its multiple definitions. However, the first definition for the word offered by the *Oxford English Dictionary* is a useful starting point: "The state or condition of being alone, undisturbed, or free from public attention, as a matter of choice or right; seclusion; freedom from interference or intrusion" (2007). This definition requires a bit of revision to more accurately describe locational privacy. While locational privacy does indeed demand being *undisturbed*, it does not require solitude or physical isolation. Rather, it is the state of being private in public, when one shuts out his or her surrounding environment. This state of being was perhaps first described by Simmel (1950) in his work "The Metropolis and Mental Life," which described the "blasé attitude" (p. 413) as a form of selective attention paid to specific stimuli. Simmel was describing an automatic phenomenon that develops in response to existence in an urban environment, full of countless distractions and demands for attention; because the human capacity to attend to stimuli is limited, the blasé attitude acts as a sort of filter that helps us to direct our limited attentional resources to the most important elements in our immediate environments.

Although this blasé attitude can and does emerge unconsciously/automatically as a consequence of day-to-day existence within a bustling environment, this does not mean that we are unable to direct our attentional resources to specific stimuli at will. On the contrary, there is a long human history of "managing and controlling our interactions" with the people around us and the places we inhabit using "interfaces" (de Souza e Silva & Frith, 2012, p. 6), defined by de Souza e Silva and Frith in their foundational work *Mobile Interfaces in Public Spaces* as "something that is between two other parts or systems [that] helps them communicate or interact with each other" (pp. 1–2). In other words, "something" (in this case, the phone) serves as a metaphorical shield against unwanted interactions with others.

While today the smartphone can be regarded as the interface of choice for those who seek to establish this type of privacy, the phenomenon is nothing new. An interface need not be electronic in nature; consider, for example, the commute of an average American worker. Today one is likely to see lots of earbuds and headphones being used aboard any given subway car or bus; certainly these count as interfaces, as they allow the commuter to escape into his or her own personal soundscape and tune out the presence of strangers who are mere feet (or less) away. But no less likely to be present in abundance are non-electronic interfaces, including newspapers, magazines, and books; these offer the same benefits and have been employed for many decades in precisely the same manner. Decorum and unspoken social covenants dictate that one should not interrupt someone who is quietly reading a book, even if they are in an otherwise public place; likewise, we have learned that it is similarly impolite to interrupt someone who is absorbed with some activity on his or her smartphone. In their essay on "Addiction and the Apocalypse" in this collection, Cole and Pulos noted the way *Pokémon Go* players (or anyone deeply engaged in something on their smartphone) are often rhetorically described like zombies, roaming the public sphere as "non-conscious, nonagentic moving bodies," consumed by technology. While hyperbolic, this characterization points to concerns that players are unapproachable and not fully present in the public sphere; they have created a private space from which others are excluded, enabled by the smartphone which functions as an involvement shield. Technology is not solely responsible for producing these zombies, though; as mentioned before, a book or newspaper can create a similar barrier. This array of interfaces, regardless of whether they are digital or analog, empower the individual with the ability to *be private in public*—in other words, locational privacy can be generated by deploying some form of interface that functions as a barrier between the individual and his or her immediate environment.

While the possible deployment of the game as a means of self-isolation is intriguing, this does not appear to be a primary motivating factor for most players. Our aforementioned survey of *Pokémon Go* players revealed that more than 14 percent of the 1,657 respondents use the game as a way to avoid interacting with other people; even if avoidance of others is not the goal, 61 percent nevertheless said that they typically play the game alone. This statistic, on its face, is peculiar, given that *Pokémon Go* seems to hold the posture of ostensibly being a social game (that is, many of its mechanics rely on inter-action between multiple players and cooperation between teams). This results in a strange tension; the smartphone, a highly individualized/personal instru-ment, serves as an interface that can produce a sense of locational privacy, while the game simultaneously promotes interaction with teammates to one degree or another. This conglomeration of factors has produced what Mey-rowitz (1985) described as "a very discernible rearrangement of the social stages on which we play our roles … [causing] a resulting change in our sense of 'appropriate behavior'" (p. 4). Playing the game with the co-present other requires a binary choice be made: interaction via the interface alone (that is, remaining in a private bubble), or interaction that is not mediated via the interface (that is, in-person, physical interaction).

Group Dynamics: Encouraging Interaction Through Competition

While the smartphone empowers users to generate this form of privacy and therefore avoid interaction with other players, there are plenty of indi-viduals who *do* choose to interact with others, though whether these inter-actions tend to produce anything that might be considered a meaningful interpersonal relationship (that is, something that extends beyond a passing acquaintanceship) is something that we probed in our player survey. The production of such relationships would give us some sense of whether Niantic has in fact succeeded in creating the parochial community that Humphreys (2016) ascribes to *Pokémon Go*. The game's requirement that one join a team upon accumulating enough experience points (XP) to reach Level 5 reinforces the perception that team- or relationship-building is implicitly expected of players. It should be noted, however, that this forced decision seems to differ from the rules of the preexisting Pokémon gaming universe. While the orig-inal games typically pitted *individual* Pokémon trainers against each other, Niantic abandoned this one-on-one approach in favor of a team-based archi-tecture more reflective of the various Pokémon anime and TV series. Players are required to select from one of three options, each with its own philosophy described:

- **Team Instinct** is represented by the color yellow, and its leader, Spark, tells players that "Pokémon are creatures with excellent intuition" [Niantic, 2018]. Spark encourages his team to trust their instincts.

- Candela is the leader for the red faction, **Team Valor**, which emphasizes the importance of strength and training as the key to a trainer's success.
- The most widely chosen team is **Team Mystic**, led by Blanche and represented by the color blue, which reveres wisdom and calm analysis.

Our survey suggested that Mystic is the most popular team by a large margin, accounting for 47.4 percent of players who responded. We were unable to corroborate these numbers directly against the limited game statistics that Niantic (2018) periodically releases, but this number seems fairly close to other estimates such as the Adobe Digital Index analysis of mentions of *Pokémon Go* teams on social media. This analysis estimated the percentage of Mystic players worldwide to be 43 percent (Martin, 2016), roughly in line with our result.

The inclusion of descriptive mythologies and various characteristic traits that aim to differentiate each of the three teams beyond a simple color code clearly implies that the game intends for players to select teams that reflect their individual value systems. Data from our survey, however, suggest that this is not in fact the manner by which most players choose which team to join. When survey participants were asked why they chose a certain team, many respondents noted that they simply liked the team's color, that they liked the legendary Pokémon bird associated with that color, or that they chose a team that their friends had already joined. Only a handful of respondents mentioned some affinity toward the given team descriptions or characteristics.

Beyond color preference, there may be an even more banal reason why so many players choose to join Team Mystic: People may simply be compromising. Consumer behavior researchers have found that when individuals are uncertain what decision to make, they will oftentimes *satisfice*, a portmanteau of satisfy and suffice coined by economist Herbert Simon ("Herbert Simon," 2009, para. 1). In other words, they compromise and choose a good-enough option that is somewhere between the extremes. In this case, when players are prompted to pick a team, they may be instinctively or unconsciously selecting Mystic—the team option that is literally displayed between Valor and Instinct—simply because it visually appears as a kind of middle ground (Fottrell, 2016). All this suggests that Niantic's attempt to draw players together through shared characteristics or goals was largely unsuccessful, eroding (at least partially) the implication that the game serves as a genuine effort to build a true community in any meaningful interpersonal sense.

While the team dynamic is not particularly relevant to advancement in the game in terms of leveling up, we could postulate that Niantic's attempt to exploit a sense of competition between groups nevertheless does serve an important function. If players were to simply accumulate Pokémon by themselves, completing no other tasks or objectives, they might quickly become bored with the game. By creating a sense of competition and completion (e.g., through filling one's Pokédex or defeating gyms held by other teams), Niantic has created a number of moving targets that players are able to pursue, either on behalf of themselves or their team. The sense of suspense that comes from working toward these constantly evolving goals, which requires competing against and cooperating with one another, is a possible reason for the visibility of occasional external displays of team loyalty (e.g., bumper stickers, t-shirts).

In order to explain this, consider Breithaupt's (2012) model of empathy in which competition plays a key factor in generating interest in other people. As an example, Breithaupt examined a soccer game:

> Whoever observes a game without specific self-interest in the outcome can certainly appreciate the performances. However, it often only becomes exciting when he or she has decided for a team and from then on lives or dies with its players. Only then can the events of the game become experienceable, only then can the attempted shot become a second of horror or a moment of hope. Every foul also becomes an emotional event, because one either feels pain with the player and curses the fouling opponent, or dismisses the player rolling around on the ground as a great melodramatic actor but no soccer player [p. 87].

In other words, joining a team, even when we have no particular initial predisposition towards it, opens the floodgates for empathy and antipathy, and it allows participants to create alliances with each other over time that allow the possibility of the development of empathy. That empathy in turn can convert apathy into interest; as a result, the game can germinate into something with a much stronger level of personal meaning and importance.

Bolstering this development of empathy is Niantic's exploitation of the minimal group paradigm (Tajfel, 1970), which suggests that even the most minimal and seemingly arbitrary distinctions between groups can be enough for members to feel animosity toward the other group and favoritism toward members of one's own group. Indeed, Mlodinow (2012) noted that there is no minimal requirement

> necessary for a person to feel a kinship with an in-group. … It is not necessary for you to share any attitudes or traits with your fellow group members, or even for you to have met the other group members. It is the simple act of knowing that you belong to a group that triggers your in-group affinity [p. 171].

Niantic makes use of this concept by creating superficial and largely arbitrary distinctions between groups: a color, a superficial declaration of team philosophy, a mascot, and not much else. Simply choosing one of three teams is sufficient to conjure an alliance between trainers. The knowledge that one is "Team Valor," for example, can provide a sense of identity within the game that makes the generic color-coded avatars seem more like individuals who belong to a very real community of other Team Valor players. Thus, the team dynamic, even if it has limited significance in terms of gameplay, nevertheless adds an additional layer of social meaning to the game, and it may reduce player attrition over time due to apathy. The popularity of Facebook groups and Discord chat channels, many of which are dedicated to specific teams, attests to players' willingness to move beyond the game to connect with fellow team members, to organize raids or meetups, and to share knowledge of rare Pokémon spawns.

Indeed, our survey participants overwhelmingly stated that they care about their team allegiances; many told us that they joined team-based social media groups after making their choices. One participant emphasized a distinct sense of "us versus them" when they noted that "[t]here is very high competition for control in my area, [sic] we do not get along with other teams" (Survey respondent #362, 2018). This tribal division is perhaps encouraged in part by *Pokémon Go* Discord chat channels that are widely used for coordinating play, which require players to declare their allegiance to a specific team before access is granted. This suggests that a desire for team coordination and bonding motivates a large part of the socialization that can occur outside of the application.

Joining a team is not the only component of the game that has the potential to produce interpersonal interactions and potential connections with other players. Seemingly in an effort to encourage more collaborative play between teams, Niantic introduced legendary raids, which usually require a minimum of four or five players, and which reward team loyalty to a certain extent; both the team that controls the gym housing the raid and the team that does the most damage to the legendary boss are awarded more chances to potentially catch the rare Pokémon as a bonus once it has been defeated. However, in order to defeat the legendary boss in the first place, players must work together in a single group regardless of team affiliation. Nevertheless, as these raids attract larger groups, players will sometimes split up by team to increase the number of bonus balls they will receive. To illustrate, an anecdotal story appeared on Reddit's /r/TheSilphRoad in September 2017 that described a group of Mystic players who went to great lengths to ensure that a gym hosting a particular raid would be controlled by Mystic at spawn time. Through an elaborate system set up via Discord, the group was able to maintain control of this particular gym for eight hours—a highly unusual feat—despite sustained and coordinated attacks by other teams. The accomplishment was celebrated by some players, while others characterized it as a waste of time. The original poster of the story criticized those who did not respect their effort, noting that "I would never dedicate years of training to climb Mount Everest but I still respect that someone else did" (Ishr5913, 2017, para. 17). This characterization suggests that at least some members of the team felt the distinct sense that this was a meaningful accomplishment that could be likened, at least metaphorically, to a physical feat of strength.

Loyalty is clearly evident in anecdotes such as this one, and it was also evident from our poll results: 73.1 percent of respondents ranked their team loyalty as 7 out of 10 or higher, although many explained that they chose their team because of friends who were already part of that same team. This suggests that this seemingly strong sense of loyalty may in fact have more to do with pre-existing friendships than any in-game competitive element. Furthermore, other comments from respondents suggested that this sense of loyalty is in fact a reflection of the potential individual gains that a team affiliation might offer to a single player—that is, loyalty functions primarily as a game mechanic that can benefit players materially while demanding minimal emotional or social investment. One statement from a survey respondent distinctly illustrates this possibility: "I love my team and will fight for them every single day, but I also enjoy players from other teams … and wouldn't side with someone just because they are mystic [*sic*] instead of valor [*sic*]" (Survey respondent #504, 2018). Perhaps the relatively underwhelming team dynamics of *Pokémon Go* simply fail to ignite the same sorts of passion that other stronger senses of team pride can produce (consider the infamous passion displayed by Green Bay Packers football fans, for example, who routinely wear "cheese head" hats to support their team).

Loyalty to one's team aside, raids also ostensibly encourage intermingling and interaction with other players while gathered together in a relatively small area, especially since some Pokémon, such as legendaries and Absol, were only accessible through raids until the quest system was introduced in April 2018. Therefore, we asked our survey participants how frequently they engage with others at raids, since our personal experience as players has been mixed. It is not uncommon to encounter familiar faces at raids in our respective neighborhoods; a casual chat with these acquaintances is not out of the norm, either, but we have also often observed players sitting in their cars while participating in the raid or standing at a distance without communicating with any other group members, even as we were all nevertheless working together to defeat a difficult raid boss.

We participated in one raid in downtown Santiago, Chile, in December 2017, that offers a stark illustration of this type of private-in-public participation. We showed up minutes before the start time of a legendary raid and wondered whether anyone else would be joining us. No group had formed as far as we could see. Yet the moment the raid opened, we watched in amazement as the lobby filled up with 20 players (the maximum number allowed) and a second lobby opened. We joined the second one and completed the raid with 16 other people. While some of those players may have in fact been spoofers playing from a remote location, closer scrutiny of our urban surroundings during the raid revealed at least a dozen people within close range tapping away on their phones, clearly engaged with the game. We did not witness a single one speaking to any other player, and once the raid finished, the players walked away without even the usual casual farewells that we had become accustomed to hearing in smaller towns. Given our informal observations over the months, our survey question about the frequency with which players engage with others at raids or events yielded mixed results, just as we expected. 16.2 percent of respondents said they rarely or never engage with others, and 11.5 percent stated that they do so less than half of the time. Approximately half of respondents said they always or almost always engage with others. This matched up with our experiences at most raids, where a majority typically engage in at least superficial communication, while one out of every three or four players will stay in their cars or try and remain inconspicuous—a minority, to be sure, but still a notable number.

Casual and informal connections between players, then, appear to be a norm, but certainly there must be stronger ties forming in some cases. When asked an open-ended question about staying in touch with others, a majority of our survey respondents indicated that they do not exchange information with other players. This echoes the findings from studies of other social games as well. For example, one study of massively multiplayer online role-playing games (MMORPGs) found that these games have the power to positively influence gamers' online bonding social capital, but there is no significant effect on offline social capital (Zhong, 2011). Another found that MMORPGs like *World of Warcraft* (2004) offer an environment in which players experience less loneliness than they do in the real world, but the study did not identify any positive effects on offline loneliness or sociability (Martončik & Lokša, 2016). Another study noted that "obsessive" players of social games tend to refer to other players as friends more frequently, but those friendships prove superficial in terms of emotional support, and these people have fewer satisfying offline friendships as well (Utz, Jonas, & Tonkens, 2012, p. 83). Nevertheless, our survey reported that a significant minority—approximately 10 percent—stay in touch with other players on a daily basis, that close friendships have developed with others, that other players have become like a second family, or even that they met a sexual partner during raids.

The range of interpersonal associations seen among *Pokémon Go* players does not appear dependent on the nature of the real-world environment in which the players interact, according to our informal survey. A chi-square test of independence conducted between likelihood of interacting with others and local population (i.e., large city of 50,000+, small city or suburb of 2,500 to 50,000, or rural area of less than 2,500) revealed no significant association between the variables: $\chi^2(6) = 5.060$, $p = 0.536$. *Pokémon Go* thus has the capacity to create a sense of a parochial community regardless of the population density of one's immediate area, yet the game does not require it, and nearly a third of players typically play "alone, together" even if they attend raids.

Conclusion

As our informal survey specifically targeted active *Pokémon Go* communities on Reddit (/r/TheSilphRoad and /r/PokemonGO), it stands to reason that less active players or those not as engaged on social media may be even more likely to play alone. This is likely all the more true for those who do not participate in raids and who only catch Pokémon, which is a solitary endeavor that requires no interaction between players, even though it is done in public view. Despite the enthusiasm for raid coordination and high team loyalty ratings, when asked how players typically play *Pokémon Go*, 61 percent confirmed that they do so alone, and those who indicated that they played with one or two other people often cited that they played with their partners or friends they already knew. This suggests that while many players expect to interact with other players or even enjoy such interactions, few of these connections ever develop into significantly meaningful relationships. This hypothesis is further bolstered by the fact that team dynamics play a relatively limited role in the game as described previously—they are mainly relevant to gym control and the outcome of group raids, and not much else. An individual player catching Pokémon in the wild is not particularly affected by their choice of team, and not all players play competitively with others via the gym system. Indeed, a player could potentially reach the maximum level without any interaction with other team members or competitors.

For more social or competitive players who do place Pokémon in gyms, their choice of team has an almost abstract effect on their choices: They can defeat and flip a gym held by a different team, or they can deposit a Pokémon from their collection in order to join one held by their own team, assuming it is not at capacity. Yet a battle in a gym is typically done alone (though two players of the same team can defeat a Pokémon faster), and beyond seeing the username associated with a Pokémon, there is no sort of profile-building capability beyond basic customization of one's avatar. Players cannot fight one another in real time, and the game does not offer an official channel for communication through which players can coordinate, though the third-party application Discord has largely filled that gap; this lack of inter-player communication within the game offers an opportunity for dynamic, somewhat unpredictable gameplay that still allows the player a sense of privacy in public, particularly for those who prefer solitary play. *Pokémon Go* thus differs greatly from many MMORPGs in which teams battle each other directly and frequently communicate with each other via built-in chat functionalities.

Pokémon Go's various shortcomings as a generator of sociality make it abundantly clear that there is no particular reason why the game can't also be used as a generator of locational privacy, and yet our survey results did not suggest that the game is used for such a deliberate purpose in any widespread fashion. However, the private-in-public nature of how many play the game *has* in fact produced a strange opacity between physically co-present players who might literally be sitting next to each other, particularly in urban settings, where interaction with other individuals is essentially inevitable. Time will tell if these trends will change, but for the foreseeable future, it seems that most *Pokémon Go* players will continue to play the game alone, together.

REFERENCES

Allan, R. (2016, December 7). *Pokémon GO* usage statistics say it's the most popular mobile game in U.S. history. *Medium*. Retrieved from https://medium.com/@sm_app_intel/pok%C3%A9mon-go-usage-statistics-say-its-the-most-popular-mobile-game-in-u-s-history-ea09ea2bf6df.

Althoff, T., White, R.W., & Horvitz, E. (2016). Influence of *Pokémon Go* on physical activity: Study and implications. *Journal of Medical Internet Research, 18*(12), e315. doi:10.2196/jmir.6759.

Amy [Amyxplier]. (2016, July 10). #PokémonGO this is actually making me want to leave my room and interact with people finally after years of depression I love this so much. Retrieved from https://twitter.com/amyxplier/status/752266024062480386.

Breithaupt, F. (2012). A three-person model of empathy. *Emotion Review, 4*(1), 84–91. https://doi.org/10.1177/1754073911421375.

Cole, K.L., & Pulos, A. (2018). Addiction and the apocalypse: The pathology of *Pokémon Go*. In Henthorn, A. Kulak, K. Purzycki & S. Vie (Eds.), in this volume.

de Souza e Silva, A., & Frith, J. (2012). *Mobile interfaces in public spaces: Locational privacy, control, and urban sociability*. New York: Routledge.

Fottrell, Q. (2016, July 31). On *Pokémon Go*, why so many people are choosing Team Mystic. *MarketWatch*. Retrieved from https://www.marketwatch.com/story/on-pokemon-go-why-so-many-people-are-choosing-team-mystic-2016–07–13.

Grebey, J. (2016, July 14). Hillary Clinton wants people to "*Pokemon-Go*-to the polls." *Business Insider*. Retrieved from http://www.businessinsider.com/hillary-clinton-wants-people-to-pokemon-go-to-the-polls-2016–7.

Grohol, J. (2016, July 12). *Pokémon Go* reportedly helping people's mental health, depression. *Psych Central*. Retrieved from https://psychcentral.com/blog/Pokemon-go-reportedly-helping-peoples-mental-health-depression/.

Heili, W., Xu, C., & Crane, N.J. (2018). *Pokémon Go*, cyborgs, and placemaking: Challenging digital-physical divide. In J. Henthorn, A. Kulak, K. Purzycki & S. Vie (Eds.), in this volume.

"Herbert Simon." (2009, March 20). *The Economist*. Retrieved from https://www.economist.com/node/13350892.

Humphreys, L. (2016). Involvement shield or social catalyst: Thoughts on sociospatial practice of *Pokémon GO*. *Mobile Media and Communication, 5*(1), 15–19. doi:10.1177/2050157916677864.

Humphreys, L., & Liao, T. (2013). Foursquare and the parochialization of public space. *First Monday, 18*(11). Retrieved from http://firstmonday.org/ojs/index.php/fm/article/view/4966/3796.

Ishr5913. (2017, September 23). My EX Raid Story: How 10 Mystics held off a combined Valor/Instinct attack for 4 hours, and why active gym defense represents the culmination of everything we have built and learned so far. *Reddit*. Retrieved from https://www.reddit.com/r/TheSilphRoad/comments/71yfcz/my_ex_raid_story_how_10_mystics_held_off_a/.

Jesse [Yourboy_jesse]. (2016, July 10). #PokémonGo has already been a better treatment for my depression than anything my doctor prescribed or therapist recommended. Retrieved from https://twitter.com/yourboy_jesse/status/752314346852589569.

Khalis, A., & Mikami, A.Y. (2018). Who's gotta catch 'em all?: Individual differences in *Pokémon Go* gameplay behaviors. *Personality and Individual Differences, 124*, 35–38. https://doi.org/10.1016/j.paid.2017.11.049.

Lara [38Violetqueen]. (2016, July 11). #PokémonGO has changed me so much for the better in only a week. Dealing with BPD, depression& anxiety it has helped me get out of the house. Retrieved from https://twitter.com/38Violetqueen/status/752488848983109632.

Lofland, L.H. (1998). *The public realm: Exploring the city's quintessential social territory*. New York: Aldine De Gruyter.

MacDonald, F. (2016, July 12). *Pokémon Go* is reportedly helping people with their depression. *Science Alert*. Retrieved from https://www.sciencealert.com/pokemon-go-is-reportedly-helping-people-with-their-depression.

Martin, J. (2016). *Pokémon Go*: Meaningless obsession or augmented reality catalyst? *Adobe Blog*. Retrieved from https://blogs.adobe.com/digitalmarketing/mobile/Pokémon-go-meaningless-obsession-augmented-reality-catalyst/.

Martončik, M., & Lokša, J. (2016). Do World of Warcraft (MMORPG) players experience less loneliness and social anxiety in online world (virtual environment) than in real world (offline)? *Computers in Human Behavior, 56*, 127–134. https://doi.org/10.1016/j.chb.2015.11.035.

Meyrowitz, J. (1985). *No sense of place: The impact of electronic media on social behavior*. New York: Oxford University Press.

Mlodinow, L. (2012). *Subliminal: How your unconscious mind rules your behavior*. New York: Pantheon.

O'Sullivan, D., & Byers, D. (2017, October 13). Exclusive: Even *Pokémon Go* used by extensive Russian-linked meddling effort. *CNNMoney*. Retrieved from http://money.cnn.com/2017/10/12/media/dont-shoot-us-russia-Pokemon-go/index.html.

"Privacy." (2007). In *Oxford English dictionary online* (3rd ed.). Retrieved from http://www.oed.com/view/Entry/151596.

Simmel, G. (1950). *The sociology of Georg Simmel* (K.H. Wolff, Trans.). Glencoe, IL: Free Press.

Tajfel, H. (1970). Experiments in intergroup discrimination. *Scientific American, 223*(5), 96–102. Retrieved from https://www.jstor.org/stable/24927662.

Tateno, M., Skokauskas, N., Kato, T.A., Teo, A.R., & Guerrero, A.P.S. (2016). New game software (*Pokémon Go*) may help youth with severe social withdrawal, hikikomori. *Psychiatry Research, 246*, 848–849. https://doi.org/10.1016/j.psychres.2016.10.038.

Tham, J., & Smiles, D. (2018). Rhetorical augmentation: Public play, place, and persuasion in *Pokémon Go*. In J. Henthorn, A. Kulak, K. Purzycki & S. Vie (Eds.), in this volume.

Turkle, S. (2011). *Alone together: Why we expect more from technology and less from each other*. New York: Basic.

Utz, S., Jonas, K.J., & Tonkens, E. (2012). Effects of passion for massively multiplayer online role-playing games on interpersonal relationships. *Journal of Media Psychology, 24*(2), 77–86. doi:10.1027/1864–1105/a000066.

Wingfield, N., & Isaac, M. (2016, July 11). *Pokémon Go* brings augmented reality to a mass audience. *New York Times*. Retrieved from https://www.nytimes.com/2016/07/12/technology/pokemon-go-brings-augmented-reality-to-a-mass-audience.html.

Yang, C.-C., & Liu, D. (2017). Motives matter: Motives for playing *Pokémon Go* and implications for well-being. *Cyberpsychology, Behavior, and Social Networking, 20*(1), 52–57. https://doi.org/10.1089/cyber.2016.0562.

Zhong, Z.-J. (2011). The effects of collective MMORPG (Massively Multiplayer Online Role-Playing Games) play on gamers' online and offline social capital. *Computers in Human Behavior, 27*(6), 2352–2363. https://doi.org/10.1016/j.chb.2011.07.014.

The World's Most Popular Fitness App

Jamie Henthorn

Pokémon Go launched in North America in July 2016, which happened to be one of the hottest summers on record. Despite an overwhelmingly popular launch that led to server crashes, login errors, and city parks being inundated with players, the augmented reality game attracted millions outside in search of wandering Gengars and Jigglypuffs. Players used their phones to find Poké Stops and gyms, often finding themselves veering outside of their routine paths through their own neighborhoods. Within the first month of the game's release, a host of articles and memes discussed, praised, and critiqued the app as a catalyst for exercise. In many ways, this makes sense. The game uses algorithms built into its mechanics, significantly a mechanism that restricts a player from collecting items from Poké Stops if they are going more than 25 miles per hour. As such, players must walk, run, bike, or scooter to play the game. While *Pokémon Go* is referred to culturally as a fitness app, it certainly doesn't fit squarely in with other fitness apps either in use or intention. In fact, the application does a great job of highlighting a population of casual athletes that in many ways reflect casual gamers.

This essay contextualizes *Pokémon Go* in a history of fitness, which gained popularity as a leisure activity in the 20th century. Casual fitness works subversively in many ways when stacked against contemporary constructions of fitness leisure time. By this I mean that 21st-century cultural narratives encourage contemporary citizens to capitalize on their leisure time. *Pokémon Go* instead delights in a relatively inefficient use of free time, which is one reason both for the game's rise in popularity and its ability to sustain the player community two years after its release. *Pokémon Go* as a fitness app is important to study for the opportunity to examine a demographic that is often ignored by the larger fitness community, even though this community frequently participates in fitness activities by using and purchasing apps, gym memberships, and athleisure wear. Looking at tertiary audiences for fitness media helps us better imagine future avenues for fitness communication. Throughout this essay, I largely compare *Pokémon Go* play to running because of running's rise over the 20th century as a dominant sport and because the running revolution paved the way for our current mindset on the use of our local neighborhoods and public spaces (even city centers) as places for personal fitness. While the majority of *Pokémon Go* players may not run while playing, these athletes have made *Pokémon Go* and augmented reality (AR) more culturally acceptable.

A Modern History of Leisure

Pokémon Go is meant to be played outside and encourages players to move distances. Poké Stops and gyms are spread across public spaces to encourage both access and movement. Niantic's crackdown on any ancillary apps that help players find specific Pokémon encourages a practice of happenstance where players wander through public areas and remap familiar spaces over and again as Pokémon nests (spaces where multiples of the same Pokémon are frequently seen) move with app updates. The algorithm for mapping, though, is meant to be kept from the user and players must remember this information and/or share it in public social media groups like those on Facebook and Discord. The outdoor-ness of the game is significant for a number of reasons, and *Pokémon Go* fits nicely into trends across the 20th and 21st centuries that promoted fitness leisure. The app has a very specific understanding of what we as a culture mean by fitness as an embedded practice of our everyday lives, a notion that increased in popularity over the 20th century. As more jobs across the world have moved from being labor-heavy to service-heavy, the expectation has been that individuals should privilege fitness activities during their leisure time.

Before the 20th century, fitness as leisure tended to be done by rather privileged classes because most people expended a lot of energy in their jobs. Running was even a job one could perform, usually as a messenger or as an employed athlete. At this time, runners and walkers were a spectacle that individuals paid money to see or gamble on, including the competitive walkers of the late 19th century. For women, domestic work was also much more physically demanding than it is today. Additionally, until the late 1950s and early 1960s, one's body type was seen as fixed, and individuals were more likely to alter their silhouettes through the clothing they wore, most obviously through the use of corsets. Fashion changes in the 50s and 60s changed perspective. Clothes with less structure that exposed more skin meant that women were expected to change their bodies to match contemporary fashions (McKenzie, 2013, pp. 62–63). As such, the idea of using fitness to attain an ideal body type is just a little over 50 years old. Combined with changes in labor, the malleable figure has significantly changed the fitness market.

State promotion of physical fitness started at the end of the 19th century but was further encouraged in the 20th century through national institutions. For instance, the United States further developed youth physical fitness programs to prepare young men for military service during the First World War (Cervantes, 2010, p. 116). Physical education became an academic discipline in the same way that English or algebra did, and degrees in recreation studies developed in the 20th century. Through the state's participation in physical education, fitness became a way to maintain good citizenship. Rampant unemployment also meant cheaper outdoor athleisure activities started to overtake gymnastics during the Great Depression. This marks a shift away from fitness as art or performance to fitness as part of a healthy civic lifestyle. Creating places where citizens of all ages could be involved in physical activity became a state priority; parks and recreation centers became important both to preserve nature and to counteract "the neurosis surrounding urbanization, industrialization, the break-up of traditional society and the presentation of relevance, competence and credibility in the self" (Rojek, 2010, p. 86). These parks and recreation centers "expanded, with more jobs for leisure and recreation graduates and eventually, more demand for university-level training in these fields" (Rojek, 2010, p. 54).

Leisure as state-sponsored physical fitness developed a market for fitness, setting a foundation for the 20th-century cultural practices that surrounded leisure. These systems resulted in a jogging and fitness revolution in the United States and Europe, and the benefits of jogging included fighting cardiovascular disease, obesity, and depression. The latter half of the 20th century saw ever-increasing numbers of individuals working in sedentary fields, developing depression and neurosis linked with affluent living. Jogging got people active and outside and experiencing public neighborhood spaces in new ways. Gotaas (2009) noted that a new running class "all knew the roads but now they were trying them without wheels and engines and discovering that everything felt completely different when travelling on foot" (p. 259). Joggers' visibility on the road helped to promote the sport and set our expectations for individuals using a variety of public spaces for exercise. Running likewise paved the way for the idea that adults should have fitness regimens and healthy hobbies.

Public fitness practices have regularly come into conflict with expected uses of public spaces. Lefebvre (1991) spoke of these as representational spaces that "need obey no rules of consistency or cohesiveness. Redolent with imaginary and symbolic elements, they have their source in history—in the history of a people as well as the history of each individual belonging to that people" (p. 41). In essence, spaces are connected to cultural expectations for use. For example, it is challenging to discuss public fitness and not single out women because their bodies have always been more closely policed. Women have been fighting this public narrative through much of the 19th, 20th, and 21st centuries. The question of adult fitness comes down to public spaces, which have often been points of conflict and contest for women. Sometimes the spatial barriers that exist are explicit, like restricting women from gym memberships, but these barriers can also be implicit.

Victorian women were the precursors of such conversations on public exercise, creating their own imaginary and symbolic spaces. In the 1800s, women were thought to be "morally fit" but to lack the strength, personality, and constitution to participate in sports and fitness into adulthood. Women were encouraged to play croquet (Gregg & Gregg, 2017) and other sports that didn't require endurance or lung capacity. These misconceptions about women's abilities were reinforced by the dress of the time, which did not encourage movement or breathing. Fashion has always been a gateway to women's fitness participation, and women's clothing has historically been designed to restrict movement for aesthetic and/or propriety reasons. In the 1800s, corsets and long skirts kept women from biking and hiking. Seeing a market, several companies created looser-fitting corsets (and in the future, the sports bra), allowing women to see themselves as athletes (Rosoff, 2006, p. 63). These technological innovations asked us to reconsider the body in space and also normalized fitness practice in community spaces. They have also helped to pave the way for a fitness market that now includes fitness wear for all genders as well as ever-expanding lines of digital technology that track and analyze individual workouts.

Since the latter half of the 20th century, running has fallen under the purview of late capital. Neoliberal running has been subject to the same market trends seen in the cultural shift toward late capital markets, which place obligation and risk on the individual, encouraging them to be entrepreneurial in all aspects of life. Leisure is adopted as a culturally moral value and physical fitness shifted from a government-provided right to a collection of moral choices and personal risk management (Lavrence & Lozanski, 2014, p. 80; Ouellette, 2014, p. 93). Remaining physically active into adulthood requires individuals to identify themselves as active people. In capitalist societies, identity is closely linked with consumptive practices. As Lavrence and Lazanski noted, "appropriate health management and the consumption of wellness lifestyles are ways in which citizens both abate and ultimately reinforce anxiety" (p. 80). Called precarity, this anxiety develops around making the so-called right choices about health by purchasing the correct attire and technologies as well as buying into the right training plan to get desired returns.

Essentially, we are a society that believe strongly in choice. We have an over-abundance of choices in work, clothes, child rearing, and fitness. However, with these choices, we as individuals take on a degree of personal risk. Where once the state felt responsible for providing green spaces for fitness leisure, this responsibility is now placed on the individual.

To not look fit (and appearance is very important here) means not making ideal use of one's leisure time even if one does not have much leisure time to begin with. One way that people navigate the expectation that they do more with their leisure time is to try to make these self-improvement activities more fun. The attempt to make less desirable activities more fun goes by many names. Gamification, for instance, is the process of turning mundane tasks into games. "Lifehack" is another term that can be used to describe making hard or ongoing tasks more fun, and lifehacks might try to help an individual complete mundane tasks faster. For instance, a lifehack article might cover how to clean your house in 20 minutes a day or the currently popular seven-minute interval workout for when one can't make it to a gym. However, lifehacks tend to try and layer one activity on top of another, preferably pairing an enjoyable activity with a more mundane one. *Pokémon Go* attempts to do just this.

By turning a daily walk or run into a game, *Pokémon Go* incentivizes the player to participate in fitness even when they do not want to exercise. The application helps the individual mitigate the responsibility and anxiety pervading contemporary fitness culture. It's important to note that this move was intentional on Niantic's part. Hanke, head of Niantic, stated in an interview with *Financial Times,* "The sad thing is we have a lot of great parks that people just don't use because everybody just goes home and puts on the TV and shuts their front doors. … We want people put back into public spaces" (as cited in Bradshaw, 2016). Hanke sees the relationship between the expansion of the park system in the 20th century and his own 21st century game. The game works within this long history of fitness and public spaces, connecting these green spaces with contemporary understandings of individualism. *Pokémon Go* is an attempt to get the individual outside while also competing to be, well, the very best at a mobile game. It moves some of that anxiety on to a productive and healthy competition.

Pokémon Go *and the Problem of Playful Spaces*

Pokémon Go is not the first running or fitness app to try and use games to get people outside or make exercise less tedious. Many of these apps focus specifically on distance sports because GPS is easy to track, backed up by the movement sensors that have become ubiquitous in most smart phones. Six to Start is one mobile game company that builds narrative-based fitness apps. The most popular one is *Zombies, Run!* (2012), a narrative-based augmented reality app where users play as a runner for a small British encampment following the zombie apocalypse. A second app, *The Walk* (2014), is an homage to Hitchcock's *North by Northwest* wherein a user's daily steps unlock an unfolding narrative about the bombing of a London train station. Fitbit uses friendly competition as a way to engage walkers and runners through its mobile app. Like Niantic's *Pokémon Go*, these apps work to keep readers engaged in walking for reasons other than actually performing physical exercise. Also like *Pokémon Go*, these apps often require individuals to leave their own homes or even gyms in order to excel at the game part of the app. For instance, *Zombies, Run!*'s most popular feature is perhaps its zombie chase. The feature is not available when a runner is on a treadmill. These apps encourage walkers and runners to get outside. As citizens begin to work more flexible hours in less physically demanding jobs, they theoretically can (and maybe need to) take up a physically demanding hobby. Running as leisure is supported by expectations, consumptive practices, and engagement through digital media. However, the practice is often discouraged by fragmented and busy work schedules.

Folding these fitness practices into physical spaces, the playfulness of *Pokémon Go* assumes a specific kind of space and a specific set of shared values between the creator of the franchise, the creators of *Pokémon Go*, the players of *Pokémon Go*, and local community members (who may have other ideas about the use of these spaces). *Pokémon Go* imagines a particular kind of safe and open space that invites everyone to play publicly. However, it's important that such spaces don't exist for everyone. Writing in the first week of the game's U.S. launch, Akil (2016) noted that playing *Pokémon Go* as a black man requires special care. He recounted his experience of wandering around his apartment complex looking for Pokémon and being met with cautious looks by his neighbors. After about 20 minutes outside playing the game, he stopped because he was too concerned that his presence might be construed as malicious, saying:

> When my brain started combining the complexity of being Black in America with the real world proposal of wandering and exploration that is designed into the gamplay [*sic*] of Pokemon GO [*sic*], there was only one conclusion. **I might die if I keep playing** [para. 8, emphasis in original].

Akil's concerns are deeply embedded in American culture where black men are often considered threats just for existing in public. As an additional example, on April 16, 2018, two black men were arrested at a downtown Philadelphia Starbucks because they were waiting for a friend before purchasing drinks. The coffee chain has a relationship with Niantic: most Starbucks are Poké Stops. It also generally advertises itself as a third space, a semi-public meeting place for the whole community. But we can see that public space might exclude whole demographics of citizens under the right circumstances.

Running also intersects with place in unique ways that add a layer to this conversation. Running is usually done outside. Most runners dislike treadmills (they are referred to as "dreadmills" by the running community). However, outside spaces for running are also marked by social and economic situations that exist outside of the game. Running is by and large performed as leisure in majority white, middle-class neighborhoods. Women make up a slight majority of the running community and report high incidents of harassment while running. In August 2016, one month after *Pokémon Go's* release, three women were killed on runs that happened in broad daylight in three different states. Many commenting on the incidents put the burden of responsibility for keeping women safe on women instead of arguing for changes (Kita, 2016). There are many examples of why people of color, particularly Black men, are uncomfortable running in public spaces and predominantly white neighborhoods due to fear of racial profiling—though they are more likely to run in Black neighborhoods (Ray, 2017, p. 4). Local races play a key role in civic participation. Black men are often particularly careful in coding themselves as participating in fitness when in public by wearing easily coded running wear or shirts that literally say "Black Man Running and It Ain't from the Police" (Hamilton, 2013).

Class mobility is a final consideration to playing *Pokémon Go*. The app relies on landmarks. In my own neighborhood, for instance, the only Poké Stop is the one by a cemetery and, yes, I continue to feel a bit bad about the fact that I look forward to passing graves because hopefully I'll get a 10K egg. When I'm on campus, however, there are many Poké Stops and rare Pokémon occasionally spawn while I'm grading in my office. The game is simply much easier to play there. I also have a $100/year membership to a local botanical garden that has dozens of Poké Stops as well as nests of rarer Pokémon. In the summer of 2016 the gardens would regularly host events where they would lure all the Poké Stops, encouraging members to come during non-peak hours. These spaces allow me the opportunity to play the game with relative convenience. The fact that I live in an urban area allows me to keep up with the game with minimal effort.

It's important to note that individuals do not have the same experience of public spaces as playful spaces because, if games like *Pokémon Go* hope to get individuals outside, we need to consider the many ways that individuals use and play with these games and how that use is often tied to their bodies and their identities. Our current cultural climate definitely puts the responsibility of being physically fit on the individual. This kind of responsibility may have us looking for ways to make fitness less tedious but also ways to create buffers between these public spaces and ourselves. I argue that when we look closer, we find many ways that our individual identities shape our experience of public spaces. *Pokémon Go* can very much feel like a solution to this issue, but by encouraging us to be active outside, it's also encouraging individuals, particularly women and people of color, to engage in spaces that can at times be hostile to them.

Casual Gaming, Casual Athletes, Casual Citizens

As already mentioned, *Pokémon Go* could serve as a good way to encourage individuals with little experience walking or running in public to be more active, though there are some obvious issues with seeing these public spaces as open and playful to all. Individuals embarking on new efforts to play and move outside are going to have their identities, based on their age, race, gender, athletic ability, weight, etc., interpreted by those around them. However, these issues are not solely the purview of society at large, but also within gaming communities. Considering the baggage that can come with fitness, finding ways to cope with that stress is important to establishing an everyday fitness practice. Exergames have been one avenue that scientists and researchers have been considering, and *Pokémon Go* might even help individuals less prone to exercise to venture out and walk more (Ying et al., 2017). However, very little research exists on the limits of how much effort should be put into these activities.

As a society, we reward dedicated athletes. Top athletes in high school often receive full or partial scholarships to attend college. Elite college players in popular sports might also later receive lucrative contracts to compete at some degree of professional play. However, participants in casual health practices are often mocked as though what they are doing is in some ways worse than not trying at all. In this way, we can draw comparisons to the divide between what we call casual and hardcore games. To different degrees, hardcore gamers are also privileged in gaming communities. As Juul (2012) described, "the *stereotype of a casual player* is the inverted image of the hardcore player: this player has a preference for positive and pleasant fictions, has played a few video games, is willing to commit little time and few resources toward playing video games, and dislikes difficult games" (p. 8, emphasis in original). We live in a culture where one cannot be seen as doing fitness unless they are all in. Marathons, high-intensity interval training workouts, and CrossFit all tell us that in order to be fit, we need to be extreme in our fitness when in actuality "exercise was imagined to be a replacement for the physical activity that had been lost to sedentary, 'desk-bound' work" (McKenzie, 2013, p. 9). Most individuals need more moderate exercise—brisk walking, swimming, mowing the lawn—in their lives. They need casual fitness in an era where the industry often promotes increasingly competitive forms of fitness. These practices show a weird relationship and an almost self-defeating psychological relationship that we have with discipline. We have to be all in, or we feel that we are not worthy of any kind of participation. Social and market pressure imply that we must work harder in our leisure time than will be beneficial to anyone. It encourages members to buy more and give more of their affective labor to these groups.

In a time when gyms, home fitness apps, and athleisure wear companies are promoting increasingly more demanding fitness regimens, being a casual athlete can be its own kind of resistance. While casual games have risen with the popularity of cell phones and tablets, casual gamers have also had to make a space for themselves within the gaming ecosystem. As Juul (2012) noted, "Casual games are positioned as a rejection of traditional hardcore game design, with its gory themes and focus on technological capabilities" (p. 25). *Pokémon Go* fits nicely within this divide for both casual players and casual gamers. The game itself encourages players to get outside. As a person who runs with the game, I can say that I can easily run with *Pokémon Go*, but the game encourages a focus on the experience instead of on running my fastest 5K. The game uses several visual and technical cues to encourage a sense of casual fitness. The game projects a pastoral interface over city streets, encouraging the user to think of public spaces in a pleasant light. The game itself can be played for a few seconds or hours at a time (phone battery and data plan willing). Poké Stops refresh every 5 minutes, encouraging players to meander and loop back to places they've already been. These mechanisms encourage a kind of casual relationship with both fitness and play. The intentionality of moving more is easily folded into the app, which encourages the player to give just as much motivation as they have at the time.

Exercise and gaming are both about incorporating a practice into the everyday and "a casual game is sufficiently flexible to be played with a hardcore time commitment, but a hardcore game is too inflexible to be played with a casual time commitment" (Juul, 2012, p. 10). These layers of discipline, particularly as they further involve community participation, create layers of community obligation that work not only as gatekeepers for a community but also to keep those with an investment to the practice even more dedicated, a dedication that often requires a certain level of established fitness. Recently in spring 2018, *Pokémon Go* introduced a very loose quest narrative that further encourages this kind of sustained play. One of the quests required players to collect five candies while walking with their buddy Pokémon, which would typically require about 25 kilometers of walking. I personally had an injury that severely limited my ability to walk when this quest came out, meaning that something that would typically only take a few days to finish took me several weeks. It was frustrating, and I wanted to quit the game. While the game can encourage invested players to get out and perform some moderate exercise, the game can also deter those who cannot make these distance dedications and/or are too far from major public areas with more Pokémon, Poké Stops, and gyms. From these examples, it is pretty easy to see why more than 100 million people downloaded the game but so many dropped the game quickly.

All this is to say that *Pokémon Go* is very much work that has few restrictions on how much time one can dedicate to play. It's work that directly ties into the same cycles of civic duty we connect with fitness. *Pokémon Go* tries to marry athleisure with the flexible work and leisure environments many 21st-century workers find themselves in. This flexibility highlights the major issues with trying to make fitness fun. *Pokémon Go* has always had a content problem in that players expect to engage with the game more often than the once-a-week they would expect from a television show, and *Pokémon Go* is quickly running out of show and manga content to adapt for the game. At its release, as the game was still managing account and server issues, many players were already barreling through the experience points required to make it to the level cap of 40. Niantic actually banned some of these over-enthusiastic players in part because it didn't understand that the concept of "casual gaming" reflects the way players play and not a certain number of hours they dedicate to a game. This is particularly apt when considering the *Pokémon* television and manga theme, a story of persistent young people competing to be the best, day and night.

Pokémon Go, *a Game for This Moment*

Keeping in mind that *Pokémon Go* imagines a casual player/athlete/citizen, *Pokémon Go* as an app often challenges and subverts common expectations for what a fitness app can or should be. Fitness apps are legion on both the Apple App Store and Google Play. There are apps that track diet and weight gain/loss. There are apps that will stream basic and trendy workouts to try at home. There are apps that will design strength-building routines for either one's home or the gym. *Pokémon Go* most closely matches mobile applications that track distance. These apps are most often used by walkers, runners, and bicyclists. While running apps and wearables seem to be declining in popularity, they remain popular apps integral to the marketing of mobile technology, like smart watches.

Based on moves in popular understandings of fitness, these apps should be teaching users how to improve at whatever exercise they try to do as well as track their ability to do said exercise. Embedded in many fitness apps is the belief that tracking and analyzing their own data helps users to make better and more informed choices with regards to their fitness and maybe even improve on their current level of fitness. Thus, tracking is important. The Fitbit app tracks steps. Other free apps like *MapMyRun*, *Runkeeper,* and *Strava* use GPS to track distance and speed. Increasing one's speed over distance is what most runners want to do, and runners can see the appeal of an app that can tell them, often in real time, if they are improving at this leisure activity. Likewise, these apps tend to track performance over time, so that individuals can see how they have progressed over extended periods of time. I'm not saying that fitness is always progressive, or even needs to progress in order for people to receive health benefits from a jogging routine. Fitness tracking falls into a particular cultural narrative that does not necessarily take into account the reality that people get injured, or that job or family changes might affect one's ability. What I am saying is that these tracking apps have embedded into them a rhetoric of progress. The assumption is that everyone will continue to improve forever, even though all bodies will break down and no amount of healthy living will make us immortal.

The thing is that *Pokémon Go* flips many of these expectations for fitness progress on their head while remaining a pretty good motivator for fitness. As mentioned, fitness trackers use GPS to locate an object. GPS devices draw lines between sequential GPS pings to determine distance. GPS is not perfect, and all running/biking apps have a bit of wiggle room for error. Applications are often more than a bit secretive about their code, and Niantic has fought hard to keep its application programming interface (API) secret. *Pokémon Go* is probably worse than most fitness apps at tracking distance. I have a five-kilometer route I do around my house all of the time that is backed up by multiple fitness apps and Google Maps, and *Pokémon Go* has never judged it to be five kilometers. *Pokémon Go* uses slightly different parameters for tracking distance. *Pokémon Go* pings GPS satellites at longer intervals than running apps and draws a straight line from the previous ping, meaning that *Pokémon Go* often records an individual who has turned a corner as having cut through a home and completely misses tracking stretches where a runner runs to the end of a street and turns around. The app is thought to be more accurate for walkers, but even this might not be true, as I've definitely turned it on to track my walk from my car to the grocery store, which was too close to be 1/10 of a kilometer, but the app recorded it as such anyway. These are personal examples, but my experiences are not unique and have been shared by many tech bloggers (Skwarecki, 2016).

The app itself does nothing to log the amount of time one spends using the app for an individual walk or run. It only tracks miles to hatch eggs (and those miles disappear as soon as the egg is hatched) and to track buddies— user-selected Pokémon that give the user a candy specific to that Pokémon every five kilometers. Finally, the app tracks how many miles total the app has been open. None of these mechanics allow runners to use the app to see if their times are improving or even how much distance they are actually covering. The app will tell users all about their progress catching and evolving Pokémon but almost nothing about whether they went faster or longer today than the day before. *Pokémon Go* privileges an ambulatory kind of fitness that might frustrate an athlete with different fitness goals.

Conclusion

All of this is to say that *Pokémon Go*, despite cultural positioning as a fitness app, might appeal, rhetorically, to a very different, more leisurely, class of fitness apps and that might be one of the reasons for the app's success. Creating a daily habit of running or walking is a challenge. It's hard to create a daily practice, whether it's eating healthier, keeping up with domestic chores, or daily writing. As a society, we have tried many ways to make these trivial but important tasks easier in a climate where we are expected to do more and more.

Pokémon Go, however, subverts that trend. The app tracks and surveils speed and distance. It uses this data to generate Pokémon and determine if someone is driving while using the app. But *Pokémon Go* likely occludes this data from users to encourage gameplay over any focus on the individual workout. It invites players to participate in the narrative of the popular television show. Success in the game is found by marrying determination and happenstance. Like with Ash, the anime's hero, most of the good stuff happens while users wander around somewhere near the right place at an opportune time. This ambulating determinism will not chisel one's abs or help one earn a personal record at a marathon, but it could help someone achieve a moderately active lifestyle.

Pokémon Go is a case study in working through the tedium: the tedium of walking the same areas every day, of maintaining some kind of fitness regimen in a world that constantly demands our time at tasks that often include a ton of sitting. Ultimately, however, *Pokémon Go* is not a magic bullet for keeping or maintaining a health habit. Popular and academic outlets have all noted both the game's popularity at launch in addition to its steep decline in monthly users only a few months after the game's release. Mentioned several times in this collection—but perhaps most clearly in Sierra and Burgoon's piece—a continued dedication to the game is greatly improved by having family and social networks who also play the game. Individuals are simply more likely to play if they have someone to play along with. This same strategy, however, is also important to starting and maintaining a gym habit. If anything, *Pokémon Go* works best when it becomes the excuse for meeting a friend downtown a few times a week for walking, chatting, and raiding. In that way, a game that does little within its game mechanics to incentivize social play is best played when the player creates that social network for themselves.

REFERENCES

Akil, O. (2016, July 7). Warning: Pokemon GO is a death sentence if you are a black man. *Medium.* Retrieved from https://medium.com/mobile-lifestyle/warning-pokemon-go-is-a-death-sentence-if-you-are-a-black-man-acacb4bdae7f.

Bradshaw, T. (2016, Nov. 25). Lunch with the FT: Pokémon Go creator John Hanke. *Financial Times.* Retrieved from www.ft.com/content/596ec790-afe8-11e6-9c37-5787335499a0.

Cervantes, R. (2010). Physical education and the labor of leisure. *Journal of Philosophy and History of Education, 60,* 110–120.

Gotaas, T. (2009). *Running: A global history* (P. Graves, Trans.). London: Reaktion Books.

Gregg, E.A., & Gregg, V.H. (2017). Women in sport: Historical perspectives. *Clinics in Sports Medicine, 36*(4), 603–610.

Hamilton, M. (2013, October 2). Black men less likely to run in white neighborhoods. *Runners World.* Retrieved from https://www.runnersworld.com/news/a20801993/black-men-less-likely-to-run-in-white-neighborhoods/.

Juul, J. (2010). *A casual revolution: Reinventing video games and their players.* Cambridge, MA: MIT Press.

Kita, M. (2016, August 11). The problem is not women running alone. *Runner's World.* Retrieved from https://www.runnersworld.com/other-voices/the-problem-is-not-women-running-alone.

Lavrence, C., & Lozanski, K. (2014). "This is not your practice life": Lululemon and the neoliberal governance of self. *Canadian Review of Sociology/Revue Canadienne de Sociologie, 51*(1), 76–94. doi:10.1111/cars.12034.

Lefebvre, H. (1991). *The production of space* (D. Nicholson-Smith, Trans.). Malden, MA: Blackwell Publishing.

McKenzie, S. (2013). *Getting physical: The rise of fitness culture in America.* Lawrence: University Press of Kansas.

Ouellette, L. (2014). Enterprising selves: Reality television and human capital. In D. Johnson, D. Kompare & A. Santo (Eds.), *Making media work: Cultures of management in the entertainment industries* (pp. 90–112). New York: New York University Press.

Ray, R. (2017). Black people don't exercise in my neighborhood: Perceived racial composition and leisure-time physical activity among middle class blacks and whites. *Social Science Research, 66,* 42–57. doi.org/10.1016/j.ssresearch.2017.03.008.

Rojek, C. (2010). *The labor of leisure: The culture of free time.* Thousand Oaks, CA: Sage.

Rosoff, N.G. (2006). "A glow of pleasurable excitement": Images of the new athletic woman in American popular culture, 1880–1920. In L.K. Fuller (Ed.), *Sport, rhetoric, and gender: Historical perspectives and media representations* (pp. 55–64). New York: Palgrave Macmillan.

Sierra, W., & Burgoon, G. (2018). Gaming across the years: Gotta catch 'em all together. In Henthorn, A. Kulak, K. Purzycki & S. Vie (Eds.), in this volume.

Skwarecki, B. (2016, July 26). How to hatch Pokémon eggs and have a great run at the same time. *Lifehacker.* Retrieved from https://vitals.lifehacker.com/how-to-hatch-pokemon-eggs-and-have-a-great-run-at-the-s-1784272881.

Ying, X., Xu, H., Xu, H., Liang, L., Hernandez, A., Wang, T., & Peterson, E. (2017). An initial evaluation of the impact of Pokémon GO on physical activity. *Journal of the American Heart Association, 6*(5), 1–7. doi:10.1161/JAHA.116.005341.

Augmented Reality Design Through Experience Architecture

JILL ANNE MORRIS

A number of researchers across many fields in the past decade have investigated teaching with augmented reality (AR), but few scholars have studied what is possible when we allow students to make their own AR art projects, games, and informatics. AR has grown immensely in its applications both inside and outside of classrooms following the release of *Pokémon Go*, and suddenly many people started playing with this technology as they never had before. Uses of AR outside of education have grown more common as the technology has become more accessible and better understood. Games like *Pokémon Go* are only one potential use of this technology. It has also been used for museum tours, locative media projects, marketing, maps, city tours, and many other projects that college graduates may one day become involved with. Within education, AR is a popular teaching tool in both K–12 and college applications—it has been shown to increase engagement with and even understanding of some topics across disciplines (Ibáñez, Di Serio, Villarán, & Kloos, 2014; Liarokapis & Anderson, 2010). As a result, in most cases when AR is used in education, it is being used by teachers for the purposes of education rather than play. AR modules are created for and by teachers and are expected to be used by students.

When cheap (or free) AR programming tools became available, I immediately wanted to start teaching them to my professional writing students at Frostburg State University. One of the skills that students must learn in order to be successful in their careers is the ability to learn new technology. As a result (and because I feel that it will be important in coming decades for students to understand), an assignment in my Applied Digital Writing class (ENGL 438) has been to develop an AR game or presentation as a class for the campus or community. In doing so, I balanced having students play AR games with having students create AR games. Thus, for the past four years, students enrolled in my ENGL 438 class were asked to first play AR games (first *Ingress* and now *Pokémon Go*) as an introduction to developing their own AR application or game for the campus community. In this part of the assignment, they were asked to play and analyze an existing game, write about the experience, and discuss it as a class. The second part of the assignment then asked them to use a simple AR tool (Aurasma, now HP Reveal) to create an AR application or game of their own as a large group project. Aurasma was recently acquired by Hewlett Packard (HP), which has made it more usable and easier to find by clients and their customers alike.

With Aurasma, anyone can create basic AR overlays, called Auras, to trigger images that appear in the offline world. Students in this class have worked with local area businesses, museums, and campus services to develop AR overlays for exhibits, menus, directions, and other publications using Aurasma (see Figure 4.1).

Overlays can be an image, video, or 3D model (and students have sidestepped this system by creating videos that contain only audio in order to create audio overlays as well). In this way, a user can look through their phone at a predetermined space in the offline world (or a trigger image that has been placed in the offline world) and listen to or view content related to that image. This is a very simple way to create WYSIWYG locative media projects.

Despite the simplicity of the tool (one can create AR applications in minutes, allowing more time to be spent on writing, investigating audience,

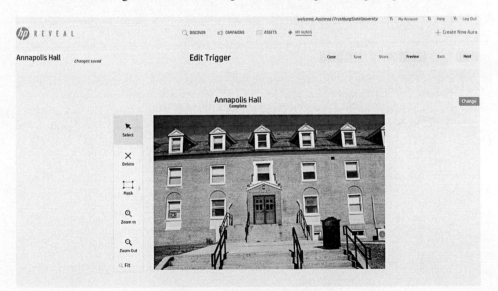

Figure 4.1. Aurasma Studio.

editing film, creating graphics, or doing archival research), students resisted this project heavily, claiming that it did not rely on a digital tool that could be added to their résumé like HTML, CSS, Adobe Photoshop, Adobe Premiere, and so on. That is, of course, until the release of *Pokémon Go*. *Pokémon Go* provided a needed entry point for students to understand how AR technologies can be engaging. Unlike its predecessor, *Ingress*, *Pokémon Go* allows users to play in a familiar universe; it remakes and rethinks public spaces into game spaces seamlessly through the use of a well-known story about collecting, competing with, and even breeding and hatching Pokémon.

Pokémon Go created a needed point of entry that allowed students to understand AR's future usefulness for employers and even themselves. It also led them to see AR as more of a storytelling medium and less one that could just be used for providing information. When students enrolled in this class first thought of AR, they thought of the heads-up displays that some vehicles use for advertising and navigational information, and certainly that is one potential way that AR can be used. However, after students played a game with a familiar story, no matter how simple that story was, I was more likely to receive projects that contained stories as well. Therefore, the implication of studying *Pokémon Go* first is that it encouraged students to develop projects that feature deeper storylines and better game mechanics when they have first played and analyzed one that does the same.

AR must be fairly simple and able to fit onto a small screen. In order to allow for complex storytelling, then, it is easier to develop a game or presentation based upon a narrative that audiences are already familiar with. *Pokémon Go* got students excited about storytelling with space and leaning heavily upon what people already knew about that space instead of relying upon lengthy exposition. These lessons could then be applied to other multimedia work like building games, multimedia poems, and websites. Fortunately, studies of space and rhetorical storytelling are already available to use through experience architecture (XA), where interaction design and experience design are studied not just in software but in offline spaces as well.

Additionally, I changed the framing of the project from a study of object-oriented ontology to framing it using XA. Object-oriented ontology would ask questions like: Why do we choose to connect a story to this object? What stories does this object want to tell? What information does it want to teach us? All of these are useful questions for museum exhibits, but less useful for games or academic projects. Potts and Salvo (2017) defined experience architecture as

> the architecture of mediated systems, resulting in a designed capability for those using those systems to communicate. Experience Architecture takes a systems approach to the reciprocal processes of analyzing and constructing social experiences in a variety of networked digital environments as well as a number of physical spaces [p. 3].

Pokémon Go uses space in a way that most other games do not—it requires players to participate physically in the offline world and maps a mediated view of the game's story onto that offline world. It succeeds where other AR games have failed—it created an engaging story that got people worldwide out of their homes and into the streets interacting with one another. It stands as an exemplary case for XA as a necessity for the design of mediated systems, and it serves as a good starting point for thinking about using XA (and not just user-centeredness) in the design of students' own projects.

Because of the game's popularity, starting in spring 2017 I had students play *Pokémon Go* as part of the class while analyzing the experience for two weeks (at least) prior to the start of the AR project. This helped to reduce student resistance to learning a brand-new technology by showing them what was possible with the technology (and how fun it could be) prior to starting their own projects. This essay traces the notable changes in storytelling and immersion in the students' own AR projects that occurred between two years—2016 and 2017—by comparing student projects that came out of playing *Ingress* or just looking at existing AR projects to those created after playing *Pokémon Go*. It uses these examples to build a theory of successful AR and successful AR pedagogy through XA. In this essay, I theorize that lessons from XA can and should be studied alongside AR applications such as *Pokémon Go* in order to rethink the ways that spaces tell stories and can be rethought of through gaming. Finally, I offer a pedagogical approach to teaching writing in public spaces when specific games (such as *Pokémon Go*) are no longer popular or available.

Literature Review

Using AR to Teach

As noted earlier, many studies have found that using AR technologies in the classroom to teach a wide variety of concepts in K–12, undergraduate, and even graduate courses can be effective (or at least more effective than traditional multimodal technologies). In AR's infancy, teachers immediately saw value in having students experience information in novel ways, and especially saw value in having students be able to see and interact with 3D models in physical space instead of on a screen. In 2002, Shelton and Hedley explored teaching geography students about how the Earth and Sun relate. They had 30 undergraduate students examine models relating to the seasons, rotation, revolution, and the equinox through ARToolkit, an open-source software development kit (SDK) for creating AR implementations (Shelton & Hedley,

2002). The ARToolkit is still available and now works on a wider variety of platforms. They found that students had a higher overall understanding of the material from participating in the AR exercise and that students' ability to look at these models whenever they wanted improved the experience versus time-constrained methods of learning from models.

While the ARToolkit has a thriving community built up around it, it is still not as easy to use for average instructors as later tools. Those tools have caused an increase in the number of studies of AR technology as time goes on. Unlike Shelton and Hedley's (2002) study that more or less proved that AR would be an adequate means of teaching, later studies focused more on the various affordances and drawbacks of this technology. For example, Dunleavy, Dede, and Mitchell (2009) documented how student use of AR can both aid and hinder teaching and learning in the 6th, 7th, and 10th grades. Both teachers and students in this study noted that AR was highly effective at sharing narrative and that they enjoyed the interactive and collaborative problem-solving that AR made possible. (Unfortunately, collaboration was not possible in *Pokémon Go* until after my students completed their projects in 2017.) Whether or not collaboration is possible directly via the software, however, AR does invite people to work together since people with their phones in hand can and do speak to one another and help each other solve problems and puzzles, provided that they are located in the same space. However, Duleavy, Dede, and Mitchell also found that AR presented unique technological challenges that other software does not—it could be noted, of course, that any new technology will present new challenges and potential issues. Rarely are new technologies so quickly developed for classroom use, so teachers have seen many potential issues that they might not when adopting older technologies: frequent software crashes, drastic updates that change interfaces significantly, and students who simply aren't familiar with new technologies and thus need more instruction about how they work.

Just a year later in 2010, Liarokapis and Anderson performed a study in Sweden to explore the advantages of using AR in higher education. They found a number of advantages, including that AR significantly improved understanding in the visualization of theoretical concepts. In some ways, this benefit can also be derived through other multimodal practices. Students can navigate through an AR lecture, for example, at their own speed and spend as much time as they need on various parts of it. However, they also noted that AR technologies need to be simple and easy to use in order to be effective (probably to avoid the technological difficulties that were noted by Duleavy, Dede, and Mitchell in 2009). In their study, Liarokapis and Anderson found that students believed that AR technology is promising for classroom use, though some of them liked it more than others. Specifically, they studied both undergraduate and graduate students, and the undergrads were impressed with the learning interface in general. Undergraduates liked to view the AR presentations on a monitor (or phone) while the graduate students preferred to wear a heads-up display and interact with the subject directly. The students overall liked using the AR to view 3D models of 3D concepts and found AR most useful in learning multimedia.

Finally, Escobedo, Tentori, Quintana, Favela, and Garcia-Rosas (2014) studied the use of AR in working with children with autism through therapy. They studied how AR can be used as an addition to traditional attention management techniques that attach verbal and visual prompts to physical objects used during therapy. Like many groups that have studied AR, they developed their own system for performing this activity, but their system allowed teachers to be the ones to put digital or textual content onto physical objects. The researchers found that their system (called Mobis, or Mobile Object Identification System) was effective in increasing the attention span of children with autism during therapy.

AR with Experience Architecture: Developing AR Systems in Classrooms

As AR systems need careful design to manage the difficulty of introducing new technology (often with different interfaces and apps from one implementation to another), they are a natural match for XA. Users have to be at the center of AR systems in order to balance difficulty, usability, and collaboration, and XA calls for user-centered design. Furthermore, Potts and Salvo (2017) noted that the use of XA in conjunction with rhetoric is especially important:

> Based in the ancient knowledge of rhetoric, performed using emergent digital tools of the current internetworked age, experience architecture is timely. This pursuit of the always-emergent is informed by ancient knowledge and by ethical action, cautioned by what we know about the problems of systems-centered and modern design [p. 7].

Anyone developing an AR technological application—whether Niantic or my students—must consider what will make a great user experience. Grice (2017) wrote that in XA, we need to build such user experiences around *people*, rather than around the product itself. These people must be actively engaged by the system in use and we "need to shift our rhetorical strategy from logos, presenting in the seemingly most logical way, and ethos, relying on an organization's reputation, to pathos, presenting in the way that most appeals to people and engages their senses" (p. 42). Grice also described two methods of designing using XA—top-down and bottom-up. From the top down, designers must "present a clear vision of what the experience will be and what it will include, carefully and fully define the entire experience space, and develop unified experience themes to tie everything together" (p. 50). When working from the bottom up, people working on the project

> may have been working towards different goals—so, for example, one part of the experience may focus on speed and efficiency at the expense of aesthetics and comfort, while another part may operate much less efficiently but be pleasant to work with. While either goal may be a good one, the combination can be distracting and annoying to users [p. 51].

Because developing a game or application for the campus or community is usually more than a single student will be willing to take on alone, students must be led to consider these XA concepts as they work in a group of 8–20 people to make the app work.

XA methodologies are also a source of inserting feminism into the process of designing apps, games, and other digital interactions. Bardzell (2010) wrote that "feminism is a natural ally to interaction design, due to its central commitments to issues such as agency, fulfillment, identity, equity, empowerment, and social justice" (p. 1301). Sano-Franchini (2017) noted that using interaction design and XA is a means of applying social justice frameworks to address "wicked problems" via feminist rhetorical approaches (p. 85). At a time when raising political issues in the classroom can be fraught, especially for graduate students and adjuncts, using XA as a means of developing assignments and having students develop projects is also a means of sneakily introducing feminist concerns. Friess (2017) wrote that XA helps us to enable "designers to create rhetorically grounded experiences that are useful, usable, and desirable" (p. 111). XA helps, then, to create AR experiences that are grounded in space, in rhetoric, and in *people*.

Assignment

In my class, the AR assignment came toward the middle of the term. Students enrolled had already completed a video project where they learned to shoot film and edit using Adobe Premiere and Adobe After Effects, had studied game design at least briefly (through reading Gee's *What Video Games Have to Teach Us About Learning and Literacy* earlier in the term) and had completed some basic readings in XA. The background in video editing allowed students to make overlays using audio and video without too much trouble. As part of the project, we also reviewed Photoshop (many students had already taken a course in graphic design where they learned some basics of using Photoshop).

At the beginning of the term, I asked students to spend at least two weeks of the class, if not more, playing *Pokémon Go*. Those two weeks started at the beginning of the project, but many students chose to play for the entire term. Previous to the release of *Pokémon Go*, I had them play an equal amount of time in *Ingress*. Students who did not own a phone compatible with the game were allowed to check out a classroom iPad for use during that part of the project (and to build their Aurasma project).

Ingress was much more difficult to get students immersed in and excited about, whereas using *Pokémon Go* in class meant that some students signed up purely to play. *Ingress* has an independent storyline that has been developing now for over five years that a player gradually discovers while playing. Players receive email updates about important changes in the plot and happenings in the game to help them keep up with the storyline. The basic storyline of the game is that scientists at CERN, the European Organization for Nuclear Research, have discovered a mysterious particle that they call Exotic Matter—or XM (Ingress, n.d.). Scientists in-game quickly found out that XM is present in larger concentrations around places with cultural significance, and somehow this led them to the conclusion that the XM was introduced by aliens. At the beginning of the game, there is an explosion that exposes all the scientists at the "Niantic Project" to high levels of XM. These scientists are then recruited by three in-game companies (Ingress, n.d.). One of the scientists loses their phone with the Ingress scanner app, which is found and distributed to other people around the game. Gamers are divided into two groups—the Enlightened, who approve the influence of XM, and the Resistance, who are against it. Players helped Niantic (in the offline world) to map areas of cultural significance around their homes. There they can interact with what Ingress calls Portals, community spots that have influence in the game. While I did have students who had played or had heard of *Ingress* before who enjoyed playing for class, most students did not care about the story and played the game by going around and doing things but not really understanding what they were doing. This emerged in classroom discussion sessions where we talked about the game. Students wanted the story explained again and again, and they did not feel like they were part of it.

Comparatively, using *Pokémon Go* to introduce AR technologies into the classroom was a lot more successful. Students spent adequate time in the game in order to analyze it, to discuss why it worked, to talk about difficulties they had (primarily with campus Wi-Fi), and to discuss how its design would influence their own ideal game. During gameplay, we discussed the game in conjunction with class readings, talked with one another about especially good finds, and talked about how the game builds a community. Additionally, *Pokémon Go* is exceptionally popular worldwide, so we were also able to discuss the responses of other countries to the game and why Pokémon as an overall concept was so successful. For example, Mr. Tarō Asō (former Prime Minister of Japan) said that he believed that *Pokémon Go* could be a solution to the problem of *hikikomori,* a severe form of social withdrawal

(Kato et al., 2017). At the same time, the game was banned in China and Korea because of concerns about the security of Google Maps (the game was released in Korea in January 2017 and is slated to be released in China, potentially as early as late 2018). Most countries, of course, have the same concerns about the game as the United States—while people leaving the house to play is good, there are worries about people wandering into unsafe areas in pursuit of Pokémon. Some individuals think that the game is potentially distracting and worry about people playing too much.

Returning to the use of *Pokémon Go* in the classroom, some students responded positively because of their nostalgia for the game. Kurlinkus (2017) argued that the most memorable designs are those that bring back past memories for us; he stated that designers should create memorable designs, plan for storytelling, and create better objects that "harness positive interaction memories—a UX concept [Kurlinkus called] *memorial interactivity* (MI)" (p. 274, emphasis in original). He included the example of a playground as a key MI since most adults have positive feelings and memories attached to playgrounds. For my students, *Pokémon Go* prompted the same sort of positive memories. They played Pokémon as children, and, as a result, they were happy to reminisce and jump back into the game as adults. They didn't need to do any background research to understand the game—it made perfect sense to them if they had played before, seen the TV show, or even watched the movies. It was familiar enough that the minimal instruction given by the game was enough to both play and understand the story. This also emerged in many of the students' classroom analyses.

One of the forms of classroom analysis used successfully in this class was autoethnography. Students were essentially asked in a brief paper to perform an autoethnography of their play and also analyze the game as an AR multimedia piece alongside their experience playing it. Their in-class discussions provided direction for these papers, and they were allowed to take notes and quote other students as well. However, the most important part of the analysis had to be their own. These autoethnographies were then shared briefly in an informal presentation so that people's overall impressions of the game could be discussed as a class.

Ethnography (and autoethnography) are useful tools for XA studies. According to Mara and Mara (2017), the philosophy of ethnography "can help UX researchers invent more useful research protocols, participant heuristics, and contextual inquiry interactions" (p. 184). They wrote that XA is concerned with users negotiating a system—in this case *Pokémon Go* and later the students' own AR creation—and thus it is useful to understand the system. By immersing oneself into the culture of the game, students became capable of identifying key concepts of successful AR and thinking about how games can be created in the image of a successful example. Much like Mara and Mara's study, I discovered that some problems—issues with Wi-Fi connectivity on campus, for example—created places for users to form a community and talk, and such "gaps and breakdowns" forced players to depend on their relationships with other players (Mara & Mara, 2017, p. 191).

The game also highlighted another of Mara and Mara's findings, which is that a player's connection to the place where a game is played can help push them to continue to play. For example, students looked forward to playing *Pokémon Go* during trips home or to favorite places on the weekends, and their connection with Frostburg, Maryland (where Frostburg State is located), led to the creation of affinity groups of play around the game. Insights that were generated during these classroom discussions and analyses were particularly helpful to students as they began to build their own AR application, which is unsurprising considering

> ethnography's dual use as a research coherency builder and an insight generator in its own right can help an experience architect connect what can feel like disparate research techniques and produced genres during a design cycle. By connecting the front-end and middle-end contextual research with the back-end usability and summative surveys, ethnography can help the XA team contextualize and integrate aspirational and instrumental data with subtle observations of more long-term participation [Mara & Mara, 2017, p. 195].

After students had thoroughly analyzed the app, the next step was building their own.

For this stage of the assignment, the constraints were largely open. Students chose via a class vote whether they wanted to work on individual projects or on a large group project. This class tended to be small, so a large group might only contain 8–10 students; students who were opposed to group projects were still allowed to work on their own in all of my classes. Each project could either be informative or a game or both. Since the project stretched over several weeks, I required that each project be made up of more than a single Aura, or AR interaction point. Students must also make use of their past skills in writing, video editing, audio editing, and photo/picture editing in order to create their projects.

Framed by XA and its focus on stories and narrative, I had students focus on what stories they wanted to share. They had the option of developing AR for community clients or campus clients. Over the years, classes have been fairly split between working with local museums and tour locations versus doing something on campus. Having spent a great deal of time playing *Pokémon Go* on campus, I was not surprised that the class in 2017 chose to develop something for the campus. During their initial discussion, they pointed out that they already knew the places on campus where phones worked well or poorly, and thus they would be able to design their AR to only rely upon areas where a signal was present.

Working with clients as a class presents its own problems. Most notably, whatever was done by the students tended to have to be cleaned up by the instructor, and this included applying updates if updates were necessary when the class was not in session. I have often been asked to update websites (developed by students in my other courses) when I or my students sincerely did not have time to perform these updates, but to keep a good relationship with these clients I updated them anyway. I have updated websites from China before, for example, in the middle of teaching a six-week intensive first-year writing course. As a result, though I love that students might create apps for a community audience that might actually use their projects, I only offered client-based projects when I thought that the necessary updates would be fairly easy to make. In this case, Aurasma was simple enough to use that changes could be made quickly.

One issue with the Aurasma software was the use of trigger images. Trigger images could be actual images placed up around the space (which was easier to do in museums) or offline places that we took pictures of. I have taken pictures using a Canon 7D Mark II camera, which enables complicated trigger images that are very high resolution; Aurasma required such high-resolution images—my initial thought was that simple trigger images like outlines and silhouettes would work best, but the software demanded complicated images for ease of recognition. However, when using offline locations such as campus buildings, changing light and seasons affected the ability of the AR to load. I have taken pictures around campus of popular locations for the students to use in a variety of seasons to try to fix this issue (the same Aura can be connected to multiple trigger images), but most of them would not load at night. Students were told this when the project began if they chose to use images of campus. Some students decided to place their own trigger images in campus spaces by putting up posters, stickers, or other game paraphernalia that would serve to bring people into the game as well as load AR information for players. However, placing these kinds of trigger images could also be difficult in public spaces as they were often taken down. Posters were usually removed within a few weeks and stickers could be removed by maintenance as early as overnight or might even be considered to be vandalism of campus property. (One of the first rules of this class was "don't get arrested.")

Students developed and tested their project over a number of weeks. Whether students were working alone (in 2016) or in a large group (2017), each day started with the students giving an oral update about what they had completed for that day. If someone had posted a video or image to the Aurasma app, we traveled to the location where that trigger image was located and tested the new Aura with our cell phones. We spent time walking around campus testing and giving feedback for the various projects, including ones that had already been tested; in some instances, we were seeing if the trigger images worked under other weather conditions, and in others we were seeing if anything had been added since we last tested them. Other days in class were simply spent producing content for their projects such as videos, images, and text. If students were working in groups, they divided themselves up based upon their specialties. Students with great graphic design skills immediately went to work creating images and titles (as well as posters and other necessary media) for the game while others checked out cameras and began filming classmates acting out various scenes from the game. The writers worked on the scripts and text that would appear on the screen, getting it to the graphic designers and movie makers as quickly as possible. Each class period was slightly different and was largely student-led other than the aforementioned testing.

Aurasma was not hosted by the university, and so information uploaded to it was bound by its terms of use that each student and user agreed to upon installing it. The current app, HP Reveal, is hosted on Hewlett Packard's servers. Students were told that since these projects were to some extent public that they should not share information that they were uncomfortable with the public seeing. Aurasma did have the option for making projects private, meaning that a project must be shared with a user and his or her account in order to view it; in this class, we kept all projects private until they were complete and had been revised several times. However, Aurasma worked by having a user add various channels in the local area. The user-side app required these channels in order to discover content. As a result, it was hard for members of the campus community to find the AR that the students created unless they were pointed to it directly. This provided additional security for students who didn't want their projects seen by a wide audience. If they did want them shared and seen, however, I recommended that students create projects where there were means to direct other people to their work—even on campus. We used links in the student newspaper and posters for this purpose.

Developing an AR Project via XA

To develop their projects using XA as well as rhetorical concepts, we followed techniques laid out in some of the articles used to frame the project; as well, we reconsidered our work with *Pokémon Go*. The most important of these pieces is Fagerjord's (2017) chapter in Potts and Salvo's edited collection on XA, which specifically looks to classical rhetoric as a way of aiding authors of "locative experiences," those experiences that tie specific places to multimedia experiences (p. 225). He wrote about the development of an application called *Musica Romana* that connected churches to important classical music that that debuted in them or had other connections to famous composers, stating that "most locative projects in the research literature seem to start from a general topic: an idea of what could be interesting to communicate in a certain spot" (p. 226). This was also the question that was posed to students in this course: what important events have happened on our campus? If we were looking at a museum, what important objects could be interesting to communicate about in our museum? History, specifically, is a common use of locative media, especially in AR, because superimposing history information over the places where history took place can be a particularly useful and educational tool. Locative media also is often used for fiction—telling a story like in *Pokémon Go* that puts the user into the story or making a fictive story more immersive by locating it in physical space.

Fagerjord (2017) began his rhetorical planning of locative media by considering *kairos*. He asked creators to consider the following:

> While *Kairos* is often described as the time and place, it is rather the audience gathered in a particular place at a certain time that should be the rhetor's concern. In locative media, however, we know *where* our audience will listen, but not necessarily *when*. And who is the audience at this spot? [p. 228, emphasis in original].

Students in this course had to consider if they were addressing everyone who visited a museum, everyone on campus, or a certain subgroup. Most classes chose to define their audience fairly narrowly, looking for a specific subgroup that might be able to download their app and use it. In museums, of course, we hoped that everyone would take advantage of the AR offered, but many times visitors simply were not interested in having their phones out all the time. Students on a campus tour, however, might be more likely to be willing to use it.

Pokémon Go is partially such a popular game because it appeals to many different audiences—people who play games as well as those who do not, and people who watched the television show and have played earlier games and those that do not. One group of students, seeing that interest was generated by attaching the game to known media, decided to base their game around the school mascot, whom they turned into a ghost (since they were sharing campus ghost stories). This was one of the most successful projects since it mixed something known with a new medium.

Secondly, Fagerjord (2017) discussed *dispositio*,

> meaning ordering the parts, [which] is the temporal dimension of a speech, but in locative media, it will also be in space…. A user interface to the navigation system guides the user from point to point, and we wanted it to be easy, logical, and as expected from earlier interfaces [p. 229].

The Aurasma interface had largely been chosen and designed for us; however, students performed this step when they decided where they were going to locate the various parts of their projects. Their first concern was Wi-Fi availability because cell service tended to be poor in the general Frostburg area for many. Other than this, the 2017 group wanted to place their story around the route that people took on campus tours. Not only were these buildings that they would come back to, but they knew that other people would walk that path and that tour guides could be told about the app. They also placed some of their trigger images where there were existing locations for *Pokémon Go* gyms and Poké Stops because students would have their phones out at those locations.

The third step is *elocutio*, or the recording of audio and other media. After students had decided what they would make and had determined the places to which their app would be linked, the next step was to make the necessary videos and recordings. This is the step where they spent a lot of class time in the lab editing audio and video, recording chunks of both, and editing photos. When working in a large group, students tended to break up these tasks so that the best photo manipulator made the images while other students worked on filming, recording, and editing. This step also bleeds into Fagerjord's fourth step, which is to put everything into the technological system which will allow it to be played back—or *actio*. I added a final step for testing and reviewing all of the work both in the classroom on a big screen and then also out in the world by walking around campus and discussing things that could be added, deleted, or that still needed revision.

Student Projects

A wide variety of projects have come out of this one assignment (which makes this my favorite kind of assignment). Previous to teaching AR as a subset of XA, a small group of students decided to take pictures of door signs around campus and connect them to brief videos about what was in the room. One good example was a gym where the video showed what equipment was inside and how to use some of it if you clicked it. The students felt that these videos would be useful for some first-year students who might be intimidated to go into new spaces that they were not invited to. Another student who worked for the campus newspaper shot video at a game one night, created a still of it, and used Aurasma to animate the newspaper. Because he worked for the paper, he gave directions for viewing the alternate content; many students said reminded them of Hogwarts, the wizarding school from Harry Potter.

A number of students worked with a local museum to do things like connect recipes to an antique stove and connect information about mining in the area to a fake mine exhibit. Other students procured recordings of records and Edison cylinders playing and had them play when users pointed their phones at the cylinders, while another took an exhibit about a local band and connected it to recordings of that band's music. Students working on their own have done things like connecting existing media (sound clips from *Welcome to Night Vale*, specifically) to images connected, which they then put up around campus to invite other students to see, hear, or read the original media.

With XA as the framing, students were more likely to work as large groups to make a bigger game or locative media exhibit for campus. I believe this is because they saw what the media could do by playing *Pokémon Go* and wanted to make something as much like it as possible. They wanted to create a game or story for students on a campus tour to find. They wanted to educate students about things they might not know. A few members of the class were interested in ghost stories; however, the rest of the group felt as if sharing real stories of people who died on campus would be inappropriate (especially after several campus deaths over the past few years). Therefore, they decided to come up with some of their own stories as well as sharing a few stories of haunted dorms that were not connected directly with student deaths. They felt that this would be fun for students who were coming to campus and might make them explore some places on campus that they would not otherwise return to after a tour. They developed a ghost version of our campus mascot and included a lot of hidden Easter eggs as part of the game. Each stop along the way gave clues to where the next stop or story might be, which also forced the potential players to learn something about campus in order to answer the puzzles.

Overall, this was the most cohesive project that involved multiple students in creating AR for the class. While not as serious as developing something for a museum, they were able to work together to tell a story and put it into place around campus. Ultimately, the process of developing an AR project based upon the XA principles that we studied as a class was effective.

Limitations of the Project

What was still missed? The primary potential use of AR games that has been missed by every class to which I have assigned this project is how much students love to play games in class. This might seem obvious—after all, who wants the teacher to know that they play games in class? However, students are primed to make this leap by being allowed to play *Pokémon Go* (and, earlier, *Ingress*) during my class as preparation for their project. They were supposed to let us know if anything good was present in the game, and my only rule was that sound be turned off. This was rarely disruptive to the class as a whole, and more than once enabled a more nuanced discussion of the game since we were playing it together and could compare experiences across phones and operating systems. As I was also playing, students were not led to believe that I was anti-game in any way, yet suggesting that students would like an AR game that could be played discreetly in class has never once been brought up as part of this project.

Every year it seems like something new becomes popular for in-class play. At one point, games that could be played in quick chunks of time during the day rose in popularity alongside smartphones and Facebook in the early 2000s— the shorter games of *Bejeweled Blitz* (2010) and the scattered (but short) playstyle of *Farmville* (2009) grew out of play being slotted between other activities like work, not out of our supposedly shorter attention spans. When these games became playable on smartphones, they only became more popular, spawning *Candy Crush* (2012) and all its imitators. Short rounds and pay-for-play systems meant these games could be played at work, in class, between classes, while stuck in traffic, and anywhere else one might be convinced to spend some time and hopefully some money. *Pokémon Go* is at least partially as successful as it is because of its playstyle that allowed it to be played as easily in a class or office as outdoors, provided that a player was near a Poké Stop or a spawn point.

However, the games that my students have designed have stayed away from classroom spaces. No trigger images have been hidden in classrooms. Without hidden surprises left for bored students, not many students have wandered into the games and AR information that were hidden in plain sight all over campus. The audiences that they have chosen were usually new students or first-years who were still learning their way around campus. These people might be interested in ghost stories on campus or the hours of the fitness center, but other students were far more plentiful and are an untapped audience for the AR games we created. Students didn't want to encourage other students to do "bad things" in class, but the actual game creators had no such limits placed upon them. In the future, I'd like to see students analyze the spaces that they use most often for game play and to apply XA concepts to those spaces by working them into their games. On our campus, people do not often stop in front of the library or many other buildings—but they do stop and spend time in classrooms before, during, and after class. These spaces have a lot of potential to be used for informational augmented placements as well as games.

Conclusion

Ultimately, I believe that projects where students make their own AR and locative media projects will gain popularity as more options are made available to create them. Aurasma was an easy-to-use tool, but it was fairly limited in ways that didn't make it appropriate for more complicated projects than those described here. XA is an excellent way to frame these types of projects, and one that more people in rhetoric and composition and gaming studies should consider. Using a mixture of rhetorical tropes and a process of carefully mediated design, student projects can improve in cohesiveness. Students can use AR to inform as well as to narrate stories, and looking at users of AR in new ways ultimately can help students create better projects from the ground up. Through using analysis and autoethnography, they can also think about the best of what is currently available in AR as a way into their own projects. (Last but not least, teachers can have a lot of fun catching Pokémon with their students!)

REFERENCES

Bardzell, S. (2010). Feminist HCI: Taking stock and outlining an agenda for design. In *Proceedings of the SIGCHI Conference on Human Factors in Computing Systems, USA,* 1301–1310.

Dunleavy, M., Dede, C., & Mitchell, R. (2009). Affordances and limitations of immersive participatory augmented reality simulations for teaching and learning. *Journal of Science Education and Technology, 18*(1), 7–22.

Escobedo, L., Tentori, M., Quintana, E., Favela, J., & Garcia-Rosas, D. (2014). Using augmented reality to help children with autism stay focused. *IEEE Pervasive Computing, 13*(1), 38–46.

Fagerjord, A. (2017). Toward a rhetoric of the place: Creating locative experiences. In L. Potts & M. Salvo (Eds.), *Rhetoric and Experience Architecture* (pp. 225–240). Anderson, SC: Parlor Press.

Friess, E. (2017). Personas as rhetorically rich and complex mechanisms for design. In L. Potts & M. Salvo (Eds.), *Rhetoric and Experience Architecture* (pp. 111–121). Anderson, SC: Parlor Press.

Grice, R. (2017). Experience architecture: Drawing principles from life. In L. Potts & M. Salvo (Eds.), *Rhetoric and Experience Architecture* (pp. 41–56). Anderson, SC: Parlor Press.

Ibáñez, M.B., Di Serio, Á., Villarán, D., & Kloos, C.D. (2014). Experimenting with electromagnetism using augmented reality: Impact on flow student experience and educational effectiveness. *Computers & Education, 71*, 1–13.

Ingress. (n.d.). *Ingress Wiki.* Retrieved from http://ingress.wikia.com/wiki/Ingress.

Kato, T.A., Teo, A.R., Tateno, M., Watabe, M., Kubo, H., & Kanba, S. (2017). Can *Pokémon GO* rescue shut-ins (hikikomori) from their isolated world? *Psychiatry and Clinical Neurosciences, 71*(1), 75–76.

Kurlinkus, W.C. (2017). Memorial interactivity: Scaffolding nostalgic user experiences. In L. Potts & M. Salvo (Eds.), *Rhetoric and Experience Architecture* (pp. 274–290). Anderson, SC: Parlor Press.

Liarokapis, F., & Anderson, E.F. (2010). Using augmented reality as a medium to assist teaching in higher education. Paper presented at Eurographics 2010, Norrköping, Sweden.

Mara, A., & Mara, M. (2017). Ethnography as research aggregator. In L. Potts & M. Salvo (Eds.), *Rhetoric and Experience Architecture* (pp. 184–196). Anderson, SC: Parlor Press.

Potts, L., & Salvo, M.J. (2017). Introduction. In L. Potts & M. Salvo (Eds.), *Rhetoric and Experience Architecture* (pp. 3–13). Anderson, SC: Parlor Press.

Sano-Franchini, J. (2017). Feminist rhetorics and interaction design: Facilitating socially responsible design. In L. Potts & M. Salvo (Eds.), *Rhetoric and Experience Architecture* (pp. 84–110). Anderson, SC: Parlor Press.

Shelton, B.E., & Hedley, N.R. (2002). Using augmented reality for teaching Earth-Sun relationships to undergraduate geography students. In *The First IEEE International Augmented Reality Toolkit Workshop, Germany.* doi: 10.1109/ART.2002.1106948.

PART TWO

Why We Play

Rhetorical Augmentation

Public Play, Place and Persuasion in Pokémon Go

JASON CHEW KIT THAM *and*
DEONDRE SMILES

A reality-shifting, experience-augmenting game, *Pokémon Go* became a sudden cultural phenomenon in July 2016. *Pokémon Go* achieved overnight popularity as all around the world, cities witnessed thousands of players congregating in public places capturing Pokémon, harvesting essential game items like Poké Balls and Pokémon eggs at Poké Stops, training and battling in gyms, and logging steps to help level up their Pokémon. Although the mobile game has since slowly lost hype, we agree with the editors that it remains a cultural artifact worthy of scholarly examination to identify how it has expanded our conversations about sociotechnological concerns such as physical and digital object representations, place-based rhetorics, and community building through gameplay.

Augmented reality (AR) arguably moved from industrial computing into the public sphere since Google announced the release of its wearable computer Google Glass in 2013, starting the trend of consumer AR as the viable next stage of development in personal computing. But AR is not all that new or novel; we show in our literature review section that many consumer technologies we encounter in our daily lives already have some sort of AR integration. However, AR can mean different things to different people. So, as a key term to this project, we subscribe to Irshad and Rambli's (2017) definition that AR is "a system that combines real and computer generated information in a real environment, interactively and in real time, and aligns virtual objects with physical objects" (p. 466).

Through the lens of *Pokémon Go*, we may understand and critically interpret a variety of issues involved in augmented public play. Liao and Humphreys (2014) concluded that AR technologies may complicate social practices, experiences, and relationships in a spatial landscape. In their examination of the AR composing app *Layer*, Liao and Humphreys have found that users create augmented content to embed communication, historicize places, and change or challenge authority. Similarly, Forlano (2013) contended that AR technologies can be used to co-produce the concept of place through visualization of digital materials, lived experience, and imagination. These observations are also made by Mejeur in this collection through the narratives of place-based play experience. Building on these findings, we provide new observations on how persuasive user engagement is produced through a sophisticated combination of the virtual and the real in *Pokémon Go* gameplay.

In this essay, we examine the intersections of the rhetorics and technologies of augmentation, with a specific investigation of how *Pokémon Go* works as a rhetorical device that manipulates public play and sense of place. We seek to build a theory of user experience that considers the marriage between physical and digital representations of location and how location-specific discourse presented through an interactive mobile application can affect a user's spatial experience. We employ rhetorical analysis of official *Pokémon Go* announcements (disseminated through subscriber emails) and qualitative interviews with a convenience sample of nine users to collect empirical data on the game's discourse and user experience. Coupled with a thematic analysis of narrative data collected from the interviews, we build a theory of rhetorical augmentation with implications for future play, practice, and pedagogy. We ground our theory in Rieder's (2017) transductive model (think both sensory processing and information flow), in which he argued that the post–PC era of ubiquitous computing can be a theoretical model for digital rhetors—and by extension, game designers, developers, and communicators—to invent persuasive experiences in a mixed reality.

Given the simple yet impressive AR capability that *Pokémon Go* affords, we argue in this essay that emerging location-based AR games can leverage virtual integration with physical places to foster public engagement with places through rhetorical transduction across physical and virtual elements. We end by providing what our observations mean for future iterations of AR technologies and game design, user participation, and pedagogical approaches to teaching students about the rhetorics of technologies.

Literature Review

AR and Human-Computer Meaning-Making

We begin by studying how AR is reorganizing our orientation to meaning-making in our immediate surroundings. To start, we look at some of the most common AR on the market today and examine the ways in which they affect how we make sense of our worlds, whether physical, virtual, or somewhere in between. Since we experience our surroundings mainly through our perception—i.e., representation and interpretation of sensory information presented to us in order to understand the environment—we enter this conversation by briefly reviewing the three most immediately accessible dimensions of perceptual augmentation, namely visual, sonic, and haptic augmentations.

Thanks to our cultural obsession with the boundary-breaking sci-fi invention that prioritizes visual feedback, the *Star Trek* Holodeck, the visual is now one of the most widely adopted sensory dimensions for augmentation. Early AR technologies such as Google Glass and Microsoft HoloLens have focused on enhancing and leveraging human visual capability in various daily life applications. Visual AR tends to either create a "third-eye" effect for the user or to increase depth perception by adding layers to a target object (Duin, Moses, McGrath, & Tham, 2016). For example, the beta version of Google Glass gave wearers a literal third layer of vision in addition to their analog sight and screen display. In the case of *Pokémon Go*, players can visually experience the intersection of their physical world and the virtual world through the overlay of Pokémon creatures on their analog world space (Figure 5.1).

Although vision is the most immediate sensory receptor for most people, sounds, for a long time, have also been used to hybridize our analog and technological worlds (Hocks & Comstock, 2017). Consider the surveillance systems for electronic articles employed by retail stores or libraries: Acousto-

Figure 5.1. A player "interacting" with a Machop as seen through another player's phone camera. Photograph by Jason Chew Kit Tham and used with permission of the person captured.

magnetic or radio frequency tags are used to mark merchandise and books, and they trigger detection systems that are usually placed at store exits if one tries to remove a tagged article from the secured premises without authorized deactivation of the tags. As a result, our shopping behaviors are shaped by the presence of these sonic surveillance technologies. Today, sonic AR is used to enhance our interaction with our physical surroundings. Sonic augmentation includes sonic installations across landmarks or travel attractions, such as the self-guided audio tours that museums use via apps like *GeoTourist*. Walking or traveling around with an earpiece that works as an electronic sensor, users may get location-specific information in tagged spaces.

Haptic augmentation (tactile or kinesthetic feedback prompted by a user's interaction with objects in the virtual world) is slowly becoming another common form of sensory augmentation. Disney Research, for instance, is developing REVEL, a tactile AR technology that "allows for change to the tactile feeling of real objects by augmenting them with virtual tactile textures using a device worn by the user" (Bau & Poupyrev, 2012, para. 1). A more common gadget, the Apple Watch, is known for integrating haptic feedback with notifications such as upcoming calendar events, scheduled exercises (reminders to wearers that it's time to stand or move), and even reminders for focused breathing. Haptic AR is proving to be one of the friendliest, least intrusive interactions a user may receive from their device since haptic feedback can be very minimalistic—like a quiet vibration on the wrist—that does not alert the surrounding public.

For the most part, AR allows the intertwining of digital elements or objects with our physical world. Such an interfacing experience invokes a new level of human-computer interactivity that was previously unavailable through 2D virtual environments. In his study of human "life" among digital objects, Liberati (2018) observed that the goal of AR is to "make our everyday world inhabited by digital objects and so to move the intertwinement between digital elements and users' everyday lives to a completely different level" (p. 213). This new level of interaction or intertwinement is immersive; AR technology merges digital objects that were once perceived as fictitious into our everyday world, allowing them to coexist with AR technology users. Scholars of human-computer interaction studies have described such experiences as similar to Schultz's (1962) phenomenology of paramount reality, where the lines between virtual and physical worlds are increasingly blurred. In 2D virtual reality, users experience their everyday lives with various finite provinces of meanings (Ayaß, 2017) generated by fantasies and games. In those worlds, users give meanings to the fictional objects they encounter with the help of augmenting technologies, albeit these objects do not have any relevance outside their virtual world. AR takes this phenomenology to a new height due to the immersive hybridization of technologized and analog experiences that AR technology affords. What AR users do via their AR applications can no longer be confined to the virtual world since "they are performed in space and time which are part of the paramount reality too" (Liberati, 2018, p. 228). This realization is key to the *Pokémon Go* experience—as many others in this collection have chosen to investigate further in their respective cases (particularly Cole & Pulos; Eanes & van den Broek; Heili, Xu, & Crane; Mejeur)—and we show later in our study that players organize their real-world community around the gameplay.

Geospatial technology in gaming has long been an object of academic study in geography and other related disciplines, with some early studies dating back to the early 1960s (Ahlqvist et al., 2012, p. 334). Much contemporary academic work has centered around collecting geospatial data as an objective of "games with a purpose," games that are intended to be educational for their players (Matyas et al., 2008, p. 244). One objective of such a game is collecting data about real-life cities (p. 244); another was a prototype game featuring the creation of a virtual board game using geospatial data (Ahlqvist, Loffing, Ramanathan, & Kocher, 2012, pp. 335–336). Augmented reality is a recent addition to this frontier of gaming, but its intellectual origins are not new— over 10 years ago, scholars hypothesized that geographic features in real life would be merged with mobile technology in order to create "cheap" augmented reality games and technologies (Ferreira, Orvalho, & Boavida, 2005, pp. 1775–1776).

Recent experiments with virtual reality/AR gaming have been used in pursuit of building sustainable, smart cities, such as a game that rewarded users for using greener, more sustainable methods of transportation (Pajarito & Gould, 2017, p. 52). With the rise in popularity of *Pokémon Go*, there is a burgeoning literature on the game itself and its geospatial impacts, whether that is rewriting explicit or implicit access to space (Mans, 2016), or even more broadly, how the game influences the mobilities of different populations through space (Colley et al., 2017). This, as a whole, demonstrates the integral connection between AR games such as *Pokémon Go* and the geospatial technologies that underpin them.

Whether through visual, sonic, and haptic augmentation, or geospatial orientation, AR is making our common lives more digitally augmented. Given such magnitude of effects, game studios like Niantic have capitalized on AR capacities to motivate *Pokémon Go* players to perform a plethora of activities—from engaging with the game to socializing with other players. In the next section, we examine a few rhetorical strategies in *Pokémon Go* that are afforded by AR technology to achieve these goals.

Rhetoric on the Go: Mobilizing Physical, Cultural and Socio-Geographical Experiences

Most game design scholars turn to Bogost as a celebrated digital rhetorician who argued that videogames are both an expressive medium and a persuasive medium. Enacting a procedural rhetorical argument, Bogost (2007) demonstrated that videogames use computational processes (if-then causal effects) and rule-based symbolic manipulation (what determines or constitutes winning or losing) to support as well as challenge existing social and cultural positions. If we use Bogost's argument as a rhetorical foundation for understanding *Pokémon Go*, we can see that the AR game is indeed a persuasive platform designed to enable multiple experiences as well as shatter some socio-cultural expectations.

First, *Pokémon Go* has been a considerably successful persuasive game, given its reported effects on players and their attitudes toward physical activity. Since its release in summer 2016, the game has piqued the interest of many clinical psychologists and medical researchers to study how players are physically impacted by gameplay. Early studies have found that *Pokémon Go* led to substantial short-term activity increases and had the potential to reach activity-poor populations (Althoff, White, & Horvitz, 2016). Some scholars called it "the Pikachu Effect" (Kaczmarek, Misiak, Behnke, & Dziekan, 2017): *Pokémon Go* has become a health motivator and a social motivator as it is related to health outcomes in players. Individuals who spent more time playing *Pokémon Go* were more physically active. They also spent more time outdoors. Players who used to be sedentary have also benefited from playing *Pokémon Go*. The game can be a starting point for sedentary people to begin a more active lifestyle (Wong, 2017).

Besides its sensory appeal, *Pokémon Go* researchers have noted that the gameplay employs narrative and social immersion strategies to keep its players engaged (Liu, Wagner, & Suh, 2017). Giddings (2017) observed how these strategies contribute to the social phenomenon of distributed imagination in *Pokémon Go*, noting that "the transmedia universe of Pokémon is a techno-aesthetic platform that facilitates particular kinds of imaginative engagement, from the rule-bound and intentional, to more unpredictable and expansive semiotic and performative play" (p. 61). Additionally, "*Pokémon Go* is integral to a rapidly changing digital economy of attention in which imagination is mobilized by, and flows through, the temporal dimensions of mobile and social media games, as well as their spatial, narrative, and economic dimensions" (p. 61). What's key in this observation is that distributed imagination is "a *social* phenomenon rather than a solitary, internal process as it is generally characterized" (p. 60, emphasis in original).

Pokémon Go also contributes to a reconfiguration of ludic culture. Since the 1960s, when the use of the word ludic became popular in western societies to designate playful behavior and artifacts, playfulness has become increasingly a mainstream characteristic of modern culture. Mäyrä (2017) contended that in modern "ludic society," or an "era of games,"

> where play and associated ludic literacies become culturally dominant ... managing and mastering games that take place in multiple layers of reality ... can create conflict with the social and cultural norms relating to proper behavior in private and public places [p. 49].

At the same time, it "means they also function as training grounds for people to evolve ludic literacies" (p. 49). In other words, AR technology and gaming make us reconsider what was familiar to us and shatter some conventional expectations about place and space in our culture.

Potentially, Mäyrä (2017) maintained, "games and play will in this broader ludification process have gradually more and more notable roles in informing our public and private behaviors, as well as in the practices of product and service design, work, learning, and multiple other areas of culture and society" (p. 49). An example of such influence can be found in nature conservation, where *Pokémon Go* is used to help establish public interest in nature and build conservation ethics. For instance, a number of conservation and nature organizations have tried making the most of *Pokémon Go* and the game's ability to motivate players to explore the natural world around them (Dorward, Mittermeier, Sandbrook, & Spooner, 2017). The journal *Nature* has publicly encouraged *Pokémon Go* players to make a contribution to real-world taxonomy by photographing and identifying real species during their Pokémon hunts ("Gotta Name Them All," 2016), and the U.S. Fish & Wildlife Service has produced a blog comparing Pokémon to the real species that occur at the National Wildlife Refuges (Brigida, 2016).

Three immersive strategies that Liu, Wagner, and Suh (2017) have identified in *Pokémon Go* as a way to engage players are tactical, strategic, and spatial. Common players know that unity is strength in the *Pokémon Go* gameplay. Typically, players would not only capture wild Pokémon alone, but also gather friends to tackle Pokémon that are high-level raid bosses or occupying gym spaces. No doubt this kind of unusual congregating in urban spaces can create inconveniences for others sharing the space. Following the innumerable stories of new friendships and experiences as a result of playing *Pokémon Go*, there have also been problematic cases of large groups of players dominating what would otherwise be semi-private spaces, such as residential streets and housing estates (Golding, 2016, p. 127). As Gong, Hassink, and Maus (2017) stated, "From a geography perspective, *Pokémon Go* and the like have provided new insights into at least two relevant topics, i.e., the perception and understanding of space … as well as [a] human's patterns of mobility" (p. 228).

Much has been written about the varied experiences associated with the act of walking and traversing public spaces. The act of walking is one where the walker may, and often does, interact with the urban spaces around them (Wunderlich, 2008, p. 125). Walking can have different purposes as well, depending on the pace or rhythm that one walks (Wunderlich, 2008; Edensor, 2010, pp. 69–70). For example, "purposive walking" means walking with a clear goal or destination in mind, while "discursive walking" is less goal-driven and more guided by observing the environments one walks in (Wunderlich, 2008, pp. 132–133). In an AR game where the environments surrounding the player come into play (whether they are large public spaces or specific urban landmarks), both types of walking come into play. The rise of pedestrian-driven urban design, such as in newer suburban "town-center" developments, or even the remaking of urban cores as walker-friendly zones, has led to the encouragement of walking and community engagement (Middleton, 2018, p. 300). A game such as *Pokémon Go* ties into this increased engagement through its promotion of walking and exploration.

The turning of serious ordinary spaces into playful spaces sheds unique light on the social construction of space. As the privatization of public spaces becomes more prominent, we begin to observe how *Pokémon Go* gameplay is more than digital. In their essay on locational privacy in this collection, Eanes and van den Broek explicated how private gameplay affects both the personal and the public. Indeed, playing *Pokémon Go* is an embodied experience associated with real-life material conditions, including the way our cities are structured and our mode of transportation (e.g., which way can I take to get to this next landmark Poké Stop? Should I take my dog along?), the weather and our clothing (e.g., is it warm enough to go outside and log some steps tonight?), and the capability of our devices (e.g., will my phone last this whole game session, or do I need a portable power bank?). We focus on these material layers in the next section.

Transductive Experience in AR Gameplay

Goggin (2017) observed a "nuanced geopolitical, transnational, regional, national, intercultural, cross-generation, and translocal framing of locations of audience" in *Pokémon Go* (p. 45). Building on the previous sections, wherein digital objects hold significant meanings in our "paramount reality" (Schutz & Luckmann, 1973) and where real (as opposed to virtual) spaces are subject to social construction, we discuss in this section a theory of transduction that can be used to describe the *Pokémon Go* experience—an experience that transcends national identities, cultures, and locational affiliation.

In *Suasive Iterations: Rhetoric, Writing, and Physical Computing*, Rieder (2017) provided a useful metaphor for theorizing AR and ubiquitous computing as rhetorical experience, and it is worth quoting in full:

> In rhetoric, there is a long tradition of calling the tropes and schemes comprising the figures of speech as the flowers of rhetoric. Traditionally, the flowers are language-based ways in which to transform (or transduce) the sound, rhythm, relationships, and meaning of words toward suasive ends. If we characterize the discovery of new flowers as a process of botanization, then as a rhetor learns how to "botanize" the transductive microcomponents on which the new era is based—identifying their affordances and constraints, and then cataloging the many ways in which the data associated with them can be transduced and allegorized—she will have taken an important step forward toward the establishment of a new canon of stylistic invention [p. 31].

Rieder proposed a transductive approach to understanding how persuasion manifests through the digital (virtual/immersive) and analog (physical/material) layers of communication. What is transduction, exactly? The prefix *trans-* denotes change from a medium to another; the postfix in *transduction* indicates "ductility," which means the ability of a material to be compressed, deformed, and transformed into a new state of being. In other words, transduction theory denotes a way of understanding communication by investigating the layered materiality through which the communication traverses.

Those who are interested in the entanglement between substantial states of being can study how movement, amplification, and reception alter our perception and reaction. Many of us may recall learning in grade school science classes how we perceive sounds. In the auditory system, sound vibrations (mechanical energy) are transduced into electrical energy by hair cells in the inner ear. Our brain detects the information transmitted to it from the cochlea of our inner ear. This transmission is a transductive process—each node (vibration, electric, information) passes on the content it received to the next node for further processing. Transduction can therefore be a useful conceptual framework for investigating the shifting of user experience from one layer of materiality (say tactile, such as a mouse click) to another (visual/cognitive sensation, like a pop-up window on the screen). For interface design and experience architecture, transduction can be represented by layers and depth, such as "the Stack" (Figure 5.2) that is illustrated in Bratton's (2015) *The Stack: On Software and Sovereignty.*

The term "stack" is borrowed from the TCP/IP or layered model of distributed network architecture. Bratton noted during an interview with Metahaven (2012) that the six interdependent layers of the stack are "an attempt to conceive of the technical and geopolitical structures of planetary compu-

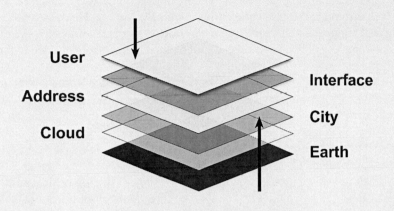

Figure 5.2. "The Stack," according to Bratton (2016), is an accidental megastructure that is both a computational apparatus and a new governing architecture (p. 66). Graphic recreated by Jason Chew Kit Tham.

tation as 'totality'" (para. 4). Traditionally, a technology stack is comprised of both hardware and software, with storage servers situated toward the bottom and end-user applications toward the top. Bratton added the city, cloud, and earth to drag computation from a mere technical ideal down to the real, the messy, and the political act of socio-cultural dominance (with geotic impact). With Bratton's model, one should no longer just look *at* a particular layer and critique its significance, but look *through* the layers by which ideas, messages, and meanings transduce and affect one another.

Pokémon Go provides similar layered effects on spatial experiences for players. Earth is no longer a habitat for humanity, flora, and fauna, but a fertile land for digital creatures to cohabitate with humankind. This cohabitation requires preprogrammed manifestation and reactivity such that the game designers must determine how players would or would not be able to interact with the in-game features on a real-time basis. For example, raid battles are pre-scheduled at specific gyms, and that determines how players decide to "prepare" the gym for the raid bosses prior to their hatches. Anecdotally speaking, as authors we have participated in what are often called gym turnarounds that were organized by the teams (Valor, Instinct, Mystic) in order to gain or regain control of a specific gym before a high-level raid battle began at the gym. These turnarounds occur because members from the team that controls the gym at the time of the raid battle receive additional Premier Balls to catch the raid boss after they have won the raid. With the introduction of the dynamic weather system in November 2017, whereby current weather conditions affect the strengths (attack and defense) of Pokémon, player bonuses, and appearances of wild Pokémon in the game, players engage not just with place but also space simultaneously. In his essay within this collection, Mejeur explicitly dealt with the notion of place and space: where a place is a physical dimension, a space is co-created by the experience of those who occupy it.

Outside the game's software design and users' interaction with their phones, researchers also observe changes in players' everyday routine. On a mammalian layer, researchers found that playing *Pokémon Go* affected the amount of time players spent with their pets. A whopping 52.3 percent of players in a study reported they spent more time with their dog as a result of playing *Pokémon Go* (Kogan, Hellyer, Duncan, & Schoenfeld-Tacher, 2017). To further investigate such real-time transduction between physical and virtual entities in *Pokémon Go*, we have conducted a study looking at how *Pokémon Go* inspired players to engage in layered locational exploration as well as gathering actual players' narratives about their gameplay experience. We describe our data collection and analysis methods in the next section.

Methods

Understanding the geospatial and embodied experiences associated with *Pokémon Go* and other augmented reality games is essential to understanding the rhetorical values that are associated with *Pokémon Go*. These experiences can tell us how one explores the spaces around them and how geospatial technology has been used to harness a sense of augmented exploration in AR games. To study the kind of social intervention *Pokémon Go* brings to public gaming, we needed methods that could capture the uptake and social effects of the game in a comprehensive manner. Recognizing the complex intervention *Pokémon Go* poses for social researchers, Clark and Clark (2016) stated that mixed-method designs are ideal for this purpose. Following their recommendation, we employed rhetorical analysis and qualitative interviews in our mixed-method study design.

Rhetorical Analysis

To understand how *Pokémon Go* engages players and motivates them to utilize its AR features, we performed an exploratory rhetorical analysis of the official announcements sent to players via subscriber emails. Since both the authors have been active players of the game since its release, we were able to archive all subscriber announcements from December 2016 to December 2017, which is when this essay was written. We decided to include emails only after December 2016 because Niantic did not send regular subscriber email under the name of "The Official Pokémon GO Team" until then. The total number of emails gathered and analyzed was 21. In our analysis, we focused specifically on the interplay between the rhetorical appeals of the email communications and the specific in-game and real-life events *Pokémon Go* held during the period of these emails. We were most interested in how these email communications stimulate a rhetorical urgency for public play and how they affect players' sense of place. Our analysis process was informed by Krippendorff's (2013) content analysis.

Qualitative Interviews

In November and December 2017, we solicited responses from *Pokémon Go* players using direct requests from our personal networks of friends and on Facebook groups that are intended for *Pokémon Go* players in a specific geographical region to share information about the games. Groups that were targeted included groups in the Twin Cities metropolitan area as well as the greater Minnesota, Columbus, Ohio, and the broader Central Ohio regions. Once players expressed interest in being interviewed, they were contacted via email with more information about this essay project and a list of questions for them to answer. The questions were as follows:

1. How long have you played *Pokémon Go* (PG)?
2. How would you describe your experience as a PG player?
3. What are the most interesting aspects of the game for you?
4. Has playing PG changed the way you interact with your surrounding community (public places, private spaces, campus areas, neighborhood, etc.)? Why/how so?
   (a) With whom have you interacted as part of playing PG?
   (b) Where have you been as part of playing PG?
   (c) What event or activity have you participated in as part of playing PG?
5. Overall, how has PG affected your perception of space, and/or social interactions between people and places?

We designed these questions to be open-ended enough to allow the respondents to elaborate upon their experiences as players. There was a wide range of interest from the *Pokémon Go* groups with which we engaged, and we collected 20 interview responses. Due to incompletion and the lack of clarity in 11 of those responses, we have included only nine of these responses for analysis in this essay. We deemed the excluded responses too ambiguous for analysis. Many of them consisted of short answers such as, "Oh, I love this game" and "I play it a lot" without substantial elaborations to justify their claims.

Findings

Rhetorical Analysis Results

Most of the official emails aimed to communicate the latest updates to the *Pokémon Go* game app by highlighting new features. Among these emails, many of them also included information about ways in which players could participate in their local community as part of their gameplay experience. In the December 17, 2016, email, for example, players were told there were "tens of millions of people in over 120 countries" playing *Pokémon Go* (para. 1), encouraging players to celebrate their membership in a global community (Figure 5.3).

Photo: Chris Collins

Did you know that tens of millions of people in over 120 countries are now playing Pokémon GO? It's fun to see so many of you getting outside with your family and friends. All of these Trainers can't be wrong, that's why Apple and Google both named Pokémon GO one of the Best Games of 2016. You can learn more about Pokémon GO and our global community on our social channels.

Figure 5.3. Screenshot from December 17, 2016, subscriber email received by Jason Chew Kit Tham (subscriber). Within the image is a promotional photograph released by Niantic.

Players were also motivated to be a part of a global movement. For example, in the May 4, 2017, email, players were motivated to contribute to a country-based contest. In the May 2017 "Eggstravaganza" event, players were inspired to compete on behalf of their respective countries. By the end of the event, Niantic shared the total number of Pokémon eggs that were hatched based on the number of steps walked during the event time frame—a whopping 87 million eggs (each takes either 2K, 5K, or 10K in steps to hatch)! The top five countries in order of distances walked by local players were the United States, Japan, Taiwan, the United Kingdom, and Germany. While this competitive event did not require players to actively seek out their local community to achieve the event goals, it was successful in fostering a communal spirit associated by country—in the sense that the players showed solidarity and national pride through collective achievements.

In the May 4, 2017, email, Niantic also shared a study from the University of Washington which found that *Pokémon Go* helps kids to spend more quality time with their parents (see also Sierra and Burgoon's essay in this collection on intergenerational gameplaying). This emotional appeal entices players who value family time or interactions with younger kids. For those who are not in a familial relationship, Niantic shared another study from the University of Wisconsin stating that playing *Pokémon Go* helps players to make friends, improves friendship, and leads to a happier state of mind.

In July 2017, Niantic hosted its first-ever real-world *Pokémon Go* event in Chicago (see a detailed account of this event by Mejeur in this collection), followed by a similar series of country-specific events in Europe and Japan. Thus, for the majority of its subscriber emails during the event periods, Niantic appealed to the fantasy of location-based game advantage—how players from different parts of the world may benefit differently from their primary geographic position. Following these festivals, Niantic launched its next location-based game feature: that is, the Legendary Pokémon appearances. While the first Legendary birds—Articuno, Moltres, Zapdos, and Lugia— were not restricted to regions, the second set of Legendary Pokémon—Entei, Raikou, and Suicune—were. The Legendary beasts rotated throughout the Americas, Europe and Africa, and Asia-Pacific regions.

These location-specific events continued through October in Europe, including Denmark, Prague, and the Czech Republic, after their major launch in July. In the October 20, 2017, email, Niantic shared how "passionate Trainers gathered to catch some awesome Pokémon, make new friends, and enjoy a fun time with friends and family" (para. 1) in their live events (Figure 5.4).

To encourage players to maximize the AR features of *Pokémon Go*, Niantic held an AR photo contest in October 2017. In an October 11, 2017, email, players were asked to share their "most epic *Pokémon Go* AR photos on Instagram with the hashtag #PokémonGOcontest." In November 2017,

POKÉMON GO SAFARI ZONE IN EUROPE

On October 7, thousands of Trainers from around the world attended Pokémon GO Safari Zone in Europe at Fisketorvet in Copenhagen, Denmark, and Centrum Cerny Most in Prague, Czech Republic. Passionate Trainers gathered to catch some awesome Pokémon, make new friends, and enjoy a fun time with friends and family. If you'd like the chance to attend our future live events, visit our events page to stay up-to-date on our event schedule.

Figure 5.4. Screenshot from October 20, 2017, subscriber email received by Jason Chew Kit Tham (subscriber). Within the image are two promotional photographs released by Niantic.

Niantic announced that they had received more than 50,000 AR photo submissions and chose ten winners for this contest. The photo contest is an exemplary instance of community building through participatory gameplay. Even if players were playing individually, they may still get a sense they are a part of a global *Pokémon Go* community through Instagram.

Breaking away from its regular country- or team-based contests, Niantic held a weeklong Global Catch Challenge in November 2017. Three social media celebrities were hired as travel hosts to tour around Japan and encourage players from around the world to help them reach their goal of catching 3 billion Pokémon in just seven days. As rewards, Niantic released double experience points, or XP (to level up players), double Stardust (to level up Pokémon), six-hour lure modules (to keep a Poké Stop active longer), and two rare Pokémon—Farfetch'd (worldwide) and Kangaskhan (in East Asia). This global event focused on creating a sense of global player membership such that each player who participated in the catch challenge felt that they held some stakes in achieving a worldwide goal.

Overall, a notable discourse produced by Niantic through the official subscriber emails is the emphasis on public rather than private play. This can be seen through the visual portrayals of players in the emails: They are always in pairs or small groups, photographed to show how the game brings people together and enhances relationships. The events held between December 2016 and December 2017 also fostered a communal rather than individual focus for the gameplay. Events like the Eggstravaganza and Global Catch Challenge helped create a collective sense of membership among players at a national as well as global scale.

Second, the subscriber emails also focused on motivating players to interact with their environment as part of the gameplay. One obvious effort is the AR photo contest that encouraged players to find creative ways to show how their surrounding environments added to the experience of the game. Another rhetorical move is seen in Niantic's effort to create a sense of location through the region-specific release of rare Pokémon (such as Kangaskhan in the Global Catch Challenge) and country-based Pokémon events (like the Safari Zone events in Europe and Pikachu Outbreak in Japan). Various countries—including the United States, France, and South Korea—have also hosted individual *Pokémon Go* Fests in conjunction with new Pokémon releases and changes to the gym battling features.

Interview Results

The responses that we received from our respondents highlighted the diversity of personal experiences related to playing *Pokémon Go*, with some threads of commonality weaved throughout. In regard to when the respondents began playing *Pokémon Go*, one immediate common factor was that all of the respondents had begun playing the game since the day it was released, or within a week afterwards, and had largely been playing continuously since then. Regarding the personal experiences from playing *Pokémon Go*, there was more diversity in the responses and more unique experiences; some played as a way to connect with their classmates, others played with their children, and some even preferred to play mostly by themselves. However, some common threads and themes that did emerge included participating in raid battles, exploring their surrounding areas, and getting out of their homes and being active in their communities. To demonstrate these observations, we provide some quotes from our interviews here under our respondents' pseudonyms.

First, many of the respondents felt that the most interesting parts of the game were catching Pokémon in real-world locations and the cooperative nature of many gameplay elements, such as the aforementioned raid battles. Andy and Naomi described how *Pokémon Go* fit into their work and personal lifestyles.

> ANDY: Around my work complex, my coworkers and I usually walk around a corporate pond where more or less the same strangers will appear around Poké Stops, gyms, and raids throughout the day.
>
> NAOMI: I got sucked into *PG* [*Pokémon Go*] because it fits into my life well. I have always been a big walker, and these days, I walk my dog and walk around the downtown Minneapolis skyway system where I work. I also take long leisure walks when the weather is nice. *PG* fits right into that.

Others praised different aspects of the real-world nature of the game, such as the prevalence of certain types of Pokémon in certain natural environments, or the new (at the time of this writing) dynamic weather feature and its effect on Pokémon appearances. For example, Megan shared how she felt playing *Pokémon Go* at night.

> MEGAN: Especially late at night, it seems clandestine to be wandering around an abandoned factory or closed churchyard looking for things that are invisible to everyone else.

When asked whether or not *Pokémon Go* had changed the ways that respondents interacted with their communities and the spaces within, all of the respondents answered in the affirmative. All of them reported becoming more active in walking or biking around their neighborhoods, campuses and cities/towns—some mentioned that they played on vacation—and they interacted with other *Pokémon Go* players, whether friends, families, or complete strangers. Megan and Ashley's responses below are particularly complementary to Cole and Pulos' essay in this collection where signs of gameplay are detectable by fellow players:

> MEGAN: Unlike a traditional game, with no social interactions or even a phone MMO where you could be sitting next to another player and never even know it, you can usually spot the signs of someone playing *PG* in the real world. It makes a nice icebreaker to know that you have something in common with people you bump into.
>
> ASHLEY: I usually felt either too sad or just introverted or shy to do a lot of talking to other people that were there, to really, you know, strike up conversations and try to actively make friends with random *Pokémon Go* players. But people were also usually really good about saying, "Oh you know there's a Vulpix over there, or there is a whatever over there," and I would have small conversations with people.

Most respondents' interaction efforts turned out to be related to game events; however, these were generally limited to raid battles. As far as how *Pokémon Go* had affected respondents' perceptions of public space and how individuals interact with said space, the majority of responses centered around the "opening up" of previously unknown places to them as a result of walking around while playing the game. Several respondents mentioned that through the act of playing the game (e.g., walking around, intently interacting with one's phone), they were able to identify *Pokémon Go* players and make contact with them, exposing them to interactions in which they might not ordinarily participate.

> DIANE: [*Pokémon Go*] has definitely helped me develop a network of people that I otherwise wouldn't have known. It's affected my perception of space by getting me to explore new areas in the Twin Cities. There are a lot of really cool places that I love going, such as Kellogg Park, that I may not have gone to if it weren't for *PG*.

One respondent made explicit references to the AR used in *Pokémon Go*, mentioning that the game's influence on being outdoors and exercising can serve as a model for future AR games.

> CAMERON: Playing *PG* has definitely changed what I do in spaces. For instance, going to new places has a new aspect of wonder, because not only am I going to a new place, but I have the chance to spin new Poké Stops and possibly find new and different types of Pokémon. Staying on campus rather than immediately heading home after class is easier because there is a reason to stay; the types of Pokémon on campus are different. The game also encourages me to go outside and exercise (an aspect I really appreciate) so I can get steps and hatch eggs.

In summary, two main themes can be parsed from these responses. The first is that *Pokémon Go* has served as a catalyst for these players to explore and investigate the public spaces around them in a way that may not have happened otherwise. The second theme is that of creating new connections among strangers based upon the simple act of playing *Pokémon Go*.

Discussion

AR Gaming as Social, Physical and Locational Experience

It is clear that AR-based games such as *Pokémon Go* involve their players in an experience that manifests itself and can be felt on social, physical, and locational levels. On the social level, a game such as *Pokémon Go* relies on building and maintaining social connections and networks in order to access certain facets of the game and to make the game more enjoyable. It is entirely possible to play *Pokémon Go* without social interaction, but events such as raid battles are nearly impossible to participate in as an individual. Additionally, social networks that are built through the game (whether they are social media groups or those informally established wherever the game is played at any given moment) provide not only the practical effects of learning the locations of Pokémon, gym battles, and raid battles but also a sense of camaraderie and community centered around catching Pokémon.

On the physical and locational levels, the experience of *Pokémon Go* is something that plays out in the real world that surrounds the player. The environments of the communities we live in are transformed into a virtual world filled with Pokémon, Poké Stops, and gyms. We travel to and through these places and spaces, becoming familiar with them not only as fields of gameplay but as part of geographies that we were not previously aware of. These geographical features and their own unique histories and identities become known to us as we interact with them. Through this increasing familiarity, we become more plugged into the amenities and settings of our communities and how we make use of them even when we are not playing *Pokémon Go*. In fact, one of the authors (Smiles) remembered being exposed to a beautiful city park in the center of downtown Columbus, Ohio, through *Pokémon Go* that he continues to use as a walking space even when he's not playing. In this way, *Pokémon Go* provides a gateway into truly becoming familiar with what has always been around us.

Rhetorical Augmentation

During our analysis of Niantic's discourse through official emails to players and the interview responses from active players, we observed a rhetorical focus on augmented user experience that leverages not just the AR technology through a smartphone but also geospatial and communal interactions. Certainly, AR technology helps create an enriched human-computer interaction (HCI) experience by expanding the user's sensory interactions with digital

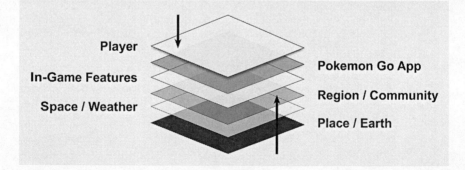

Figure 5.5. Bratton's "Stack" as reimagined in *Pokémon Go* layers. Graphic created by Jason Chew Kit Tham.

content. These additional simulations add new layers to the meaning-making process—users could now create, express, and exchange meanings through multiple dimensions that aren't traditionally afforded by 2D screen media. We use Rieder's (2017) theory of transductive rhetoric to zoom in on these dimensions. Coupled with earth, space, and interface layers, we can see how each *Pokémon Go* experience layer transduces from one to another (Figure 5.5).

Each is not only significantly linked to its adjacent layer but also trickles up and down among other layers that make up the overall experience of AR gaming. Given the emphasis on communal gaming in *Pokémon Go* and the success it garnered from large-scale community gaming events, we should also focus on the interactivity between the individual user and the surrounding community at local, regional, national, and global levels. The stack analogy might be a useful starting point for us to re-envision user experience in an age of augmented reality. The focus on the human and social elements—not just the physical environments—helps us to continue to engineer interfaces that pay attention to how design facilitates individual as well as community interactions. Rhetorical augmentation is thus a heuristic framework for designing augmented user experience with regard to sensory expansion and community organizing using rhetorical strategies such as simulating geotic relations (e.g., AR photography in *Pokémon Go*) and collective membership across regions or even worldwide (e.g., Pokémon Eggstravaganza and Global Catch Challenge).

Conclusion

In this essay, we have reviewed literature relevant to the emerging trends of AR in HCI and social computing, which informed our study of *Pokémon Go* as a rhetorical device for augmented public play. Based on our analysis of the game creator's email announcements and interview responses from *Pokémon Go* players, we observed an emerging theory of rhetorical augmentation that can be illustrated by Rieder's (2017) transductive model of digital rhetoric. We discussed this model as a heuristic framework for future interface design that pays attention to interactivity between humans as well as humans and environments.

For future AR game systems, we urge developers and designers to prioritize the aforementioned interactivity such that users can realize a fuller experience through sensory stimulations and communal participation. The dimensions of place and space are more valuable if they are experienced within the social dimension. Based on our observation, the *Pokémon Go* design has been successful in terms of integrating these dimensions with their overall game strategy. We encourage game developers and designers to follow suit for their future systems. Rhetorical augmentation improves not only individual user experience but also the social wellbeing of a community since it motivates communal effort in achieving a common goal. Certainly, this assertion would hold more weight if it is tested with a larger data set (more participants) in the future. Future game studies researchers may also consider studying the ethical dimensions of such augmentation and how it may affect user participation and their experience with AR gaming.

Pedagogically, the implications for AR gaming to inform and assist geospatial education are quite exciting. Imagine a course of study where students use an AR game, whether it is *Pokémon Go* or another game, to learn more about important sites and spaces in their cities or towns. Educators will no longer need to rely on textual accounts of these sites, nor will they need to arrange costly and time-prohibitive fields trips in order for students to interact with these spaces, which is of benefit to K-12 educators, and even college instructors and professors, for whom such trips may be impossible to coordinate. The possibilities for AR games to teach basic principles of qualitative fieldwork are also quite broad in a number of fields of study. For example, a rhetoric instructor may use the social aspects of such games to show students how discourse communities are created, both in cyberspace and in offline space. In her essay on teaching experience architecture in this collection, Morris showed some example applications in rhetoric and writing, too. For a geography instructor, having students go out into the community and observe the patterns through which players move through and interact with space can help to bring to life concepts such as the geographic imaginary or analyses on public space usage. Certainly, other disciplines could also benefit from AR gaming as the possibilities are only limited by the instructor's imagination.

REFERENCES

Ahlqvist, O., Loffing, T., Ramanathan, J., & Kocher, A. (2012). Geospatial human-environment simulation through integration of massive multiplayer online games and geographic information systems. *Transactions in GIS, 16*(3), 331–350.

Althoff, T., White, R.W., & Horvitz, E. (2016). Influence of *Pokémon Go* on physical activity: Study and implications. *Journal of Medical Internet Research, 18*(12), e315. Retrieved from https://www.ncbi.nlm.nih.gov/pubmed/27923778.

Ayaß, R. (2017). Life-world, sub-worlds, after-worlds: The various "realnesses" of multiple realities. *Human Studies, 40*(4), 519–542.

Bau, O., & Poupyrev, I. (2012). REVEL: Tactile feedback technology for augmented reality. *ACM Transactions on Graphics, (31)*4, article 89. Retrieved from http://doi.acm.org/10.1145/2185520.2185585.

Bogost, I. (2007). *Persuasive games: The expressive power of videogames.* Cambridge, MA: MIT Press.

Bratton, B.H. (2015). *The stack: On software and sovereignty.* Cambridge, MA: MIT Press.

Brigida, D. (2016, July 14). The Pokémon around us. Retrieved from http://www.fws.gov/news/blog/index.cfm/2016/7/14/The-Pokémon-Around-Us.

Clark, A.M., & Clark, M.T.G. (2016). *Pokémon Go* and research: Qualitative, mixed methods research, and the supercomplexity of interventions. *International Journal of Qualitative Methods,* 1–3. https://doi.org/10.1177/1609406916667765.

Colley, A., Thebault-Spieker, J., Yilun Lin, A., Degraen, D., Fischman, B., Häkkilä, J., ... Schöning, J. (2017). The geography of *Pokémon GO*: Beneficial and problematic effects on places and movement. *Proceedings of the 2017 CHI Conference on Human Factors in Computing Systems, USA,* 1179–1192.

Dorward, L.J., Mittermeier, J.C., Sandbrook, C., & Spooner, F. (2017). *Pokémon Go*: Benefits, costs, and lessons for the conservation movement. *Conservation Letters, 10*(1), 160–165.

Duin, A.H., Moses, J., McGrath, M., & Tham, J. (2016). Wearable computing, wearable composing: New dimensions in composition pedagogy. *Computers and Composition Online.* Retrieved from http://cconlinejournal.org/wearable/.

Edensor, T. (2010). Walking in rhythms: Place, regulation, style and the flow of experience. *Visual Studies, 25*(1), 69–79.

Ferreira, P.M., Orvalho, J., & Boavida, F. (2005). Large scale mobile and pervasive augmented reality games. *Proceedings of EUROCON 2005–The International Conference on "Computer as a Tool," Serbia,* 1775–1778.

Forlano, L. (2013, November 4). Making waves: Urban technology and the co-production of place. *First Monday, 18*(11). Retrieved from http://firstmonday.org/ojs/index.php/fm/article/view/4968/3797.

Giddings, S. (2017). *Pokémon GO* as distributed imagination. *Mobile Media & Communication, 5*(1), 59–62.

Goggin, G. (2017). Locating mobile media audiences: In plain view with *Pokémon GO*. In C. Hight and R. Harindranath (Eds.), *Studying digital media audiences: Perspectives from Australasia* (pp. 30–59). New York, NY: Taylor and Francis.

Golding, D. (2016, December 22). Gotta (publicly) catch 'em all: *Pokémon GO*. *Metro Magazine, 190,* 127.

Gong, H., Hassink, R., & Maus, G. (2017). What does *Pokémon Go* teach us about geography? *Geographica Helvetica, 72,* 227–230.

Gotta name them all: How Pokémon can transform taxonomy. (2016, July 21). *Nature, 535,* 323–324. Retrieved from http://www.nature.com/news/gotta-name-them-all-how-pok%C3%A9mon-can-transform-taxonomy-1.20275.

Hocks, M.E., & Comstock, M. (2017). Composing for sound: Sonic rhetoric as resonance. *Computers and Composition, 43,* 135–146.

Irshad, S., & Rambli, D.R.A. (2017). Advances in mobile augmented reality from user experience perspective: A review of studies. In H.B. Zaman, P. Robinson, A.F. Smeaton, T.K. Shih, S. Velastin, T. Terutoshi, ... N.M. Ali (Eds.), *Advances in Visual Informatics: 5th International Visual Informatics Conference, IVIC 2017, Malaysia,* 466–477.

Kaczmarek, L.D., Misiak, M., Behnke, M., Dziekan, M., & Guzik, P. (2017). The Pikachu effect: Social and health gaming motivations lead to greater benefits of *Pokémon GO* use. *Computers in Human Behavior, 75,* 356–363.

Kogan, L., Hellyer, P., Duncan, C., & Schoenfeld-Tacher, R. (2017). A pilot investigation of the physical and psychological benefits of playing *Pokémon GO* for dog owners. *Computers in Human Behavior, 76,* 431–437.

Krippendorff, K. (2013). *Content analysis: An introduction to its methodology* (3rd ed.). Thousand Oaks, CA: Sage.

Liao, T., & Humphreys, L. (2014). Layar-ed places: Using mobile augmented reality to tactically reengage, reproduce, and reappropriate public space. *New Media & Society, 17*(9), 1418–1435. Retrieved from http://nms.sagepub.com/content/17/9/1418.

Liberati, N. (2018). Phenomenology, *Pokémon Go*, and other augmented reality games: A study of a life among digital objects. *Human Studies, 41*(2), 211–232.

Liu, L., Wagner, C., & Suh, A. (2017). Understanding the success of *Pokémon Go*: Impact of immersion on players' continuance intention. In D.D. Schmorrow & C.M. Fidopiastis (Eds.), *Augmented Cognition: Enhancing Cognition and Behavior in Complex Human Environments* (pp. 514–523). Cham, Switzerland: Springer International Publishing AG.

Mans, S. (2016). Who owns the playground?: Urban gamification and spatial politics in *Poké-*

mon GO [Blog post]. *Masters of Media: New Media & Digital Culture M.A., University of Amsterdam*. Retrieved from https://mastersofmedia.hum.uva.nl/blog/2016/11/14/who-owns-the-playground-urban-gamification-and-spatial-politics-in-Pokémon-go/.

Matyas, S., Matyas, C., Schlieder, C., Kiefer, P., Mitarai, H., & Kamata, M. (2008). Designing location-based mobile games with a purpose: Collecting geospatial data with CityExplorer. *Proceedings of the 2008 International Conference on Advances in Computer Entertainment Technology*, Yokohama, Japan, 244–247.

Mäyrä, F. (2017). *Pokémon GO*: Entering the ludic society. *Mobile Media & Communication, 5*(1), 47–50.

Metahaven. (2012, December 16). The cloud, the state, and the stack: Metahaven in conversation with Benjamin Bratton [Blog post]. *Metahaven* [Tumblr blog]. Retrieved from http://mthvn.tumblr.com/post/38098461078/thecloudthestateandthestack.

Middleton, J. (2018). The socialities of everyday urban walking and the "right to the city." *Urban Studies, 55*(2), 296–315.

Pajarito, D., & Gould, M. (2017). Smart mobility, the role of mobile games. In M. Alcañiz, S. Göbel, M. Ma, M.F. Oliveira, J.B. Hauge & T. Marsh (Eds.), *Serious Games: Third Joint International Conference, JCSG 2017, Valencia, Spain*, 44–59.

Rieder, D.M. (2017). *Suasive iterations: Rhetoric, writing, and physical computing*. Anderson, SC: Parlor Press.

Schultz, A. (1962). *Collected papers I: The problem of social reality*. (M. Natanson, Ed.). The Hague, Belgium: Martinus Nijhoff.

Schutz, A., & Luckmann, T. (1973). *The Structures of the life-world* (vol. 1). Evanston, IL: Northwestern University Press.

Wong, F.Y. (2017). Influence of *Pokémon Go* on physical activity levels of university players: A cross-sectional study. *International Journal of Health Geographics, 16*(8). Retrieved from https://www.ncbi.nlm.nih.gov/pmc/articles/PMC5322678/.

Wunderlich, F.M. (2008). Walking and rhythmicity: Sensing urban space. *Journal of Urban Design, 13*(1), 125–139.

To Be the Very Best …
You Gotta Pay

Motivation, Resources and Monetizing Frustration

Eric Murnane

Much of the success of *Pokémon Go* can be attributed to Niantic's selection of a globally familiar franchise. Jenkins (2006) noted that many American children are more aware of Pokémon than they are of traditional Western fairy tales. Thus, a game which is ostensibly free to use and allows individuals to interact with these creatures has considerable draw. Players are encouraged to venture into the world and catch Pokémon in their own neighborhoods. The premise is simple and built right into the name: Go catch Pokémon. The exigence of *Pokémon Go* appears clear given the presence of monsters appearing in specific locations, the existence of Poké Stops and gyms that must be visited, and eggs that hatch after a specified amount of walking. On the surface, the message being sent by the game, and by extension its developers, is to explore the world. Given the bad reputation that gaming often gets for keeping people inside (Rey-López, Vincente-Rodrígez, Biosca, & Moreno, 2008; Vandewater, Shim, & Caplovitz, 2004), a walking game appears to be a welcome change.

However, even in the earliest stages of the game, it became clear that individuals who were willing to invest in the game's currency would receive considerably more payoff for each step. This essay investigates these in-game resources as well as resource nodes in order to get to the heart of the argument being made by *Pokémon Go*. Over the course of my analysis, I demonstrate the key clusters of in-game resources as they align with effort, time, and money to highlight the rhetorical message which is being implicitly sent by the game. Additionally, I perform a comparison to test how well that implied message lines up with the explicit message of health that a social walking game such as *Pokémon Go* sends through marketing materials and public-facing direct communications.

Using Burke's (1941) cluster criticism, I analyze the clusters surrounding what I identify as three key inputs for the player: walking, time, and money. The first two inputs are finite. The player can only walk so far and only dedicate so much time to the game itself. Just as importantly, the player can experience a limited scope of the gameplay relying solely on walking and time. While this has certainly been true since the beginning, the implementation of Raid Passes (of which the player receives one for free per day) serves to highlight this trend well. However, should the player so desire, they can purchase Raid Passes up to their inventory capacity (at the time of this writing, a player can hold 1,500 items). The same can be said for other items in the game such as egg incubators, lure modules, and lucky eggs. Essentially, the player can achieve more in the game with a higher degree of frequency if they invest in the game's currency. The core of this argument is that such key input moments create player frustration, which is a key component of Niantic's revenue stream. To be clear, frustration in and of itself is not necessarily a problem. Gee (2003) described games as "long, hard and challenging" (p. 6), and he is not wrong. However, he is discussing challenges inherent in a game to institute learning. These are frustrations to be overcome. My key contention here is that the act of monetizing frustration is not about a struggle to become proficient at a game so much as it is a marketing strategy in which companies offer players the opportunity to pay their way out of a particular headache. This analysis showcases an inconsistent message on the part of *Pokémon Go*, which ultimately compromises the core premise to get out there and catch them all in favor of pay to catch them all.

Design Affordances

In order to appreciate how these clusters send messages to an audience, it is useful to begin by discussing how the design of *Pokémon Go* influences actions. We can see the design at the level of interface. Juul (2011) noted that rules, and by extension the games themselves, *"set up potential actions"* within the play space (p. 58, emphasis in original). In essence, the player is constrained by the possibilities given in the code. He furthered this notion, explaining that the design of the space explicitly determines which actions can be taken in a given moment and which ones cannot (p. 163). This is to say that developers exercise control over the kinds of experience that players can have within a given game. On the surface, this is intuitive. Players can only throw a Poké Ball if they have one. Additionally, they can only do so during an encounter with a Pokémon. This is present at every level of the design process and has considerable impact on the player's experience of the game. Thus, we can see that potential actions (things to do in a game) are often rigidly determined, allowing the player to only play the game in the manner in which it was intended. Credible actions are made clear through the directions that a game sends the player. Aarseth (2005) noted that games generally apply three different categories of activities which are oriented by place, objective, and time, which will be discussed below.

Within *Pokémon Go*, the place-oriented aspects of the game are perhaps the most obvious. Players must venture into the world in order to get much of anything done. Poké Stops and gyms are at fixed locations, and individual Pokémon appear at specific (albeit random) GPS coordinates. Because the game is so largely oriented by place in the physical world and its correlation to the player's location within the game world, players must move around in order to accomplish most in-game goals. Obvious exceptions occur when in-game objects are within the range of a player's home or work, but this certainly cannot be counted upon, as will be demonstrated later in the essay. Typically, these actions are repeatable every few minutes, with new Pokémon appearing periodically. Thus, the player is encouraged to keep moving within a play session, traversing the space in order to get the most out of a given session.

Bogost (2007) pointed out that "exergames with rhetorics of training … tend to recontextualize the idea of exercise by creating repeating incentives to continue physical exertion" (p. 313). Here, the movement between different tasks which regenerate over time asks players to exert themselves in a repetitive fashion in order to achieve in-game goals of acquiring resources. Certainly, this call to keep moving is most in line with the overall message being sent by the game. The official launch message on the *Pokémon Go* website from July 2016 was titled "Break out the sneakers and Poké Balls!" while another update from five months later announced "200,000 trips around the Earth!" (Hanke, 2016; Pokémon Go Team, 2016a). That the place-oriented aspect of the gameplay is so foregrounded is not surprising. The game's central exigence is ostensibly to get players moving, and in-game items such as incubators certainly incentivize this activity.

If place-based activities represent the core mission of the game, one could argue that objective-oriented portions provide the player-specific activities that make it enjoyable. The most basic task of this kind is the act of catching a Pokémon. In what can best be described as the core essence of Pokémon, players have a specific task at hand (catching the monster) with tools (berries and balls) that they use to accomplish this. More complicated objectives are certainly present, such as taking and holding gyms. Here, a player arrives at a gym, and if it is controlled by an opposing faction, she proceeds to remove all opposing Pokémon and take over said location with one of her own Pokémon. This type of activity, in which players interact with one another indirectly and over diffuse time periods, is what Bogost (2004) called asynchronous gameplay. There is a persistent game world in which players' actions can have a meaningful impact, but the level of interaction in controlling a gym is always distributed. After leaving a Pokémon at a gym, the monster acts autonomously, battling new players who arrive without any input from the player. Here, the objective of taking and holding a gym is twofold. On the one hand, players (by virtue of selecting a team) control gyms as a matter of pride. The more gyms controlled by one's faction, the better. However, there is the additional resource component to such an objective. Over time, a Pokémon will earn Poké Coins for the player, up to fifty in a given day, thus encouraging the player to continue controlling these installations. These objective-oriented activities represent the core of "things to do" in terms of *Pokémon Go*. Certainly, tasks such as visiting Poké Stops represent credible actions, but they are largely transactional. Players visit these locations in order to acquire resources.

Lastly, there are time-oriented activities. While these are somewhat less common in the game, they do represent significant opportunities for motivating players into taking action. In a broad sense, the implementation of weather in *Pokémon Go* serves as one such example. Depending on the weather conditions outside (clear, partly cloudy, cloudy, rain, snow, fog, windy), either two or three of the Pokémon types will appear more frequently as well as with improved stats. In addition to longer-term phenomena such as these, there are raids. These events are temporal by design, asking players to gather around a gym with an egg while a counter ticks down until a powerful Pokémon emerges. Players then have a limited timeframe to catch it. The Pokémon that emerge during these raid events are typically powerful and, just as importantly, rare. Legendary creatures only appear in raids, thus encouraging players to participate in raids.

The point then is that each of these ways to operate within the game (place, objective, time) represent different actions that the player can take while playing the game. It is thus the responsibility of the designers to create a game that manages the player's attention effectively. In his discussion on how procedural rhetoric influences player action, Bogost (2007) noted that "the total number of and credibility of user actions is not necessarily important; rather, the relevance of the interaction in the context of representational goals of the system is paramount" (p. 46). In this case, there are certainly things a player could be doing rather than participating in the raid. However, since raids (by their nature as time-oriented events) represent credible actions which will shortly disappear, the player is motivated by the system to participate, especially if other players are present and the task feels surmountable.

This push for time as a factor in play only intensified with the introduction of EX Raids, invitation-only raids with incredibly difficult and rare Pokémon that "happen randomly and with little notice" (D'Anastasio, 2018, para. 8). In EX Raids, players who frequently participate in regular raids are given a location and time in which the EX Raid will occur. The expectation is that enough players invited will attend and the Pokémon will be defeated and subsequently caught. The temporality of many events in *Pokémon Go* adds a sense of urgency, but it simultaneously imposes constraints. Players have their own schedules to keep, and appetizing as that Zapdos is, one would have a hard time using it as an excuse to be late for work.

When taken together, the three ways that a player can orient himself with respect to the game simultaneously represent finite resources within the game's space. Players must walk from one Poké Stop to the next in order to acquire the resources that they need to accomplish in-game goals. Balls and berries allow the player to catch more Pokémon. Raid Passes (given once a day at a gym or purchased) are the only way that players can participate in raids. As will be demonstrated later, these three orientations are intrinsically linked within the game in a symbiotic relationship. One must invest time, resources, and energy into the game in order to play it effectively. However, built into the game is a shortcut. Simply invest some real money in the game.

Free to Pay

While there are numerous types of games available on mobile platforms, the most striking dichotomy in the current industry is the monetization strategy. Using this characterization schema, games can be divided into two classes: games which use the standard gaming marketing of pay once (the minority) and games which accumulate microtransactions over time (the majority). *Pokémon Go* falls firmly into the latter category. In games such as these, players download the game for free and have the option to spend money in order to make the gameplay process easier. Alha, Koskinen, Paavilainen, Hamari, and Kinnunen (2014) described the process as follows:

> F2P [free to play] games often feature the double currency model where players can earn soft currency via completing gameplay tasks and buy hard currency with real money. More often than not, the player can convert hard currency to soft currency but not vice versa [p. 3].

In *Pokémon Go*, this is executed through purchasing Poké Coins. These are resources used to acquire in-game items that can be used by the player. This relationship between soft and hard currency is illustrated in Figure 6.1.

Figure 6.1. Making Change.

On the left are in-game items that can be purchased by the player, while the right represents the conversion ratio. The items represented here are quite useful to the player, offering some kind of advantage during play. Super incubators hatch eggs with fewer steps, and free Raid Passes are only given to the player at a rate of one per day.

Certainly, players can collect Poké Coins in the game, but only at a rate of fifty per day. Thus, at this rate, players would take at least two days to get even one paid Raid Pass and four days to get a single super incubator. Evans (2016) referred to this process as "monetizing player impatience" (p. 565). The logic is simple to unravel. Wait a few days or spend a couple of dollars and get those items right now. Not uncommon in free-to-play games, purchasing larger sums of the soft currency creates a savings in the price point. Of note, it would take 290 days to accumulate the 14,500 coins that one can purchase for a hundred dollars. This process of getting players to invest in the game is the subject of considerable research in both the academic and corporate communities. Companies estimate a "Customer Lifetime Value" (Sifa et al., 2015, p. 79), a term that uncomfortably reduces players to values on a spreadsheet. The games themselves are fine-tuned to extract that value. Jin (2017), drawing on Mirrlees (2016), used the term "playbour" to describe the free time invested in a game to earn these in-game currencies (p. 57). The move on the part of the companies is to make the process just irritating enough that spending money feels like the right move while not making gameplay so frustrating that the player quits the game entirely. Of note, designers know that this process is not the same for each player. Soroush, Hancock, and Bohns (2014) explained that players with lower levels of self-control (those most likely to spend while playing) are also more likely to quit a game when experiencing frustration. Thus, designers must strike a balance in the approach. This stems from delicate psychological processes which are built right into the game. Kimppa, Heimo, and Harviainen (2015) demonstrated that one of these strategies is the sunk-cost fallacy. Essentially, if players have invested a lot of time in a game, then quitting the game feels like wasting that time. Thus, they begin to spend money in order to proceed because they do not wish to lose the effort that they have already expended. This is in turn supple-

Figure 6.2. Raid Battling.

mented with the social aspects of play. Shi, Xia, and Huang (2015) noted that players who have a circle of friends who also play the game tend to invest in gameplay items in increasing quantities to keep up with their peer group (p. 184). This becomes all the more important when one considers the implicit requirement for players to play the game socially, especially with regard to endgame content such as raiding.

The raiding system in *Pokémon Go* is tiered, with level one and two raids being relatively easy for a single player to handle and each successive additional level requiring an increasing number of players to participate. The difference in power between a single player and a legendary raid (level five) is apparent in Figure 6.2.

Here, Kygore, a legendary Pokémon who can only be acquired through raiding, has a combat power (CP) which is nearly twenty times that of my strongest Pokémon. The implicit message is that players must team up with one another in order to get the opportunity to catch this Pokémon. By itself, this makes sense given the general messaging of the game as a social activity through the inclusion of raids and gyms as end-game content. However, the concept of teamwork as a monetization strategy is clearly embedded in this process. Getting ten or more people together to participate in raids such as this is a labor- and time-intensive activity. Thus, coordinating all of these people in order to participate in just one raid feels like a waste. Certainly, players can augment the number of raids per day in which they can participate by purchasing additional Raid Passes. Or so the logic goes. This social aspect of the game operates in tandem with the sunk cost fallacy. Early content is relatively easy to achieve alone and without investing money. Players tend to level up quickly (getting rewards for doing so) and can acquire the items they need exclusively from Poké Stops. When players reach a higher level, endgame content is more difficult, requires increasing resources and time, and, importantly, all but necessitates players to spend within the game. Certainly, they can quit, but (as demonstrated above) every part of the design process has been set up to discourage them from wanting to do so.

The preceding sections have outlined some of the key operations within *Pokémon Go*. In one sense, the game can be described as a social exergame that encourages players to use a familiar franchise as a way to get out into the world with friends and get healthy. However, another view of the game is that it is a carefully designed Skinner box which consistently encourages players to invest larger and larger sums of money in order to stay competitive. These two competing messages are incongruent. It is therefore useful to deeply interrogate how the game sends signals to the player. The following section does just that.

Clusters of Pokémon, or, Trudging Through the Pokédesert

One of the principal purposes of this essay is to establish exactly what kinds of messages *Pokémon Go* is sending to its players. In order to get to the heart of this message, I have selected cluster criticism as outlined by Kenneth Burke (1941) in the middle of the twentieth century. In his book *Philosophy of Literary Form*, he demonstrated how one can examine parts to better understand the whole. Burke explained:

> It should be understandable by now why we consider synecdoche to be the basic process of representation, as approached from the standpoint of "equations" or "clusters of what goes with what." To say that one can substitute part for whole, whole for part, container for the thing contained, thing contained for the container, cause for effect, or effect for cause, is simply to say that both members of these pairs belong in the same associational cluster [p. 77].

Taking a moment to unpack this, Burke outlined clusters as a way to group like ideas. Associational clusters are grouped according to what kinds of ideas they have in common. It was with this in mind that I grouped information presented within the game itself. I found that themes within the gameplay can be isolated in this fashion into one of three categories: effort that the game expects the player to expend, time the game expects the player to wait, and money the game expects the player to invest.

The individual units that demonstrate these characteristics can, through synecdoche, teach us about the overall value system that the game presents to the player. In describing how to interpret these clusters, Burke asked one to look for "critical points" (p. 78). These points are critical precisely because the work only functions with these considerations in mind. As a free-to-play game, time and money are always a factor, and as an exergame, effort is added to this discussion. I posit that *Pokémon Go* is indeed asking the player to do or think something particular through the act of play. Bogost (2007) noted that games achieve this via the use of procedural rhetoric, "the practice of authoring arguments through processes" (p. 29). The theories of Burke and Bogost, in turn, work in tandem with one another, with Burke's cluster criticism functioning as a means to isolate individual ideas and their effect on the audience and Bogost's procedural rhetoric functioning as a way to understand the arguments that these clusters come together to make. The union of the two ideas allows for a deep analysis that still considers the holistic message. Using this framework of analysis, I demonstrate that *Pokémon Go* is undermining its stated goal of encouraging health by creating a system which ultimately foregrounds revenue over exercise. I demonstrate this below by discussing the reward systems that are interwoven in everything the player does.

Effort

When I describe effort within the space of the game, I am principally discussing the amount of walking that the game asks the player to perform. One can look at this in a number of ways. Players must move from location to location to perform the credible actions outlined in the earlier section on design affordances. The act of playing the game consists largely of four distinct activities that revolve around the central exigence of the franchise, "Gotta catch 'em all." Players catch Pokémon in the wild using berries and Poké Balls. The resources to do so are received through the second expenditure of effort, visiting Poké Stops. While Pokémon will largely appear throughout the world, they are typically concentrated in specific areas (nests). Thus, effort must be expended to find and exploit the nests just as effort must be expended to visit Poké Stops in order to receive the supplies necessary to do the catching. Theoretically, nests can occur anywhere, but the usefulness of one is often directly linked to its proximity to one or more Poké Stops. This proximity as it impacts effort can be seen in Figure 6.3.

Figure 6.3. Effort and Resources.

The left image is at the University of Central Florida in Orlando, Florida, in the middle of the day. Note that Pokémon exist near my location, and the nearby indicator demonstrates that even more are close. Just as importantly, twenty Poké Stops and three gyms are within a reasonable walking distance. It is in areas such as this that the game's core claim as an exergame is the strongest. A player can walk around catching Pokémon and replenishing resources as she goes. Effort is not a negative aspect of play. In fact, it is one of the core premises of *Pokémon Go*. The other things to do in the game are also available to the player. One can visit gyms in order to take down opposing factions (all three are represented in Figure 6.3), participate in raids (there is a legendary Pokémon about to hatch), and install a Pokémon in one of these gyms. These activities would require potions, revives, and Raid Passes, but the area is littered with opportunities to get these items. Lastly, players can expend effort in order to hatch eggs. This activity gives players difficult-to-obtain Pokémon and candies, which are used to make individual Pokémon stronger or evolve them. Ideally, a player is working on whichever eggs he has in incubators while doing other activities, as every step taken by the player works towards those eggs eventually hatching.

However, the right image in Figure 6.3 tells a very different story. This image was captured in southwest Louisiana, outside of the city limits. At the bottom right of the image, one can see the end of the road. The lack of topographic features in the right image is telling. It does not show the lush forest that spans for miles, for example. While there is much to say about the messaging which is inherent in this game with respect to urban versus rural areas, I limit my interpretation to how this impacts the discussion of what the game values and what options it presents the player. In the right image in Figure 6.3, the player can catch Pokémon and hatch eggs. The nearest Poké Stop is miles away and the nearest gym is even further. This is all to say that while the surprising number of Pokémon present at this location is intriguing, when one runs out of Poké Balls, the road to getting more is somewhat longer and more labor intensive. In his later work, *Grammar of Motives*, Burke (1950) noted that there is a correlational, but not necessarily one-to-one, relationship between imagery and ideology. He explained, "As the imagery would be a translation of the idea into sensory terms, criticism might conversely propose to retranslate this sensory version back into purely dialectical or ideological terms, abstractions transcending sheer sensory experience" (p. 89). It is with this in mind that one can evoke a particular ideology from the imagery. When examining these two images side by side, it becomes clear that in some cases, there is a balance between effort and resources, and in others, there is not. This discussion is further illuminated by examining additional clusters.

Time

Within the game, time can be considered to occur concurrently with time in the real world. This is demonstrated in a few ways. Poké Stops take about five minutes before they will allow a player to spin them again and release more items. Raid Passes are given to a player for free once per day (however, a player cannot possess more than one free pass at a time). Pokémon stationed at gyms will give players a maximum of fifty coins per day. In each of these instances, the time elapses regardless of whether or not the player is logged into *Pokémon Go*. In addition to these static measurements of time, there is the somewhat more ephemeral time it takes to accomplish any given task. Sometimes, this time is limited by the system. For example, a raid battle will become available when the countdown reaches zero. There is nothing the player can do about this. Similarly, the raid will expire at the appointed time regardless of player input. The time it takes to accomplish goals such as defeating a raid or overthrowing a gym largely depends on the presence of other players. Opponents can use berries to bolster Pokémon in their own faction, making the process of taking over a gym take longer. Similarly, the number of players participating in a raid decreases the amount of time it will take. In these cases, one can look at the game functioning as advertised. As a social game, players can expect other people to have an impact on the play experience.

However, time is also a factor in resource collection. Referring back to Figure 6.3, players in areas with fewer Poké Stops can expect to receive fewer resources for time invested. In this sense, time is not equal across the board. Players with access to resources can expect to receive more benefits for less time. On the other hand, players with less access can expect to experience resource scarcity. In this sense, time must be divided. Players spend part of their time catching Pokémon (playing the game), and part of their time going to the nearest Poké Stop (doing a chore). This creates a frustrating choice for players in these situations. If the core goal of *Pokémon Go* is to have fun while getting exercise, then situations such as this demonstrate a clear problem. They can either drive, get a ride, or use public transit to get to these resources, violating the explicit purpose of the game, or they can make the walk without the necessary resources to catch the Pokémon they encounter on the way, thus causing the game to not live up to its promise to be enjoyable. Returning to Burke's dichotomy between ideology and imagery, the image of a person choosing between two key aspects of a game in order to receive anything demonstrates a key flaw in the idea. Unless, of course, exercise and fun are not the core ideals for which the game is striving in the first place.

Money

As described earlier, the player is always given the option to spend money within the game. Often this is downplayed in the marketing materials. With over fifty updates on the *Pokémon Go* Live website, only a handful explicitly address this with one advertising "limited-time holiday item packs!" (Pokémon Go Team, 2016b) and another announcing "new avatar items" (Pokémon Go Team, 2017). This, in theory, demonstrates that the company really is including the hard currency transactions as a convenience to the players. After all, most of their announcements showcase new content that they are adding which is completely free to the player. However, Burke (1945) pointed out that "many people would vote for cities—but only a few real estate men would vote *explicitly* for slums" (p. 169, emphasis in original). This holds true in this analysis. The hook in free-to-play games often lies explicitly in burying the revenue strategy in such a way that it is all but invisible to the player. However, the implicit messaging buried in the game tells a different story. Figure 6.4 demonstrates this phenomenon.

This is the menu that showcases possible options available to the player. Settings, tips, and news are in the top right corner. This makes sense. They are visible, but because they would be used less often, they are unobtrusive. However, the main options are considerably more telling. In-game options that are critical to play are moved to the periphery of the frame. Players can easily find their own Pokémon, access their Pokédex, and view their items, but these options are clearly not the main event. The game shop is in the center. Additionally, it is made distinctive with red font and a red circle, furthering its quest for the player's attention. The logic and appeal of this formatting is clear. The game is never directly telling the player to go to the shop. It is never telling the player that he must make purchases. However, by positioning it in the menu in this fash-

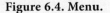

Figure 6.4. Menu.

ion, the messaging is still clear. This is important. It is this kind of messaging that informs the previous sections. Every inconvenience that is built directly into the design of the game makes sense only if money (as it is in the game's menu) is at the center of the messaging. In essence, money becomes a stand-in for time and effort. The player who has run out of Poké Balls in a rural setting *could* go all the way to the nearest Poké Stop, get two or three and wait five minutes to get some more. A player could participate in just one free raid battle per day. However, it would be much easier to simply spend a few dollars. Ease is key in how the logic is structured here. The reason that Raid Passes are given at a rate of one per day, and, for that matter, why a player cannot possess more than one free pass at a time, is that it is frustrating to gather up a group of friends for one raid. So frustrating, the developers bet, that the player will spend a little money to alleviate this frustration. That players, especially high-level players, must invest money to play the game without interruption demonstrates the core conceit that is baked into every interaction within *Pokémon Go*. It is first an enterprise for profit, and second an exergame.

Conclusion

The above discussion highlights the core issue with the monetization strategy inherent in *Pokémon Go*. While marketing materials outline a message of health and friendship, every aspect of the design is created to frustrate the player into investing money into the game. This is not to say that games should not have a revenue stream. Rather, this discussion serves to highlight the problem of monetizing frustration. Video games should not be chores. Life is filled with plenty of chores, and many already view exercise as one. That a game exists that asks people to go out into the world with friends and do something enjoyable while also getting healthy is inherently positive. This highlights the central issue, though. When games such as this put barriers in place that inhibit a person's ability to meaningfully engage with the game unless they pay, they undermine the central argument that players should be getting this exercise. Thus, the move going forward is to highlight aspects of play that encourage getting out into the world while minimizing paywalls. Models such as the free/premium model implemented by games such as *Super Mario Run* could be useful in solving this issue.

The point, then, is not that games should not cost money. It is instead that money as a substitute for frustration undermines the positive potential of *Pokémon Go*. If it is the case that this game, and those that come after it, are to meaningfully improve player's health goals (as claimed in marketing materials), then designing systems with transparent monetization structures is important. Moreover, as scholars, it is our responsibility to deconstruct the messages being sent by designers. By carefully deconstructing the messages explicitly created by companies and comparing them to the implicit messages being sewn into the design process, it becomes possible to make those implicit messages clear and ultimately hold their creators responsible for incongruities.

REFERENCES

Aarseth, E. (2005). From *Hunt the Wumpus* to *Everquest*: Introduction to quest theory. In F. Kishino, Y. Kitamura, H. Kato & N. Nagata (Eds.), *International Conference on Entertainment Computing—ICEC 2005* (pp. 496–506). Berlin, Germany: Springer. Retrieved from http://dl.ifip.org/db/conf/iwec/icec2005/Aarseth05.pdf.

Alha, K., Koskinen, E., Paavilainen, J., Hamari, J., & Kinnunen, J. (2014). Free-to-play games: Professionals' perspectives. *DiGRA Nordic '14: Proceedings of the 2014 International DiGRA Nordic Conference.* Retrieved from http://www.digra.org/wp-content/uploads/digital-library/nordicdigra2014_submission_8.pdf.

Bogost, I. (2004). Asynchronous multiplay: Futures for casual multiplayer experience. Paper presented at the Other Players Conference on Multiplayer Phenomena, Copenhagen, Denmark. Retrieved from http://bogost.com/downloads/I.%20Bogost%20-%20Asynchronous%20Multiplay.pdf.

Bogost, I. (2007). *Persuasive games: The expressive power of videogames.* Boston: MIT Press.

Burke, K. (1941). *The philosophy of literary form.* Berkeley: University of California Press.

Burke, K. (1945). *A grammar of motives.* Berkeley: University of California Press.

Burke, K. (1950). *A rhetoric of motives.* Berkeley: University of California Press.

D'Anastasio, C. (2018, January 26). Rampant hacking is hurting *Pokemon Go*'s EX Raids. *Kotaku.* Retrieved from https://kotaku.com/rampant-hacking-is-hurting-pokemon-gos-ex-raids-1822466052.

Evans, E. (2016). The economics of free: Freemium games, branding and the impatience economy. *Convergence, 22*(6), 563–580. doi: 10.1177/1354856514567052.

Gee, J.P. (2003). *What video games have to teach us about learning and literacy.* New York, NY: Palgrave Macmillan.

Hanke, J. (2016). Break out the sneakers and Poké balls. *Pokémon Go Live.* Retrieved from https://pokemongolive.com/en/post/launch/.

Jenkins, H. (2006). *Convergence culture: Where old and new media collide.* New York, NY: New York University Press.

Jin, D.Y. (2017). Critical interpretation of the *Pokémon GO* phenomenon: The intensification of new capitalism and free labor. *Mobile Media & Communication, 5*(1), 55–58. doi: 10.1177/2050157916677306.

Juul, J. (2011). *Half-real: Video games between real rules and fictional worlds.* Boston: MIT press.

Kimppa, K.K., Heimo, O.I., & Harviainen, J.T. (2016). First dose is always freemium. *ACM SIGCAS Computers and Society, 45*(3), 132–137. doi:10.1145/2874239.2874258.

Mirrlees, T. (2016). Pokémon GO's precarious "play-bour": Real work, augmenting the economy. Retrieved from http://www.durhamregion.com/opinion-story/6787664-pok-mon-go-s-precarious-play-bour-real-work-augmenting-the-economy/.

The Pokémon Go Team. (2016a). 200,000 trips around the Earth! *Pokémon Go Live.* Retrieved from https://pokemongolive.com/en/post/milestones/.

The Pokémon Go Team. (2016b). Limited-time holiday item packs! *Pokémon Go Live.* Retrieved from https://pokemongolive.com/en/post/holiday-packs/.

The Pokémon Go Team. (2017). New avatar items inspired by the Alola region available in *Pokémon Go. Pokémon Go Live.* Retrieved from https://pokemongolive.com/en/post/ultrasunmoon/.

Rey-López, J.P., Vicente-Rodríguez, G., Biosca, M., & Moreno, L.A. (2008). Sedentary behaviour and obesity development in children and adolescents. *Nutrition, Metabolism and Cardiovascular Diseases, 18*(3), 242–251.

Shi, S., Xia, M., & Huang, Y. (2015). From minnows to whales: An empirical study of purchase behavior in freemium social games. *International Journal of Electronic Commerce, 20*(2), pp.177–207.

Sifa, R., Hadiji, F., Runge, J., Drachen, A., Kersting, K., & Bauckhage, C. (2015). Predicting purchase decisions in mobile free-to-play games. *Proceedings of AAAI AIIDE, USA.* Retrieved from https://www.aaai.org/ocs/index.php/AIIDE/AIIDE15/paper/viewFile/11544/11359.

Soroush, M., Hancock, M., & Bonns, V.K. (2014). Self-control in casual games: The relationship between *Candy Crush Saga*™ players' in-app purchases and self-control. In *2014 Games Media Entertainment IEEE, Canada,* 131–136. Retrieved from https://touchlab.uwaterloo.ca/testing/wordpress/wp-content/uploads/ieee-gem2014_submission_56.pdf.

Vandewater, E.A., Shim, M.S., & Caplovitz, A.G. (2004). Linking obesity and activity level with children's television and video game use. *Journal of Adolescence, 27*(1), 71–85. doi:10.1016/j.adolescence.2003.10.003.

Addiction and the Apocalypse

The Pathology of Pokémon Go

Kristen L. Cole *and* Alexis Pulos

The summer of 2016 may be remembered by many as the season of *Pokémon Go*, but for the majority of non-players, this memory is likely tinted with sentiments of danger and distrust. This is because, within days of its release, the popularity of *Pokémon Go* not only inspired intense fandom but also a litany of critiques regarding its potential negative social effects. Media sites and news outlets at the time littered the public sphere with clickbait-worthy headlines that warned of the game's threats to cybersecurity (e.g., Allen & Corse, 2016; also see Eanes & van den Broek's discussion of Russian hacking in their essay in this collection), military secrets (e.g., Carsten, 2016), and personal safety (e.g., Costa-Lima & Hudetz, 2016). Experts in various fields cautioned about game play overuse by highlighting the signs and potential effects of *Pokémon Go* "addiction" and offering suggestions for how to intervene in (e.g., Grant, Odlaug, & Chamberlain, 2016) or overcome this affliction. Critics of the *Pokémon Go* craze (Hern, 2016; Robinson, 2016; Tsukayama & Guarino, 2016) were quick to draw similarities between the game's players and the walking dead, citing their aimless wandering and fixed attention to a screen, even going as far as using the term "zombie apocalypse" (e.g., Landau, 2016, para. 1).

In this essay, we question what these criticisms reflect about dominant cultural norms and social expectations. Using metaphoric criticism (Ivie, 1997), we explore how *addiction* and the *apocalypse* are employed in criticisms of *Pokémon Go* and what they reveal about contemporary social anxieties surrounding technology. We argue that, as metaphors of pathology, these media representations assume a clear distinction between self and technology, subject and object, which promulgates an anthropocentric definition of social interaction. Anthropomorphism privileges human-to-human interaction over human-object or human-technology interaction. This privileging precludes the possibility of conceiving of objects and technologies as part of or as an extension of social interaction and, in doing so, constructs *Pokémon Go* users as anti-social rather than differently social. Narrowing, rather than broadening, what counts as social interaction carries implications for contemporary notions of pathology and citizenship.

New Technology Panics

Pokémon Go is certainly not the first technology to elicit distrust and panic and it will also not be the last. Early concerns over new technologies date as far back as Plato (360 BCE/2006) and the written word, which was considered a new technology during his time. In the *Phaedrus*, Plato asserts that letters and the written word "will create forgetfulness in the learners' souls, because they will not use their memories; they will trust" the written word over their memory (Plato, 360 BCE/2006, p. 66). In general, the written word created a sense of panic and concern over what this new technology would do to the capacity of the human mind. More than a millennium later, the printed word—made possible by the Gutenberg press—created a new sense of panic. Critics claimed that the overabundance of new information made available by the printing press would be confusing and harmful to the mind. Conrad Gessner, a Swiss physician, even called on the state to intervene in and regulate how much content could be produced (as cited in Blair, 2003). Later, 18th-century newspapers were credited with isolating readers and distracting them from church. These anxieties were followed by the creation of school literacy programs in the 19th century, which were accused of ruining children's bodies by protracted imprisonment, exhausting their nervous systems, and giving rise to a state of madness (Bell, 2010). Panic over the written word and its many subsequent mediums and implementations illuminates the ways new technologies generate uncertainty when they are integrated into society.

Concerns about and resistance to new technologies are often couched within a framework of threat and risk as it intersects with economic, social, and cultural norms. For example, when the telephone was introduced in 1876 as a tool for business productivity, businessmen prohibited their wives from using the device because they feared it would lead to idle gossip (Thompson, 2016). This perceived side effect fueled patriarchal concern over the technology's threat to domestic productivity among homemakers. According to Juma (2016), "the more valuable a thing being made obsolete, the stronger the challenge … or the greater the benefit the more the innovation is promoted" (p.

29). In other words, the greater threat a technology poses to business prosperity or dominant social expectations, the greater the associated anxieties. For example, recently, "in almost every market that the app-based car service Uber has entered" the company has been met with some resistance (Alderman, 2015, para. 6). The taxi industry has persistently sought to defend itself from the economic threat of this new technology, claiming that Uber participates in illegal business practices (para. 5), and calling on policymakers to defend their traditional business practices.

Technological anxieties also correspond with sociocultural perceptions of risks versus benefits. Juma (2016) argued that "society is most likely to oppose a new technology if it perceives that the risks are likely to occur in the short run and the benefits will only accrue in the long run" (p. 7). This claim undoubtedly manifested in initial reactions to home computers. In the early 1980s, when personal computers entered the mass market, anxiety over the device created "computerphobia," giving rise to a variety of resistances, fears, anxieties, and hostilities (Jay, 1981). According to Grundy and Grundy (1996), anxiety over the computer included fear of damaging it by touching it, fear of human beings being replaced by computers, and fear of humans becoming slaves to computers (p. 20). Opposition to computers was fueled by an overall fear that they would cause people to lose themselves in machine worlds, thereby distracting users from facing problems in the real world (Turkle, 2011, p. xi). This made the immediate risks of computers more threatening than their long-term benefits.

Nearly forty years later, the computer has not only demonstrated its long-term benefits, it is now fundamentally ingrained in the fabric of society. Turkle's (2011) research has shown that computers were not isolating devices but evocative objects that fostered new reflections about the self (p. xi). However, recent developments in networked systems, social networks, untethered connection, and developments in robotics has given her pause. She asserted that

> these days, insecure in our relationships and anxious about intimacy, we look to technology for ways to be in relationships and protect ourselves from them at the same time ... we fear the risks and disappointments of relationships with our fellow humans. ... [we] expect more from technology and less from each other [xii].

Building on these concerns, Carr (2011) argued that persistent interactions through computer-mediated systems like Google are shaping their users in their image as efficient, consuming, and unreflective shallow thinkers. What both authors have asserted is that the technologies we are using, and will be using, are disrupting dominant understandings of human interaction and changing the cultural milieu in which we currently live. Juma (2016) claimed that innovations that threaten to alter culture tend to generate intense social concern and video games have become the most recent lightning rod for these anxieties.

Video games are frequently presented in media as creators of violence, moral unbalance, and social ineptitude. For example, a 1982 article in *The New York Times* ("The battle for," 1982) asserted that an onslaught of new arcade machines "are corrupting our youth" (para. 2), "teach gambling and breed aggressive behavior" (para. 7), "and drive young people to crime" (para. 8). In early video game research, Dominick (1984) noted that psychologists "think that habitual videogame players may be pushed closer to performing real life violence," stating that most games are focused only on masculine fantasies of power, control, and destruction, and asserting that even the surgeon general feels that there is "nothing constructive in the games" (p. 136). Concerns about video games are not simply about content but are about the environments and spaces where people play and the act of playing a digital technology. These anxieties have fueled cultural debates for decades. Video games have played the role of scapegoat for social problems ranging from violence perpetrated by teenagers to socially awkward tendencies and weight-related epidemics across populations. In sum, what we can learn about past technology panics is they often reflect attitudes, values, and beliefs that support the dominant social, cultural, and political ideologies of their time. In some cases, these panics and anxieties are evoked or represented by the public to discourage change or encourage regulation. Many of these historical debates and trends are resurrected in recent media discussions of *Pokémon Go*, this time through the metaphors of addiction and the apocalypse.

Metaphoric Criticism: Addiction and the Apocalypse

Metaphoric criticism illuminates how two distinct realms of experience and meaning interlock and filter reality, thus affecting how audiences perceive a particular context. Metaphors are "nonliteral comparisons in which a word or phrase from one domain of experience is applied to a different domain" (Foss, 2018, p. 285). In rhetorical criticism, Ivie (1997) explained, "the value of locating underlying metaphors is in revealing their limits or untapped potential as sources of invention" (p. 59). Not all metaphors are explicit and, in fact, many of them operate implicitly and routinely to the extent that they become naturalized or literalized in speech. When this happens, Ivie suggested that speakers and audiences "become accustomed to routine extensions of images no longer serving their original purposes" and "lose sight of alternatives" (p. 59). In other words, commonly circulated metaphors suggest a shared reality when they actually represent a particular interpretation. Therefore, it is the responsibility of the rhetorical critic to strip away "the outer layers of literalized metaphors" in order to expose them to "closer scrutiny and possible reconstruction" (p. 59). Doing so allows the critic to interpret how these metaphors operate, meaning what and how they argue, how they construct a particular "way of knowing the world" (Foss, 2018, p. 288), and how they can be altered to conceive of different realities.

To conduct a metaphoric criticism of mass media reactions to *Pokémon Go*, we conducted a Google search for Internet content related to the broad search term "Pokémon Go" that was published between July 16, 2016 (the initial release date of *Pokémon Go* in the United States), and August 16, 2016 (a one-month range). Although there was a lot of neutral and positive content published about *Pokémon Go* during this time period, because we were specifically interested in understanding cautionary reactions, we chose to focus our analysis on content that warned of or alluded to the game's potential negative impacts and consequences. A broad-brush coding of these media texts revealed two predominant metaphoric themes: addiction and the zombie apocalypse. Narrowing our analysis to focus specifically on media content that evoked these themes, we found that the term *addiction* is utilized metaphorically insofar as it originates in the domain of chemical dependence but is applied in the case of *Pokémon Go* to a domain of behavioral repetitiveness. The term *zombie apocalypse* is a metaphor insofar as it is a fictionalized event being applied to real-life cases of playing *Pokémon Go*. In the following analysis, we begin by exposing the outer layers of each of these metaphors in more depth and then we move into unraveling the basic assumptions upon which they rely, which reproduce and bolster dominant views of technology and social interaction.

Gaming Addiction

In the wake of *Pokémon Go*'s popularity, some mental health professionals reacted by claiming that "research shows those with a behavioral addiction—including gaming addiction—have similar brain dysfunction as those with cocaine or gambling addiction" (Grant, Odlaug, & Chamberlain, 2016, para. 3). However, the existence of gaming addiction, including its psychological and physiological manifestations, is heavily debated among addiction researchers and specialists. Although Internet Gaming Disorder (IGD), which encompasses computerized and non-computerized gaming habits (Carbonell, 2017), was included in the fifth edition of the Diagnostic and Statistical Manual of Mental Disorders (DSM-5), not all practitioners embrace it as a legitimate pathology (Billieux, Schimmenti, Khazaal, Maurage, & Heeren, 2015; Carbonell, 2017; Kuss, Griffiths, & Pontes, 2017; Turner, 2008; Wood, 2008).

Billieux et al. (2015) suggested that many behavioral addiction diagnoses, which are non-chemical addictions, tend to follow an "atheoretical and confirmatory approach" based on "anecdotal observations" (p. 121), thus invalidating them. Carbonell (2017) elaborated upon these concerns, suggesting "most studies on behavioral addiction do not address two mandatory factors: functional impairment and stability of the dysfunctional behavior" (p. 124). In terms of functional impairment, "the consequences of playing video games are lesser in severity than those of abusing substances" and video games do not cause the same physiological harm as chemical substances (pp. 124–125). In terms of stability of behavior, the diagnosis of addiction requires "a 12-month duration of symptoms" but video game use changes frequently over shorter periods, making it difficult to identify (p. 125). Because of these inconsistencies with validity and reliability, there is currently "no consensus on an operational definition of video game addiction" (van Rooij, Schoenmakers, Vermulst, van den Eijnden, & van de Mheen, 2010, p. 206). Researchers may "choose to utilize the term 'addiction' for the sake of consistency with other studies" but van Rooij et al. admitted that a more precise description would be "heavy online gamers" (p. 206). Since most research conducted in the area of gaming addiction focuses primarily on online gaming, its transferability to mobile gaming behavior is also questionable.

In the context of media use, LaRose, Lin, and Eastin (2003) pointed out that lack of chemical impairment and dependence in relation to technology renders the term addiction a metaphor rather than a literal indicator of habitual or unregulated use. McIlwraith, Jacobvitz, Kubey, and Alexander (1991) explained that, as a vehicle to explain technology use, the term addiction reflects one of two dominant beliefs: 1) technology as "mere entertainment … not an important use of time" or 2) entertainment as "morally suspect and unproductive" (p. 105). When employed in discussions of *Pokémon Go*, the addiction metaphor mobilizes these beliefs as well as the underlying assumptions that 1) technology is necessary and positive in contexts of capitalistic production and consumption—such as work activities but 2) technology is unnecessary and negative in contexts of social interaction—such as spending time with family and friends.

Pokémon Go Addiction

Reactions to *Pokémon Go* that employ the metaphor of addiction assume that healthy social interaction is predicated on a distinction between self and technology, with the self occupying a superior role. To understand how the vehicle of addiction constructs the game and its users in this way, it is useful to understand what generally characterizes addiction. According to the American Society of Addiction Medicine (ASAM) (2011), addiction is identified by an "inability to consistently abstain, impairment in behavioral control, craving, diminished recognition of significant problems with one's behaviors and interpersonal relationships, and a dysfunctional emotional response" (para. 2). These characteristics often present as loss of control, neglect of other activities, secrecy, relationship issues, and continued use despite negative effects. When mapped onto discussions of *Pokémon Go*, these characteristics manifest through mockery and trivialization of heavy game use and we highlight in this essay the ways the game hijacks face-to-face relationships and overtakes offline interactions.

Two media texts that employ the metaphor of addiction that have gained significant social media traction and are offered here as analytic examples are a comedy sketch by SketchSHE (2016), "*Pokémon Go* Addiction Kills Relationship," and an article by Healey (2016) on CNET, "*Pokémon Go* Out of Control? Here's How to Kick the Habit." The SketchSHE video comically represents a married couple at odds over *Pokémon Go* use. The video starts with a husband walking in the front door of his house, holding and looking down at his phone. When he looks up, his wife is sitting on the couch, waiting for him, and the following exchange occurs:

> WIFE: "Where have you been?"
> HUSBAND: (answers tentatively): "Having sex with someone."
> WIFE: "Where have you been, Paul?"
> HUSBAND: "I was having sex with a prostitute."
> WIFE: "Tell me the truth."
> HUSBAND: "I told you, I was having sex with a prostitute."
> WIFE: "Show me your phone! Show me your phone!" (takes the phone out of her
>   husband's hand)
> HUSBAND: "Give me the phone back! That's my property!"
> WIFE: (sighs and rolls her eyes with disappointment)
> HUSBAND: "It's the hooker's phone."
> WIFE: "How did you get a hooker's phone?"
> HUSBAND: "Murdered the hooker. I didn't want to have to tell you that but I murdered the hooker, so…"
> WIFE: (speaking to the camera) "It's frustrating. I feel so powerless within my
>   own relationship. I feel like my husband's already gone."
> NARRATOR: "Lana is a victim of *Pokémon Go* addiction. Her husband, Paul, [is] a
>   current user … for weeks now he has been battling the constant urge that has
>   taken full control of his life and relationships."

In this scenario, the husband is depicted as exhibiting classic signs of addiction, including loss of control—an inability to abstain from playing the game—and secrecy—hiding his use to avoid negative relational consequences. The comedy evoked by this sketch depends on the audience's assumptions that *Pokémon Go* is not a serious addiction—it is trivial in comparison to more recognizable addictions—but hyperbolizing the scenario through this frame resonates with audiences because it carries with it a kernel of truth. This kernel is the belief that *Pokémon Go* is mere entertainment and not an important use of time. This belief assumes that Paul's engagement with *Pokémon Go* is not necessary for sustaining his life and relationships but rather an external inhibitor to these entities. The self is constructed as a distinct entity, defined by its relationship to other people but separate from technology. Anything that does not serve to uphold or sustain this distinction is an unimportant, even frivolous, urge to be battled.

Healey's (2016) CNET article also highlights characteristics of addiction but in a more serious tone. He lists the following signs of *Pokémon Go* addiction, urging users to be reflective of their gaming habits:

- It's the last thing you do at night, it's the first thing you do in the morning, and it's what you wake up in the middle of the night to do.
- You're playing at work (and not just on your breaks), you're taking an extended break from work … to play.
- You're playing instead of spending time with friends and family.
- You wish you could spend a little less time playing, but you keep finding yourself opening the app even when you don't mean to [para. 3].

This list is almost identical to the list of addiction symptoms outlined by ASAM, including a loss of control, neglecting activities, relationship issues, and continued use despite negative consequences. Contextualized in this way, these "symptoms" proffer the belief that *Pokémon Go* is morally suspect and unproductive. Specifically, the game and its technology are presented as inhibiting the self from getting enough sleep, producing enough work, developing meaningful relationships, and managing time appropriately. The underlying assumption is that *Pokémon Go* can only facilitate play but the self can facilitate life, capitalism, and social interaction. In other words, a hierarchy is clearly established, which separates and distinguishes the self—the productive—from gaming technology—the unproductive.

Elaborating on the morally suspect nature of technology, LaRose, Lin, and Eastin (2003) suggested that "the term 'addiction' may be abused to generate a sense of urgency about psychological problems" (p. 227). These problems may not be clinically and diagnostically valid but instead serve to draw lines between good and bad citizens, dependent on their productive or unproductive uses of technology. These uses are largely predicated on an anthropocentric view of social interaction, which privileges human-to-human interaction except in the case of economic value. This is particularly evident in Healy's (2016) tips for overcoming *Pokémon Go* addiction, which included "only play outside; play with friends; don't take a spare battery pack; and turn off AR (augmented-reality) mode" (para. 6–9). In other words, *Pokémon Go* is only productive if the background of the activity is not technologically mediated—playing outdoors—and if interaction with other humans is the primary motivation—playing with friends. In the latter two suggestions, he even explicated an anthropocentric plea for separating self from technology by suggesting that users take away the agency of the technology (drain its life, or make it mundane) in order to give agency back to the human user. This perspective of human agency and appeals to its supremacy are not just the underlying assumptions of technology addiction; they also fuel metaphors of the zombie apocalypse.

The Zombie Apocalypse

The zombie apocalypse is one of the most prevalent science fiction sub-genres in popular culture today. Zombie mythology derives much of its power and ideological force from the cultural history of imperial repression and enslavement on the island of Haiti. While the origins of the zombie narrative originated in West Africa, the Haitian discourse around zombification is "associated with compromised subjectivities that resulted from imperialism and slavery" (Thomas, 2010, p. 2). Zombies represented the post-slave subject who, without connection to a group, wandered the earth looking for a home or resting place, unable to generate a sense of subjectivity or a consciousness of the self, making the metaphor of the zombie a particularly potent cultural reference (Thomas, 2010, p. 2). At the fore, "the zombie is a folkloristic manifestation of a colonial or postcolonial society's greatest fear: subjugation, marginalization, and enslavement" (Bishop, 2010, p. 59). Lauro and Embry (2008) explained, "in its history, and in its metaphors, the zombie is most often a slave" (p. 87). To become a zombie is to become subjugated, marginalized, and enslaved.

The cultural mythology and fear of zombification was terrifying to early Hollywood audiences who understood slavery "as a violation of the Christian ideals of personal agency" and feared the uprising of the repressed Other (Bishop, 2010, pp. 59–60). In their contemporary manifestations, zombies have become "important representations of what Americans fear, or desire" (Poole, 2011, pp. 196–197). In fact, as Drezner (2014) pointed out, "more than one-third of all zombie films have been released since the September 11, 2001, terrorist attacks" (p. 825). During times of war, viral outbreak, and changing cultural landscapes, "the zombie offers a talisman, a laughably horrific symbol about a fake apocalypse that keeps at bay real fears about social degeneration and collapse" (Poole, 2011, p. 203). Beginning in the 1980s, the zombie apocalypse began to intertwine "with technological fears regarding the new millennium" (p. 217). Fears of Y2K and cyberterrorist attacks have found symbolism in zombie narratives, which represent "for many Americans the current state of their own society or its eventual direction" (p. 217). As liminal creatures, dead yet animated, the zombie offers audiences a useful metaphor for exploring and envisioning the limits and possibilities of the human body and subjectivity.

In contexts of technological anxiety, the zombie apocalypse metaphor reflects apprehension surrounding the convergence of subject and object, and ultimately the erasure of the self. The zombie is depicted by its lack of "cognitive processing, subverted animation, and dormant consciousness" (Lauro & Embry, 2008, p. 86) while "the zombie horde is a swarm where no trace of the individual remains" (p. 89). The fear of zombies, and the use of the zombie apocalypse to elicit panic, ultimately reveal "the primal fear of losing the 'self'" (p. 89) and becoming repressed or enslaved.

Moral panic over the shambled horde of homogenous citizens is most evident in discourses around youth who—through the loss of their social skills, identity, and energy—are routinely depicted as "inert, unresponsive and either/both aggressive or lethargic" zombies addicted to technology (Carrington, 2016, pp. 29–30). Specifically, their video game playing activities are "constructed in the media as the cause of sleep deprivation and declining social skills that serve to zombify young people, while technologies such as mobile phones are linked to youth isolation and alienation" (p. 29). The merging of these technological activities (video game play with mobile phone use) further heightens social anxieties surrounding the convergence of the subject with the object. In discussions of *Pokémon Go* that employ the zombie apocalypse metaphor, this belief in and fear of losing the self represents an underlying assumption that 1) technology is a threat to human agency and human social interaction, and 2) social interaction and human agency are appropriate and meaningful only within certain social and cultural boundaries.

The *Pokémon Go* Apocalypse

Many of the articles that characterize the widespread popularity of *Pokémon Go* as a zombie apocalypse tap into and exploit the fear of losing one's self due to objectification. They often suggest that humans are mindless slaves to a game on their phones, which is a symptom of interacting with technology rather than other humans. Lauro and Embry (2008) claimed that this terror of losing one's self comes from "a fear of the loss of consciousness" (p. 90). This is because "humanity defines itself by its individual consciousness and its personal agency: to be a body without a mind is to be subhuman, animal; to be a human without agency is to be a prisoner, a slave" (p. 90). Through the metaphor of the zombie apocalypse, *Pokémon Go* users are characterized as non-conscious, non-agentic moving bodies, which critics argue is evident based on their lack of social interactivity.

For example, an article from the *Huffington Post* (Landau, 2016), titled "*Pokémon Go*: It Might Be the Zombie Apocalypse," explicated this scenario clearly in their description of encountering *Pokémon Go* players in the streets:

They stagger around waving their phones in the air, or stare off at the landscape, with a feverish look: zombie. They cluster together, and non-players have to jump out of their way, zombie. They touch you, and show you their screen, and next thing you know, you're playing too, zombies [para. 4].

A letter to the editor from the *Los Angeles Times* (Rouse, 2016), titled "Hey, '*Pokémon Go*' Zombies, Put Down Your Phones and Experience Reality," similarly described the apocalyptic scene as:

A boy and a girl walking together, texting and not talking to one another. A father and son walking together, both texting, not talking to each other…. At least I thought they were texting. I was told that they were actually playing *Pokémon Go* [para. 2–4].

Both of these articles emphasize the role of *Pokémon Go* players' bodies—walking, staring, jumping, touching—while simultaneously highlighting, or rather presuming, their verbal communication deficiencies—not talking. In other words, they are constructed as bodies without minds, humans without agency, which is assumed to be a byproduct of the game and its technology.

The fear of being consumed by, and reduced to, an object is a useful tool for making humans aware of and invested in their subjectivity. As Lauro and Embry (2008) claimed, "when we feel threatened by a force external to our bodies" this fear "heightens our awareness of ourselves as individuals" (p. 89). In this case, the medium of *Pokémon Go*—the smartphone or personal computerized device—is an external, threatening object, which we must resist in order to secure our individual subjectivity. There is even more at stake than individual subjectivity though because a threat to stable subject and object positions also "risks destroying social dynamics that have remained … largely unchallenged" (Lauro & Embry, 2008, p. 90). The social dynamic at risk, in this case, is not only the centrality of the human subject in dominant understandings of appropriate and meaningful social interaction but also the cultural and regulatory systems of knowledge and power to which those understandings are bound.

For example, during a press conference following the release of *Pokémon Go*, former New York Police Department (NYPD) Commissioner William Bratton condemned the game and commented: "I think too many people have been watching the zombie shows on TV and basically our millennials seem to be fascinated with making themselves walking zombies" (Diamond, 2016, para. 6). He followed up these statements by claiming players are putting themselves at "great risk" (para. 7) by playing the game, citing instances of victim luring, robbery, trespassing, and other examples of law breaking. In his statements, lack of agency is linked to the technology of a generation, *Pokémon Go* being its latest incarnation. Appropriate and meaningful social interaction is implicitly and explicitly depicted as occurring in the absence of this technology and within the confines of socially and legally sanctioned uses of space and place.

Places are "bordered, specified and locatable" through the process of being named and defined, whereas a space is "open, undifferentiated, undesignated" (Blair, Dickinson, & Ott, 2010, p. 23). The authors, drawing on Tuan (1977), noted that places can elicit a sense of "security and stability" among visitors while space can elicit a sense of "openness, freedom, and threat" (as cited in Blair, Dickinson, & Ott, 2010, p. 23). Commissioner Bratton's statement implied that *Pokémon Go*, its technology and its players, violate the security and stability of named and bordered places (i.e., robbery and trespassing), while also manifesting the ever-present threat of undefined space (i.e., victim luring). The implication is that zombie-like game players are threatening figures because they cede control to objects. In doing so, they are incapable of traversing the defined and undefined borders of space and place in ways that mirror the social and legal expectations set forth to contain and maintain the visitor's subjectivity.

All of these examples use the zombie apocalypse metaphor to highlight the underlying threat of technology to the individual, the subject. This metaphor is provocative and popular in this context because a threat to subjectivity is also a threat to unquestioned and unchallenged social structures and dynamics. Zombies are "destructive rather than productive [and they resist] the rational" (Lauro & Embry, 2008, p. 106). If *Pokémon Go* users are categorized as such, then the stability of the subject-object dialectic can persist. Technology can remain seen as a tool controlled by humans and necessary primarily when it supports the stability of society and its economy; social interactivity can remain seen as the domain of face-to-face interaction and appropriate primarily for the purposes of cultural stability, within the purview of the law. However, these beliefs and assumptions come at a cost.

Implications: Overpathologization and Regulation

In both metaphors, addiction and the zombie apocalypse, social interaction is considered most successful when separated from technology and when the human subject is centered and distinct from the technological object. *Pokémon Go* is seen as contrary to this and thus socially negative. These metaphors construct *Pokémon Go* players as anti-social rather than differently social. The implications of these media representations are twofold: 1) they bolster a trend of overpathologizing everyday behaviors, especially as they intersect with digital worlds and technological objects and 2) they serve to separate good citizens from bad citizens by inciting panic about the potential problems of unregulated technology use.

Overpathologization is a phenomenon in which everyday activities or habits that are perceived as negative by health professionals are labeled, diagnosed, and treated as a medical condition without "external or clinical validity" (Billieux et al., 2015). Although pathologizing conditions can be beneficial when it legitimizes a person's condition and grants them access to necessary medical care, it can also, and often does, create damaging stigma and misunderstandings. Billieux et al. (2015) suggested that a major consequence of overpathologization is that it encourages practitioners to offer standardized treatment that "might lead to neglecting the key psychological processes" involved in the person's behavior (p. 122). In the case of *Pokémon Go*, the public is quick to pathologize players. This not only encourages a culture that stigmatizes gamers (particularly individuals who play casual games and may not choose to label themselves as gamers; e.g., Vie, 2014) but it also makes the process of identifying and intervening into legitimate and significant health concerns more complicated.

Another consequence of overpathologization is that it can cause unwarranted panic and confusion that leads to uninformed (re)actions, which can have significant consequences for those who engage in the scrutinized behavior (Wood, 2008). Wood (2008) reminded us that "despite the panic that has ensued we should not forget that millions of people play video games and only a tiny minority appear to experience any kind of problem" (p. 172). It is important that the public remain accurately informed on public health issues rather than being motivated by a sense of urgency about psychological problems that, broadly, may not exist. Because of the intimate relationship between public health concerns and public policy, constructing *Pokémon Go* players, and gamers more generally, as pathological opens the doors for conceiving of them as bad, unhealthy, unproductive citizens in need of regulation.

Although the popularity of *Pokémon Go* generated many reactions that also addressed and advocated for its benefits, these perspectives still tended to emphasize the game's potential to separate humans from technology and reaffirmed the significance of human-to-human interaction. For example, *Forbes* listed the benefits of the game as "1) lots of walking! 2) You get some fresh air and sunlight; 3) it's educational; and 4) It brings people together—literally, in real life" (Haelle, 2016). Recent scholarly perspectives and studies that discuss the benefits of *Pokémon Go* also defined these positive consequences as the ability to "conduct interpersonal relationships in the real world" (Kato et al., 2017, p. 75), improve social relationships (Ruiz-Ariza, Casuso, Suarez-Manzano, & Martínez-López, 2018), maintain friendships (Yang & Liu, 2017), and increase physical activity (LeBlanc & Chaput, 2017; Wong, 2017). Regardless of whether *Pokémon Go* is viewed as socially and culturally positive or negative, it is still predominantly discussed within a paradigm of anthropocentrism.

Objects are not separate from human social interaction. They are necessary for and constitutive of social interaction. Nevile, Haddington, Heinemann, & Rauniomaa (2014) pointed out that "studies have begun to reveal how objects, as an important part of people's lives, can be tied to and constituent of the situated, embodied, material and spatial circumstances of social interaction" (p. 12). Gaming technologies facilitate, extend, and interact in contexts of human communication, not only making them inseparable in these situations but integral to human experience. Acknowledging and understanding how technological objects play a substantial role in social interaction disrupts and problematizes the pathologization of *Pokémon Go* players as addicted zombies. If these objects are seen as facilitating and extending, rather than inhibiting and obstructing, all facets of life, *Pokémon Go* players (and gamers more generally) emerge as differently social rather than anti-social.

We see two potential ways that *Pokémon Go* and other augmented reality mobile games produce differently social interactions. First, the technological platform encourages users to see and engage with the world through a more playful lens. Rather than acquiescing to a world constrained by linearity and institutional regularities, *Pokémon Go* can turn even the most mundane environments into sources of play rather than objects of utility or passive consumption. *Pokémon Go* facilitates engagement with bordered places and undifferentiated spaces in ways that encourage users to explore and interact with materiality in spontaneous and unpredictable ways. Even though these acts may be considered deviant or disruptive in some cases, they are significant moments of interaction in which the technological object co-constitutes the agency and legitimacy of play (see, for example, Andrade's discussion of actor-network theory in this collection).

Second, the technology and objectives of play embedded in the game structure enable collective convergence, which produces differently social interactions among players. Individuals can collectively gather within proximal range to accomplish gaming tasks, sometimes without ever seeing each other or communicating verbally (see, for example, Eanes & van den Broek's discussion of playing the game "alone together" in this collection). Regardless of a player's social predisposition, the game facilitates a unique relational leap, one that thrusts players into a context of trust and cooperation that defies the subtlety and linearity of anthropocentric social interaction. Whereas many theories of social interaction suggest that trust and cooperation are built and enacted through actions of the self, such as verbal communication and self-disclosure, *Pokémon Go* facilitates an emergence of interactions that do not rely solely on human communication and contact. Instead, they are co-constructed through the knowledge and processes embedded in the objects and mechanics of the game.

In sum, *Pokémon Go* should not be a cautionary tale about the dangers of gaming technology but about the dangers of moral and ideological myopia. Metaphors of addiction and the zombie apocalypse illuminate dominant social anxieties as much as they reveal alternative ways of seeing what counts as social. As this analysis reveals, disrupting the persistent threat of subjectivity in the face of emerging technology holds the potential for expanding our assumptions about who counts as a good, healthy, and productive citizen.

REFERENCES

Alderman, L. (2015, June 3). Uber's French resistance. *The New York Times Magazine*. Retrieved from https://www.nytimes.com/2015/06/07/magazine/ubers-french-resistance.html.

Allen, S., & Corse, A. (2016, July 11). *Pokémon Go* is a hacker's dream. *Daily Beast*. Retrieved from https://www.thedailybeast.com/pokemon-go-is-a-hackers-dream.

American Society of Addiction Medicine. (2011, April 12). Definition of addiction. Retrieved from https://www.asam.org/quality-practice/definition-of-addiction.

The battle for America's youth. (1982, January 5). *New York Times*. Retrieved from http://www.nytimes.com/1982/01/05/nyregion/the-battle-for-america-s-youth.html.

Bell, V. (2010, February 15). Don't touch that dial! A history of media technology scares, from the printing press to Facebook. *Slate*. Retrieved from http://www.slate.com/articles/health_and_science/science/2010/02/dont_touch_that_dial.html.

Billieux, J., Schimmenti, A., Khazaal, Y., Maurage, P., & Heeren, A. (2015). Are we overpathologizing everyday life? A tenable blueprint for behavioral addiction research. *Journal of Behavioral Addictions, 4*(3), 119–123.

Bishop, K.W. (2010). *American zombie gothic: The rise and fall (and rise) of the walking dead in popular culture*. Jefferson, NC: McFarland.

Blair, A. (2003). Reading strategies for coping with information overload ca. 1550–1700. *Journal of the History of Ideas, 64*(1), 11–28.

Blair, C., Dickinson, G., & Ott, B.L. (2010). Introduction: Rhetoric/Memory/Place. In G. Dickinson, C. Blair, & B.L. Ott (Eds.), *Places of public memory: The rhetoric of museums and memorials* (pp. 1–54). Tuscaloosa: University of Alabama Press.

Carbonell, X. (2017). From *Pong* to *Pokémon Go*, catching the essence of the Internet Gaming Disorder diagnosis. *Journal of Behavioral Addictions, 6*(2), 124–127.

Carr, N. (2010). *The shallows: What the Internet is doing to our brains*. New York, NY: W.W. Norton & Company.

Carrington, V. (2016). The "next people": And the zombies shall inherit the earth. In V. Carrington, J. Rowsell, E. Priyadharshini & R. Westrup (Eds.), *Generation Z: Zombies, popular culture and educating youth* (pp. 21–36). New York, NY: Springer.

Carsten, P. (2016, July 15). In China, fears that *Pokémon Go* may aid locating military bases. *Reuters*. Retrieved from https://www.reuters.com/article/us-nintendo-pokemon-china/in-china-fears-that-pokemon-go-may-aid-locating-military-bases-idUSKCN0ZV0YD.

Costa-Lima, B., & Hudetz, M. (2016, July 15). The '*Pokémon Go*' files: 10 tales of trespass, robbery, murder and more. *Insurance Journal*. Retrieved from https://www.insurancejournal.com/news/national/2016/07/15/420198.htm.

Diamond, M. (2016, July 14). NYPD Commissioner Bratton calls *Pokémon Go* "stupid." *CBS New York*. Retrieved from http://newyork.cbslocal.com/2016/07/14/nypd-bill-bratton-pokemon-go/.

Dominick, J.R. (1984). Videogames, television violence, and aggression in teenagers. *Journal of Communication, 34*(2), 136–147.

Drezner, D.W. (2014). Metaphor of the living dead: Or, the effect of the zombie apocalypse on public policy discourse. *Social Research: An International Quarterly, 81*(4), 825–849.

Foss, S.J. (2018). *Rhetorical criticism: Exploration and practice* (5th ed.). Long Grove, IL: Waveland Press.

Grant, J.E., Odlaug, B.L., & Chamberlain, S.R. (2016, July 19). *Pokémon Go*—Addiction to mobile tech no laughing matter: Reclaiming your life from a behavioral addiction. *Psychology Today*. Retrieved from https://www.psychologytoday.com/blog/why-cant-i-stop/201607/pok-mon-go-addiction-mobile-tech-no-laughing-matter.

Grundy, A.F., & Grundy, J. (1996). *Women and computers*. Exeter, England: Intellect Books.

Haelle, T. (2016, July 11). Five ways *Pokémon Go* is actually good for you. *Forbes*. Retrieved from https://www.forbes.com/sites/tarahaelle/2016/07/11/five-ways-pokemon-go-is-actually-good-for-you/#9cad75f3f29b.

Healy, N. (2016, July 12). *Pokémon Go* out of control? Here's how to kick the habit. *CNET*. Retrieved from https://www.cnet.com/news/pokemon-go-tips-to-play-less/.

Hern, A. (2016, July 12). *Pokémon Go* becomes global craze as game overtakes Twitter for US users. *The Guardian*. Retrieved from https://www.theguardian.com/technology/2016/jul/12/pokemon-go-becomes-global-phenomenon-as-number-of-us-users-overtakes-twitter.

Ivie, R.L. (1997). Metaphor and the rhetorical invention of Cold War "idealists." In M.J. Medhurst, R.L. Ivie, P. Wander, & R.L. Scott (Eds.), *Cold War rhetoric: Strategy, metaphor, and ideology* (pp. 103–130). East Lansing: Michigan State University Press.

Jay, T.B. (1981). What to do about computerphobia. *Educational Technology, 21*(1), 47–48.

Juma, C. (2016). *Innovations and its enemies: Why people resist new technologies*. New York, NY: Oxford University Press.

Kato, T.A., Teo, A.R., Tateno, M., Watabe, M., Kubo, H., & Kanba, S. (2017). Can *Pokémon Go* rescue shut-ins (hikikomori) from their isolated world? *Psychiatry and Clinical Neurosciences, 71*(1), 75–76.

Kuss, D.J., Griffiths, M.D., & Pontes, H.M. (2017). Chaos and confusion in DSM-5 diagnosis of Internet Gaming Disorder: Issues, concerns, and recommendations for clarity in the field. *Journal of Behavioral Addictions, 6*(2), 103–109.

Landau, D.Q. (2016, August 1). *Pokémon Go*: It might be the zombie apocalypse. *Huffington Post*. Retrieved from https://www.huffingtonpost.com/dawn-q-landau/pokemon-go_b_11199526.html.

LaRose, R., Lin, C.A., & Eastin, M.S. (2003). Unregulated internet usage: Addiction, habit, or deficient self-regulation? *Media Psychology, 5*(3), 225–253.

Lauro, S.J., & Embry, K. (2008). A zombie manifesto: The nonhuman condition in the era of advanced capitalism. *Boundary 2: An International Journal of Literature and Culture, 35*(1), 85–108.

LeBlanc, A.G., & Chaput, J.P. (2017). *Pokémon Go*: A game changer for the physical inactivity crisis? *Preventative Medicine, 101*, 235–237.

McIlwraith, R., Jacobvitz, R.S., Kubey, R., & Alexander, A. (1991). Television addiction: Theories and data behind the ubiquitous metaphor. *American Behavioral Scientist, 35*(2), 104–121.

Nevile, M., Haddington, P., Heinemann, T., & Rauniomaa, M. (2014). On the interactional ecology of objects. In M. Nevile, P. Haddington, T. Heinemann & M. Rauniomaa (Eds.), *Interacting with objects: Language, materiality, and social activity* (pp. 3–26). Philadelphia: John Benjamins Publishing Company.

Plato. (2006). *Phaedrus*. (B. Jowett, Trans.). Teddington, England: Echo Library. (Original work published 360 B.C.E.)

Poole, W.S. (2011). *Monsters in America: Our historical obsession with the hideous and the haunting*. Waco, TX: Baylor University Press.

Robinson, P. (2016, September 7). Remembering "*Pokémon Go*," the craze that swept July 2016. *Vice*. Retrieved from https://www.vice.com/en_uk/article/xdmpgq/remembering-pokemon-go-the-craze-that-swept-july-2016.

Rouse, M.B. (2016, July 11). Hey, "*Pokémon Go*" zombies, put down your phones and experience reality. *Los Angeles Times*. Retrieved from http://www.latimes.com/opinion/readersreact/la-ol-le-pokemon-go-zombies-20160713-snap-story.html.

Ruiz-Ariza, A., Casuso, R.A., Suarez-Manzano, S., & Martínez-López, E.J. (2018). Effect of augmented reality game *Pokémon Go* on cognitive performance and emotional intelligence in adolescent young. *Computers & Education, 116*, 49–63.

SketchSHE. (2016, August 2). *Pokémon Go* addiction kills relationships. *YouTube*. Retrieved from https://www.youtube.com/watch?v=kslRkOuxefM

Thomas, K. (2010). Haitian zombie, myth, and modern identity. *Comparative Literature and Culture, 12*(2), pp. 2–9. Retrieved from https://docs.lib.purdue.edu/clcweb/vol12/iss2/12/.

Thompson, C. (2016, March). Texting isn't the first new technology thought to impair social skills. *Smithsonian Magazine.* Retrieved from https://www.smithsonianmag.com/innovation/texting-isnt-first-new-technology-thought-impair-social-skills-180958091/.

Tsukayama, H., & Guarino, B. (2016, July 12). What is really behind the *Pokémon Go* craze. *The Washington Post.* Retrieved from https://www.washingtonpost.com/news/the-switch/wp/2016/07/12/what-is-really-behind-the-pokemon-go-craze/?utm_term=.71179b537058.

Tuan, Y.-F. (1977). *Place and space: The perspective of experience.* Minneapolis: University of Minnesota Press.

Turkle, S. (2011). *Alone together: Why we expect more from technology and less from each other.* New York, NY: Basic Books.

Turner, N.E. (2008). A comment on "Problems with the concept of video game 'addiction': Some case study examples." *International Journal of Mental Health and Addiction, 6*(2), 186–190.

van Rooij, A.J., Schoenmakers, T.M., Vermulst, A.A., van den Eijnden, R.J., & van de Mheen, D. (2010). Online video game addiction: Identification of addicted adolescent gamers. *Addiction, 106*(1), 205–212.

Vie, S. (2014, November 12). Casual surveillance: Why we should pay attention to *Candy Crush Saga* & other casual games. *First Person Scholar.* Retrieved from http://www.firstpersonscholar.com/casual-surveillance/.

Wong, F.Y. (2017). Influence of *Pokémon Go* on physical activity levels of university players: A cross-sectional study. *International Journal of Health Geographics, 16*(8). Retrieved from https://www.ncbi.nlm.nih.gov/pmc/articles/PMC5322678/.

Wood, R.T.A. (2008). Problems with the concept of video game "addiction": Some case study examples. *International Journal of Mental Health and Addiction, 6*(2), 169–178.

Yang, C.-C., & Liu, D. (2017). Motives matter: Motives for playing *Pokémon Go* and implications for well-being. *Cyberpsychology, Behavior, and Social Networking, 20*(1), 52–57.

PokéStories

On Narrative and the Construction of Augmented Reality

Cody Mejeur

On July 22, 2017, Niantic hosted the first *Pokémon Go* Fest: an event that would celebrate the game in Chicago's Grant Park with "thousands of Trainers from the community!" (Niantic, 2017). The event featured increased encounters with Pokémon in the park, trainers working together to overcome challenges and earn rewards, and team lounges so players from the game's Team Instinct, Team Mystic, and Team Valor could meet up, relax, and swap stories of their *Pokémon Go* experiences. The overarching narrative of the day was supposed to be one of players coming together as a community in order to get outside, explore, play, and enjoy each other's company. However, as Farokhmanesh (2017) narrated in her article, "I Went to *Pokémon Go* Fest, and It Was a Disaster," things did not go as planned: "As connectivity problems and in-game crashes made *Pokémon Go* unplayable for attendees, the day spiraled into a large-scale echo of the game's earliest problems." Eventually, Niantic announced refunds and special rewards for everyone who attended the festival, but that did little to assuage frustrated and disappointed players who left with negative experiences and stories of the day.

While *Pokémon Go* Fest was a failure as a celebration, it is an excellent example of how the game spawns narratives of play experiences. Each player had a different experience of the event, such as driving all night to get there from Ohio, flying from Atlanta, or winning tickets in a raffle so they could attend, and this meant that every player had a different story to tell about it. When the game became unplayable that day, many players gathered in areas around the main stage to swap these stories and commiserate about how disappointing the event was (Farokhmanesh, 2017). As these stories came together, they contributed to the larger, collective narrative of the event as a failure, a rip-off, a fiasco. Narratives like these shape how players, both as individuals and communities, understand the game and their experiences with it, and they emerge through players' multivalent interactions with the game and with each other.

The stories players tell about *Pokémon Go* and their experiences playing it—their PokéStories—demonstrate how narrative is more than a written or programmed series of events related by a text (Eskelinen, 2012, p. 111). While narrative can certainly take that form, it is also an aspect of player experience and cognition. In this sense, narrative is an ongoing process in *Pokémon Go* that constructs the stories that we tell each other about the game, and these PokéStories are a crucial part of how we make sense of the game, relate to it, and even navigate it in each moment of play. As we play *Pokémon Go*, we link the signs, experiences, and events we encounter in it together into meaningful sequences that are narrative in terms of Sanford and Emmott's (2012) definition of narrative: They are chronologically ordered, proceed from one event to the next, and earlier events in the sequences contribute to later ones (p. 1). Upton (2016) described how this narrative process of sequencing events actively structures our experiences of the game, and helps us assess and choose our next actions, which will become the next events in the sequence (p. 223). As the narrative sequences that emerge in the playing of *Pokémon Go* extend and accrue, they become the PokéStories that players use to understand and relate their experiences with the game, such as the stories of frustrated players who failed to play at Pokémon Go Fest. These stories both affect and, to some extent, effect players' realities while playing the game, because they organize and mediate players' experiences. In doing so, PokéStories construct a sense of reality for each player, one that takes place within the larger augmented reality (AR) of *Pokémon Go*. Thus, an AR such as *Pokémon Go* requires narrative and the stories that it produces in order to make its reality possible, and narrative is a powerful tool for shaping (and reshaping) these realities in games.

Of course, there are many factors that affect narrative in *Pokémon Go*. The process of generating stories is emergent and playful and contributes to an AR that is as rich and varied as the people who play it all around the world. In order to account for these shifting qualities of narrative in the game, this essay develops a model of narrative based on the complex interactions of game system, player experience, and social and cultural context. All of these considerations are present in the narrative processes of *Pokémon Go*, and indeed it would be impossible to have a PokéStory that did not involve each of them in some way. By building this model of narrative, we can gain a better understanding of how *Pokémon Go* constructs its AR, and we better grasp narrative as a living and playful process that structures our experiences and realities.

Pokémon Go *and the Ludification of Narrative*

Narrative in *Pokémon Go* is established and constrained in part by the game's systems, including its hardware, software, and rules, and any model of narrative in the game must account for these systems. *Pokémon Go* is commonly described as an AR game, a game that, as Peddie (2017) described it, provides "a real-time view of information overlaid on a view of the real world" (p. 20). In the case of *Pokémon Go*, the game creates an AR by projecting digital representations onto actual space, and uses the GPS, mapping, and camera functions of a smartphone in order to allow players to find digital Pokémon in the spaces around them. As such, *Pokémon Go* is both an AR game and a location-based mobile game (LBMG), a "melding of virtually delivered information and physical sensory experience" (Bunting, 2014, p. 165). *Pokémon Go* further connects many different domains of experience, including the digital, the fictional, the social, the political, and, of course, the economical, among many others. The many intersections present in the game have even prompted some scholars to claim it heralds a new category of "supercomplexity," a phenomenon that "moves fully across physical, social, and virtual spaces" (Clark & Clark, 2016, p. 2). This supercomplexity that defines the game's melding of the digital and the actual, the technological and the human, and the individual and the social also defines the game's narrative processes. One cannot look to the game's representations, players, or social elements alone to explain the existence and meaning of PokéStories. All of these domains play a role in narrative, and in shaping *Pokémon Go's* AR for players.

Pokémon Go's ability to mobilize multiple technologies and domains of experience so effectively (or not, as seen during *Pokémon Go* Fest) is itself the result of a confluence of cultural trends in recent years. As Keogh (2017) has argued, the technological capacity for AR is not new, and *Pokémon Go's* success with it is due more to the "Pokémon franchise's sheer brand power and the ubiquity of the smartphone" than it is to AR as a novel or meaningful possibility (p. 41). Neither AR, the Pokémon franchise's popularity, nor the prevalence of the smartphone emerged suddenly. Each of these things has a history that reaches back at least to the 1990s, and in their current intersections in games like *Pokémon Go*, we can see how emerging technologies and transmedia franchises have affected how we interact with our environments, each other, and even reality itself. For example, Mäyrä (2017) posited that *Pokémon Go* reveals the "ludification" of society, wherein our social structures, institutions, and daily experiences are becoming increasingly playful, and rely on gaming complex systems of rules, strategies, and possibilities (p. 49).

I would add to Mäyrä's argument that *Pokémon Go* points us to the ludification of narrative itself: No longer completely linear or fully determined, narrative is increasingly mediated by many technologies, platforms, bodies, and spaces, and its variable and emergent forms demand recognition of narrative as a living and playful process. Game studies has long defined narrative as a static linear or multilinear series of events (Aarseth, 1998, p. 43), as events, settings, and rules that build a sense of a world or storyworld (Ryan, 2014, p. 34), or as a set representation of events, such as a game's "cutscenes and backstories" (Eskelinen, 2012, p. 224). Central to all of these definitions is the idea that narrative is a relatively stable and established series of events and representations, even if games sometimes allow the player to choose between different series. Yet, as Roine (2016) argued, this understanding of narrative, largely borrowed from other media such as literature or film, fails to account for how a game's story "is not monolithic" but rather "a result of many small fragments used in the performance" of playing the game and the interaction between player and system (p. 83). A ludified understanding of narrative, then, accounts for how players are constantly assembling and interpreting their own stories as they play. While ludic narrative in a game like *Pokémon Go* is experienced as linear, it is much more playful, variable, and emergent than existing models account for. *Pokémon Go* provides an excellent opportunity to build a new model of narrative that addresses this issue and highlights how games and other contemporary media "now appear to us as phenomena to be cut, pasted, reassembled, and distributed with ease" (Roine, 2016, p. 83).

Given the need for a ludified understanding of narrative, I offer the following definition of narrative in order to build a model of narrative based on *Pokémon Go*. Narrative is the process of storytelling, of organizing signs and events into meaningful sequences. Narrative often involves a storyteller (author or narrator), an audience (narratee), and a message (a story), though it can sometimes be difficult to distinguish these in games, where different stories emerge through players' interactions with game systems and each other. The interplay between player and game system means that gameplay involves several interrelated narratives and produces stories such as those written into the game by developers and those that the player develops of their own play experiences (Journet, 2007, p. 93). These narratives are made of signs—representations, information, and sensory inputs, including haptic, auditory, and especially visual stimuli. Players experience, interpret, and organize signs as they navigate a space, whether that be a virtual space or actual space as in *Pokémon Go* (Journet, 2007, p. 113). Navigating a space also requires action and motion, suggesting that movement itself is part of the narrative process, and that activities like walking around in *Pokémon Go* are laden with at least basic meaning that become part of the game's stories and drive them forward. Galloway (2006) explained the significance of movement by comparing action to language when he wrote, "Video games create their own grammars of action," including "physical vocabularies" that players use to play a game and create meaning in it (p. 4). Motion, images, sounds, feelings, and other sources and forms of meaning come together in a type of "narrative accrual" during the experience of play and are structured by narrative into what we perceive as reality (Bruner, 1991, p. 18).

Recognizing game narrative as the interaction between player and system is not new, and the idea that the player is active in it is well-trodden ground. Yet, as Hetland, Hughes, and Bunting (2012) argued, mobile AR games like *Pokémon Go* further alter our understanding of narrative because they take it on the road, as it were: They take gameplay and its narratives beyond the constraints of traditional gaming consoles or PCs and mingle virtual spaces with many more spaces in the actual world where new possibilities can emerge. They wrote, "By extending the game beyond the screen and into the physical world, these games co-opt the player's sensory experiences of real-world places as potential storytelling tools, mixing the physical and virtual to create immersive hybrid gameworlds" (Hetland et al., 2012, p. 144). Further, as Eanes and van den Broek (in this collection) noted, the game actually cannot be played effectively while sitting still; it requires movement and has resulted in significant increases in physical activity amongst players. The player's body as well as the game system mediate the narrative process and create a sense of a world or a reality wherein play takes place. By recasting narrative as the gradual construction of meaning resulting in a world, we can arrive at "a storytelling model in which the story of import is the nonlinear, non-narrative unfolding of a player's experience of a gameworld as it is co-created by the gamemaker and the player" (Hetland et al., 2012, p. 148). Hetland et al. (2012) referred to this process as non-narrative because they argue that narrative and story exist on different levels or scales. My view is different: Narrative is the process that creates a story, rather than a larger category or type of story. We identify similar processes here but differ in calling them narrative based on these definitions.

With a ludified understanding of narrative in place, it is possible to develop a model of narrative processes in *Pokémon Go* and other games (see Figure 8.1). *Pokémon Go*'s narrative is the confluence of multiple processes proceeding from different sources and through various mediations. The first process emerges from the team (or teams) that makes the game, in this case Niantic and, to a lesser extent, their telecommunications partners (such as Sprint and Boost Mobile for *Pokémon Go* Fest). The narrative laid down by the developers of a game is generally scripted, and players cannot do much to change it, though they may be able to make decisions within it. I call this *determined narrative*. This narrative consists of the lore and backstory embedded in the virtual world of the game, such as the world of Pokémon, trainers, professors, and teams in the case of *Pokémon Go*. Determined narrative is distinct from, but intricately tied to, the stories that the players can produce for themselves within the game. I call the stories created by players *personal narrative*. Personal narrative emerges through the stories players attach to their characters, stories enabled by the customization and choices allowed for by the developers in the determined narrative. Finally, an additional narrative

Figure 8.1. The interwoven narratives that create game narrative.

emerges when multiple players come together in groups, as with *Pokémon Go* Fest or when players undertake a raid against a legendary Pokémon. The interactions between players tell stories that I term *collective narrative*. Collective narrative is active when players interact, either helping or hindering each other as they adventure in the virtual world. It can be seen on smaller scales, such as a family playing together and sharing stories of their play (see Sierra & Burgoon in this collection), and it is especially apparent when players band together during large events. In working together, the players create a collective story, one that is comprised of players but at the same time irreducible to the sum of individual experiences. Determined, personal, and collective narrative are interrelated and codependent, and it is only together that they construct AR.

In order to put this model of narrative processes into action, the following sections provide close examinations of each in *Pokémon Go*. Each section explains what that type of narrative contributes to the game and what it means, and, further, how the different types come together. By developing this theory of ludic narrative and highlighting the playful confluence of different narratives, we can gain new understanding of what narrative is, how it operates, and why it matters. These questions have been at the center of ongoing discussions in fields such as literary theory and psychology. Literary theorists Palmer (2008) and Zunshine (2006), for example, argued that we read fiction and engage in narrative because they allow us to encounter the minds of others in characters or authors; in other words, narrative is a social activity (Zunshine, 2006, p. 162). Oatley (2002), a cognitive psychologist, claimed that narrative is an emotional stimulus, and it is important for its ability to make its audience feel something (p. 39). These theories are not mutually exclusive, and indeed fit well within the larger theory developed by Bruner (1990) that argued that narrative is one of the primary processes we use to understand and navigate the world: "The system by which people organize their experience in, knowledge about, and transactions with the social world ... is narrative rather than conceptual" (p. 35). In this sense, narrative shapes our realities because it produces stories that help us understand ourselves and the world around us. Narrative, then, is an organizing principle that does more than merely represent reality; it actively constructs it (Bruner, 1991, p. 5). As the following sections demonstrate, this same process is active in our experiences of AR. By bringing together the different narrative processes created by developers, produced by the game system, or experienced by players, *Pokémon Go* affords players the opportunity to create and play their own PokéStories and to thereby shape the game's AR.

Determined Narrative

Determined narrative is the first narrative players encounter in *Pokémon Go*, and it is put forward by the developers in order to establish the world of Pokémon in the game and give all players a common ground for their stories. The first time players begin the game, they are introduced to Professor Willow, a fictional Pokémon professor who tells the player that the world is filled with Pokémon and he needs their help to research them: "You'll need to find and collect Pokémon from everywhere!" The introduction proceeds to allow players to choose their avatar's style from a number of preset options, help them catch their first Pokémon from three options (with a fourth hidden one!), and pick their nickname in the game. Once the player reaches level 5, they can join one of the three teams directed by Professor Willow's assistants: Team Instinct (led by Spark), Team Mystic (led by Blanche), and Team Valor (led by Candela). While there are choices built into this narrative, each player is going to have a similar experience. The game's determined narrative does not change much if a player picks a different starting Pokémon or joins a different team, though their personal and collective narratives can change based on with whom they align themselves and whom they end up fighting.

The determined narrative of the game is significant because it establishes the content of its AR, and it does so by drawing on the lore, mechanics, and player expectations established throughout the Pokémon franchise. Pokémon is a transmedia story, and the narratives of Ash and the other protagonists journey from region to region of the Pokémon world across video games, television, films, comics, manga, toys, and other merchandise (Geraghty, 2017, p. 4). Each installment of the transmedia universe involves collecting, battling, trading, or even dressing up Pokémon, and further explores a world where Pokémon and humans live alongside each other. By drawing on the expansive narratives of earlier games and other media, *Pokémon Go* quickly taps into a recognizable world that AR can mix with our own. For example, when the player starts the game and encounters a professor who studies Pokémon, they know they are at the start of an adventure because every major installment of the Pokémon franchise (including the main games, the anime, etc.) has started the same way. Similarly, when they are handed their first Poké Balls, they know that they need to throw them at the Pokémon they want to catch, likely without the attendant tutorial telling them so. The continuation of these earlier narratives and mechanics provides the virtual spaces of AR with a sense of time and existence beyond the player—Pokémon have a history without the player, and presumably a present and a future which the player will affect somehow. All of this combines to make the virtual world feel real, and gives the player a sense of presence, or of "being there" (McMahan, 2003, p. 68). *Pokémon Go*'s AR coheres because of determined narrative, and it is determined narrative that provides the initial reasons for players to explore that reality and interact with each other.

The determined narrative also establishes *Pokémon Go*'s themes, meanings, and values, though players also bring their own to the game once they start playing. As Geraghty (2017) has argued, the adventures of Ash and other protagonists in the franchise play out in conjunction with their emotional and personal journeys, wherein the characters learn about friendship, cooperation, perseverance, and being true to oneself (p. 4). *Pokémon Go* continues this trend and places the player in the role of a young adult venturing into the world to discover, learn, and overcome challenges in what is in many ways a typical hero's quest narrative. Pokémon's quest narrative valorizes a particular set of values, the first of which is curiosity and exploration. McCrea (2017) noted this: "The playing subject of Pokémon is interpellated as a relentless explorer and opportunist, who gains from consistent movement and methodical approaches over long periods" (p. 43). In *Pokémon Go* this is seen in how the game pushes players outside to find more Pokémon, Poké Stops, and gyms. The mobility and challenges of exploration lead to the second value, which is progression, leveling, training, or getting stronger—the "progressive digital revelation" of a developing character realizing their destiny as the greatest Pokémon trainer (McCrea, 2017, p. 45). In *Pokémon Go*, this value manifests in either catching stronger Pokémon or leveling up existing ones so they are more capable of fighting in battles at gyms. The final value is combat and competition, evident in how the games, including *Pokémon Go*, encourage players to either battle each other's Pokémon or to participate in raids against rare and powerful Pokémon at a gym.

While *Pokémon Go*'s determined narrative contributes a great deal to the content, coherence, and values of the game's AR, it remains a relatively simple narrative. Once the player enters the game and begins to explore the actual world within it, they are mostly left to experience their own stories without further intervention from the characters in the determined narrative. Professor Willow and the team leaders rarely make appearances in the game outside of offering tips occasionally or, in Professor Willow's case, allowing you to trade in Pokémon for candy. The great benefit of this limited determined narrative is that it opens more space for players' personal narratives. Jagoda, Gilliam, McDonald, and Russell (2015) noted this in their work on alternate reality games: Open-ended play allows for more variance and emergence in player experiences and thus more room for the players to play with their own experiences and understandings of the game (p. 91). To see what they do with this, I turn now to personal narrative, the stories that emerge from players' experiences of the game. As Cardoso and Carvalhais (2013) noted, this is representative of the relationship between hardcoded, scripted events and procedural, emergent occurrences in games: As the events become more determined, there is less emergence, and vice versa (p. 26).

Personal Narrative

The determined narrative that establishes *Pokémon Go*'s AR for the player is the first narrative in the game, but it would not be successful (narratively or financially) without the player's further input in the form of personal narrative. Personal narrative begins with the player's initial choices within the determined narrative, including the process of creating a character, wherein the player authors their own representation in the game within a set of constraints. Each character will be at least slightly different from other players' characters, but always within the limits of the customization options the game provides. This freedom-within-constraints situation is representative of every interaction the player has with the game, but especially the limited choices presented to them initially. It isn't that personal narrative does not exist in these early decisions (a player choosing Bulbasaur has a different story with different possibilities, experiences, and meanings than one choosing Squirtle) but rather that the determined narrative takes the lead in introducing the player to the game.

Personal narrative is much more prevalent once players are free to actively explore the world on their own. As players move around the actual world with the game, they encounter different Pokémon based on where they are (their biome) and which Pokémon randomly appear near them. In some cases, Pokémon are only found in specific regions of the actual world, such as Tauros (found only in North America), or Lunatone and Solrock (currently rotating between the western and eastern hemispheres, respectively). The Poké Stops and gyms that players have access to also affect their stories of the game, particularly by determining the difficulty they have in obtaining the game's resources. Finally, *Pokémon Go*'s use of AR is founded on interaction with the actual world, meaning that anything that happens in the world around players can impact their stories in profound ways. These are the small but constant occurrences that Shivel (2009) stated can "subtly but irrevocably change one's gameplay," and I add that they subtly alter a player's personal narrative (p. 211). There are many examples of how players share their experiences as stories, ranging from players' forum posts to blogs to social media to news articles. For a particularly humorous example, consider Favis' (2016) article, "The Most Bizarre *Pokémon Go* Stories We've Heard Thus Far," which detailed players' escapades searching for Pokémon in caves, over cliffs, or even running into parked cop cars (a less humorous narrative is people finding Pokémon at the Holocaust Museum). The different experiences players have give life to personal narrative and encourage players to share their stories with each other—a phenomenon I will return to shortly with collective narrative.

All of these examples demonstrate the importance of space to personal narrative in a location-based mobile game like *Pokémon Go*. Sierra and Burgoon noted in their essay that "knowledge of and means to successfully navigate the local environment are essential to *Pokémon Go*," and that knowledge and navigation will vary greatly based on where players live, travel, and play. Players play in different spaces, and as a result they have different encounters and tell different stories. This is because the relationship between actual and virtual space in AR shifts with location. As AR overlays actual space with virtual spaces and objects, actual space also writes itself onto virtual space. The actual space determines what appears on the screen for the player, including the environment and the Pokémon that appear, yet what appears on the screen also determines a player's perception of the actual world around them. In other words, AR is more than a digital projection or representation—it's an active construction of reality based on the interplay of actual and virtual space. Hjorth and Richardson (2016) addressed this in their discussion of how play adds meaning to space and turns it into place: "Place, as it is enacted through play, highlights the collaborative, performative, and creative dimensions of cartography" (p. 6). As players navigate space with *Pokémon Go*, they are mapping and shaping spaces into places as part of an AR.

While this process is a technological and cognitive one, it is also a narrative: It involves the constant organizing of signs and events into meaningful sequences that may or may not be shared with others. One can see this in players' personal narratives of where they went and what they did there: They generated narrative as they moved through and experienced spaces. Walsh (2011) discussed this with what he called "emergent narrative," the idea that narrative develops simultaneously with sequences of events. He argued that events and phenomena in a game become narrative when the player attaches semiotic meaning to them and they become representative or communicative (p. 79). This is a continuous process as players navigate space in the game and strategize what to do or where to go next; it is the "development and exchange" between player and space that constructs "lived experiences of places" (Ruston, 2010, p. 115).

The massive number of places players can go with *Pokémon Go* and the choices they make while navigating spaces makes personal narrative a source of nearly infinite variation. Some of this variation has to do with the players themselves because different players focus on different things and experience things differently. For example, players who value the competition and combat of *Pokémon Go* over its story often narrate their experiences more in terms of gameplay decisions than an elaborate story. Other players are more likely to focus on developing narratives or roleplaying (Lindley, 2004, p. 190). Beyond explicitly narrative considerations, players have many different motivations—Yang and Liu (2017) identified seven motivations specific to *Pokémon Go*: exercise, fun, escapism, nostalgia, friendship maintenance, relationship initiation, and achievement (p. 55). All of these are various reasons for and ways of playing, and each affects the narrative construction of AR for the player.

As important as different playstyles are to narratives in AR, intersectional identity categories are even more so because they determine who gets to access AR and in what ways. As Thornham (2011) argued, as players play, "a certain type of gamer is being constructed," a gaming identity that exists in relation to power (p. 19). GamerGate—the online harassment campaign targeting women and feminist game critics that began in 2014—and toxic gaming communities have made it clear how players have to exhibit certain qualities in order to be fully accepted in some gaming cultures. Namely, players should be white, straight, and male, and exhibit qualities of mastery and dominance. Those who do not meet these ideals (or who only meet them in part), such as women, players of color, LGBTQ folk, and players with disabilities, often have to hide or diminish parts of themselves and accept that they are the butt of jokes. While this pertains especially to online communities, it is also written onto every experience that players have with *Pokémon Go*: "The culture, place, identity, and embodiment of the player all inform their experience of *Pokémon Go*, highlighting the uneven politics of mobile games and everyday play and their intrinsic relationship to power" (Hjorth & Richardson, 2017, p. 4). For example, consider how a person with a disability might experience navigating space in the game differently, how someone living in a neighborhood deemed as dangerous (often based on race and class in the United States) might be less able to explore with the game at night, or how a queer player might have to avoid certain spaces while playing. Intersectional identities and sociocultural contexts can also make it very easy for some to participate, as Sierra and Burgoon discuss in their essay in the context of large, affluent suburbs near metropolitan cities. Thus, when players are generating their personal narratives of the game, "the prioritization offered within the narrative is as much to do with the narrator's own performed identity and the socio-cultural moment and context of that performance, as it is to do with the narrated events" (Thornham, 2011, p. 22). Ultimately this demonstrates a crucial truth about the narrative construction of AR: Narratives are not neutral or objective, and not everyone has equal access to them. If we truly want to make AR available and welcoming to everyone, then we have to confront social, cultural, and institutional power structures and the narratives we have about them.

Already one can sense that personal narrative is never separate from collective narrative, the stories players tell when they come together in groups. Collective narrative demonstrates the same balancing act between individual difference and group commonality that determined narrative and personal narrative have to navigate. In other words, it has to bring players together as a recognizable whole while also providing space for interesting and meaningful difference in players' experiences. This is especially true in mobile games like *Pokémon Go*, where there is a constant tension between public space and private experience, between "individual and community interfaces" as we navigate public spaces with our personal devices (Farman, 2012, p. 116). Eanes and van den Broek (in this collection) discussed this tension at greater length in terms of "locational privacy," the phenomenon of being alone in public spaces that many *Pokémon Go* players experience. To see how players come together and construct group experiences and stories, I turn to the collective narratives of *Pokémon Go*.

Collective Narrative

In *Pokémon Go*, players are constantly interacting with each other through battling, messaging, or talking to each other when they are in the same place. In doing so, players bring their personal narratives into contact with each other, resulting in collective narrative. Collective narrative is thus tied to individuals and their personal narratives, but it also becomes its own distinct narrative because it is irreducible to the mere sum of its parts and it is not attributable to individual players. For example, the narrative of how terrible *Pokémon Go* Fest was emerged from thousands of individual players' stories, but the larger, group narrative of the day could not be traced back to any one individual.

In order for a collective narrative like *Pokémon Go* Fest's to happen, there has to be a shared experience, feeling, or sense of events amongst players. As multiple people experience the same thing (even if their experiences of that thing are different), a curious form of intersubjectivity emerges that could be described as a distributed imagination or collective consciousness. This group imagination or consciousness is created by the shared experience and a willingness to participate in the same fiction (or AR) that results from it. Giddings (2016) argued that this imagination in *Pokémon Go* is a "social phenomenon rather than a solitary, internal process as [imagination] is generally characterized" (p. 60). The content for this shared imagination, and the collective narratives it produces, is the common stories, mechanics, and values provided by the determined narrative of the game, combined with elements of each person's personal narrative. In contributing to the shared imagination and collective narrative, however, no one individual can claim ownership of it—the narrative belongs to the group and is a shared reality. Further, players have to rely on each other in collective narrative because, as Jagoda et al. (2015) explained, "no single player can experience every event, solve each puzzle, or know every narrative detail" (p. 78). Players can thus refer to the collective narrative in order to find both shared experiences and parts of the experience that they may have missed.

What really necessitates cooperation and forges collective narrative, however, is combat and competition. In raids or group gym battles, for example, the players must use their Pokémon to support each other because it would be impossible to overcome the challenges alone. As more players become involved in a challenge, the collective narrative shifts in order to accommodate them. In raids against legendary Pokémon, players and their Pokémon appear on each other's screens and become part of the group story. This happens dynamically as players join or leave the raid and as their Pokémon faint and are replaced by other Pokémon. In effect, this means collective narrative is constantly shifting according to player interaction and producing a story that is irreducible to any individual player's experience. In working and struggling together, the players form communal bonds of shared identity based on their experience, and a shared consciousness emerges when players narrate themselves together as "we" (Krzywinska, 2007, p. 112). Included in the collective consciousness can be a sense of belonging built on the knowledge that one is contributing to the success or failure of the group. This also appears outside of raids and gyms in player associations, such as the teams from the determined narrative: Instinct, Mystic, and Valor. The teams are networks of players who infrequently perform group activities together, often in emergent situations where team members happen to be in the same place at the same time. The teams promote player affiliation to a group and encourage a collective identity defined against other groups. While members of the same team might not be close to each other, they contribute to the same cause and collective narrative.

The shift away from personal narrative means the individual loses some power to affect AR in a collective narrative, but this also has the advantage of making the individual part of something greater than their self. Golub (2010) described the moment of overcoming a group challenge in online games as "a collective accomplishment that creates social solidarity and can even serve as an important moment in the biographies of individual players" (p. 17). Raids in *Pokémon Go* accomplish this by making battling and capturing a rare Pokémon a collective effort that forces players to rely on one another and builds community, even if only temporarily. Similar to what Golub noted with the biographies of individual players, the personal narrative of a character can be shaped by what collective narratives that character has or has not participated in. Some players even define themselves in the game by not participating in collective narratives and instead creating their own. For example, players who were tired of the fighting between teams Instinct, Mystic, and Valor created their own Team Harmony, a team whose narrative emphasizes balance, harmony, and avoiding conflict with others (Fahey, 2016).

Finally, collective narratives can emerge outside of the game as well, often in online forums, blogs, and social media where players gather to discuss the game. For example, Geraghty (2017) documented how some *Pokémon Go* players gather on forums to share secrets or promote conspiracy theories about the game. In doing so, he argued that they "are attempting to engage with and enhance the metatext (the established game universe, characters and backstories alongside fan fiction and theories) beyond what is allowable in the virtual gaming environment" (p. 6). Another prominent example of collective narrative outside of the game is The Silph Road, the largest grassroots network of *Pokémon Go* players. The Silph Road is an online hub for players to read the latest game news, connect with other players (including local groups), and access a number of tools that help players play the game and find the Pokémon they want to catch. The Silph Road generates collective stories about the game by allowing players to contribute their experiences and data to the network's tools and social media, and players that do so become part of a larger community that generates and distributes stories about the game. Both of these examples demonstrate how players are using the flexibility provided by a limited determined narrative to create their own stories and meanings in the game and to share these with each other. This makes the AR of the game "more tangible, complete and real" (Geraghty, 2017, p. 11).

Of the three narrative processes in *Pokémon Go*, collective narrative is the most difficult to contain in a neat description. This is because it blurs distinctions between the individual and the collective: Remove the individuals and one loses the collective, but at the same time the collective is more than the sum of individuals. It is also worth noting that collective narratives are not always positive ones. The difficulties that require group play also present a very real possibility of failure, and in failure it is easy for players to get frustrated and blame each other. In such cases, the collective narrative is not one of overcoming, but rather one of disjunction and resentment. Collective narratives can and sometimes do fall apart, just as the groups that create them also fall apart. Despite these complexities, collective narrative produces shared, distributed identities and stories that are essential in constructing *Pokémon Go*'s AR.

Narrative Realities, Present and Future

The narrative processes of *Pokémon Go* proceed from developers and players, taking the forms of determined, personal, and collective narrative. None of the three narratives ever exists entirely on its own, and each contributes to a player's experience of AR. No player of *Pokémon Go* can completely avoid determined narrative (could they be a player if they didn't play the game?), personal narrative (could a player play without having their own experiences while doing so?), or collective narrative (even alone, aren't players always part of some social system?). Further, if the narratives conflict, such as when players' expectations are dashed, then the experience of the game can become inconsistent in a way that the player finds jarring and unenjoyable (Juul, 2007, p. 192). At worst, such conflicts could cause players to cease playing entirely, or at least threaten to do so in social media posts. A coherent and welcoming AR is only possible when determined, personal, and collective narrative flow together.

The narrative construction of AR is significant for several reasons. First, recognizing these narrative processes helps us see how *Pokémon Go* constructs AR and affects its players. The game draws on the determined narrative of a world filled with fictional (and often adorable) monsters and uses that narrative to promote values of exploration, friendship, and competition. Yet the game keeps this narrative simple in order to allow space for emergent experiences that become personal narratives and for players to bring their own narratives into the game and make them part of its AR. When players come together in groups, this takes on a social dimension and makes AR a shared experience that many players can be a part of. These same narrative processes are present in other games and potentially other media as well, and help us understand how meaning is created and shared by players and audiences.

Second, the narrative construction of *Pokémon Go* and other AR can reveal a great deal about our cultures. By seeing how players (as individuals and as groups) play in various places and how they use those experiences to craft their own narratives, we can better account for how we understand ourselves and the worlds around us. Better yet, we can see more clearly how we do these things differently. Our PokéStories provide textual cues of what we value, what we like and dislike, and who we think we are, including all of the attendant ideologies that inform these categories. In other words, by looking at how narratives operate and produce stories in *Pokémon Go*, we can see more clearly which ideas, beliefs, and aesthetics are built into our AR. As a game, *Pokémon Go* excels at this because play has a long history as an inter-disciplinary and poetic "cultural probe"—a site where cultural values and contemporary social trends become more apparent and observable (Hjorth & Richardson, 2016, p. 7). Its complement here, narrative, is equally inter-woven with culture. As Graesser, Olde, and Klettke (2002) noted, "perhaps the easiest way to understand the mind of a culture is to understand its sto-ries" (p. 229). Together, narrative and play provide a unique and powerful lens for understanding *Pokémon Go* and contemporary popular culture.

Finally, the narrative construction of AR gives us the tools to imagine how we could create AR in different and potentially transformative ways. We could, for example, use narrative as part of a "playful resistance" or "critical play," reshaping events and our understandings of them to be explicitly anti-normative or unexpected (Hjorth & Richardson, 2016, p. 10). Many players at the margins are already doing this, engaging in what Chang (2017) called "queergaming" by challenging the stereotypical and the status quo and instead building their own narratives and embracing the "heterogeneity of play" (p. 15). For example, LGBTQ *Pokémon Go* players have developed narratives of one or more of the team leaders (Candela, Blanche, and Spark) being LGBTQ, including that Candela and Blanche are in a relationship, or that Spark is a trans man, or a gay or asexual cisgender man (LGBTQ Video Game Archive, 2018). These players are essentially playing with narrative—putting the lud-ified understanding of narrative into practice to reorganize and reshape their experience of the game and creating their own version of its AR in the process. Of course, narrative is no panacea, and AR such as *Pokémon Go* have inherent problems such as the commodification of digital games and the use of players as free laborers (Jin, 2017, p. 56). Yet narrative can be a place to start, and it can contribute, even if slowly and incrementally, to changing our realities. It does so in *Pokémon Go* and elsewhere by telling us about ourselves and by giving us the opportunity for "encountering, processing, and testing the pres-ent" (Jagoda et al., 2015, p. 75). The narratives of *Pokémon Go* are our stories, and they can reveal parts of who we are, how we play, and what we can imag-ine.

REFERENCES

Aarseth, E.J. (1997). *Cybertext: Perspectives on ergodic literature*. Baltimore: Johns Hopkins University Press.

Bruner, J. (1990). *Acts of meaning*. Cambridge, MA: Harvard University Press.

Bruner, J. (1991). The narrative construction of reality. *Critical Inquiry*, *18*(1), 1–21. Retrieved from https://www.jstor.org/stable/1343711.

Bunting, B.S., Jr. (2014). The geocacher as placemaker: Remapping reality through location-based mobile gameplay. In J. Farman (Ed.), *The mobile story: Narrative practices with locative technologies* (pp. 161–174). New York, NY: Routledge.

Cardoso, P., & Carvalhais, M. (2013). Breaking the game: The traversal of the emergent narrative in video games. *Journal of Science and Technology of the Arts*, *5*(1), 25–31. Retrieved from http://artes.ucp.pt/citarj/article/view/87/47.

Chang, E. (2017). Queergaming. In B. Ruberg & A. Shaw (Eds.), *Queer Game Studies* (pp. 15–24). Minneapolis: University of Minnesota Press.

Clark, A.M., & Clark, M.T.G. (2016). *Pokémon Go* and research: Qualitative, mixed methods research, and the supercomplexity of interventions. *International Journal of Qualitative Methods*, *15*(1), 1–3. https://doi.org/10.1177/1609406916667765.

Eskelinen, M. (2012). *Cybertext poetics: The critical landscape of new media literary theory*. New York, NY: Continuum.

Fahey, M. (2016, July 13). *Pokémon Go* fans seek to end cross-faction hostility via Team Harmony. *Kotaku*. Retrieved from https://kotaku.com/pokemon-go-fans-seek-to-end-cross-faction-hostility-via-1783607654.

Farman, J. (2012). *Mobile interface theory: Embodied space and locative media*. New York, NY: Routledge.

Farokhmanesh, M. (2017, July 25). I went to *Pokémon GO* Fest, and it was a disaster. *The Verge*. Retrieved from https://www.theverge.com/2017/7/25/16019404/pokemon-go-fest-refunds-disaster-review.

Favis, E. (2016, July 30). The most bizarre *Pokémon Go* stories we've heard thus far. Retrieved February 13, 2018, from http://www.gameinformer.com/b/features/archive/2016/07/30/the-most-bizzare-pokemon-go-stories-we-have-heard-thus-far.aspx.

Galloway, A.R. (2006). *Gaming: Essays on algorithmic culture*. Minneapolis, MN: University of Minnesota Press.

Geraghty, L. (2017). Can Pikachu die? Online fan conspiracy theories and the Pokémon gaming universe. *The Journal of Fandom Studies*, *5*(1), 3–20. https://doi.org/10.1386/jfs.5.1.3_1.

Giddings, S. (2017). *Pokémon GO* as distributed imagination. *Mobile Media & Communication*, *5*(1), 59–62. https://doi.org/10.1177/2050157916677866.

Golub, A. (2010). Being in the World (of Warcraft): Raiding, realism, and knowledge production in a massively multiplayer online game. *Anthropological Quarterly*, *83*(1), 17–45.

Graesser, A.C., Olde, B., & Klettke, B. (2002). How does the mind construct and represent stories? In M.C. Green, J.J. Strange & T.C. Brock (Eds.), *Narrative impact: Social and cognitive foundations* (pp. 229–262). New York, NY: Psychology Press.

Hetland, T., Hughes, J., & Bunting, B.S. (2012). The player as author: Exploring the effects of mobile gaming and the location-aware interface on storytelling. *Future Internet*, *4*(1), 142–160. https://doi.org/10.3390/fi4010142.

Hjorth, L., & Richardson, I. (2017). *Pokémon GO*: Mobile media play, place-making, and the digital wayfarer. *Mobile Media & Communication*, *5*(1), 3–14. https://doi.org/10.1177/2050157916680015.

Jagoda, P., Gilliam, M., McDonald, P., & Russell, C. (2015). Worlding through play: Alternate reality games, large-scale learning, and *The Source*. *American Journal of Play*, *8*(1), 74–100. Retrieved from https://eric.ed.gov/?id=EJ1080017.

Jin, D.Y. (2017). Critical interpretation of the *Pokémon GO* phenomenon: The intensification of new capitalism and free labor. *Mobile Media & Communication*, *5*(1), 55–58. https://doi.org/10.1177/2050157916677306.

Journet, D. (2007). Narrative, action, and learning: The stories of *Myst*. In C.L. Selfe & G.E. Hawisher (Eds.), *Gaming lives in the twenty-first century: Literate connections* (pp. 93–120). New York, NY: Palgrave McMillan.

Juul, J. (2007). Without a goal: On open and expressive games. In B. Atkins & T. Krzywinska (Eds.), *Videogame, player, text* (pp. 191–203). New York, NY: Manchester University Press.

Keogh, B. (2017). *Pokémon Go*, the novelty of nostalgia, and the ubiquity of the smartphone. *Mobile Media & Communication*, *5*(1), 38–41. https://doi.org/10.1177/2050157916678025.

Krzywinska, T. (2007). Being a determined agent in (the) *World of Warcraft*: Text/play/identity. In B. Atkins and T. Krzywinska (Eds.), *Videogame, player, text* (pp. 101–19). New York, NY: Manchester University Press.

LGBTQ Video Game Archive. (2018). Candela, Blanche, and Spark in *Pokémon GO!* Retrieved June 8, 2018, from https://lgbtqgamearchive.com/2017/02/11/candela-blanche-and-spark-in-pokemon-go/.

Lindley, C.A. (2004). Narrative, game play, and alternative time structures for virtual environments. In S. Göbel, U. Spierling, A. Hoffman, I. Iurgel, O. Schneider, J. Dechau, & A. Feix (Eds.), *Technologies for interactive digital storytelling and entertainment 2004* (pp. 183–194). Berlin, Germany: Springer.

Mäyrä, F. (2017). *Pokémon GO*: Entering the ludic society. *Mobile Media & Communication*, 5(1), 47–50. https://doi.org/10.1177/2050157916678270.

McCrea, C. (2017). Pokémon's progressive revelation: Notes on 20 years of game design. *Mobile Media & Communication*, 5(1), 42–46. https://doi.org/10.1177/2050157916678271.

McMahan, A. (2003). Immersion, engagement, and presence: A method for analyzing 3-D video games. In M. Wolf & B. Perron (Eds.), *The video game theory reader* (pp. 67–86). New York, NY: Routledge.

Niantic, Inc. (2017). *Pokémon GO Fest*. Retrieved February 11, 2018, from https://www.pokemongolive.com/events/fest/chicago/.

Oatley, K. (2002). Emotions and the story world of fiction. In M.C. Green, J.J. Strange, & T.C. Brock (Eds.), *Narrative impact: Social and cognitive foundations* (pp. 39–69). New York, NY: Psychology Press.

Palmer, A. (2008). *Fictional minds*. Lincoln: University of Nebraska Press.

Peddie, J. (2017). *Augmented reality: Where we will all live*. New York, NY: Springer.

Roine, H.-R. (2016). How you emerge from this game is up to you: Agency, positioning, and narrativity in *The Mass Effect Trilogy*. In M. Hatavara, M. Hyvärinen, M. Mäkelä, & F. Mäyrä (Eds.), *Narrative theory, literature, and new media: Narrative minds and virtual worlds* (pp. 67–86). New York, NY: Routledge.

Ruston, S.W. (2010). Storyworlds on the move: Mobile media and their implications for narrative. *Storyworlds: A Journal of Narrative Studies, 2*, 101–120. https://doi.org/10.1353/stw.0.0001.

Ryan, M.-L. (2014). Story/Worlds/Media: Tuning the instruments of a media-conscious narratology. In M.-L. Ryan & J.-N. Thon (Eds.), *Storyworlds across media: Toward a media-conscious narratology* (pp. 25–49). Lincoln: University of Nebraska Press.

Sanford, A.J., & Emmott, C. (2012). *Mind, brain and narrative*. Cambridge, UK: Cambridge University Press.

Shivel, G. (2009). *World of Warcraft*: The murloc is the message. *Symploke, 17*(1–2), 205–213. https://doi.org/10.1353/sym.2009.0026.

Thornham, H. (2011). *Ethnographies of the videogame: Gender, narrative and praxis*. Farnham, England: Ashgate.

Upton, B. (2015). *The aesthetic of play*. Cambridge, MA: MIT Press.

Walsh, R. (2011). Emergent narrative in interactive media. *Narrative, 19*(1), 72–85. doi:10.1353/nar.2011.0006.

Yang, C., & Liu, D. (2017). Motives matter: Motives for playing *Pokémon Go* and implications for well-being. *Cyberpsychology, Behavior, and Social Networking, 20*(1), 52–57. https://doi.org/10.1089/cyber.2016.0562.

Zunshine, L. (2006). *Why we read fiction: Theory of mind and the novel*. Columbus: Ohio State University Press.

PART THREE

The Impact of Play

Raid Pass

Constitutive Capital Flows
for Augmented Reality

PETER SCHAEFER *and*
MARGARET SCHWARTZ

On September 9, 2017, Niantic scheduled a field test for the *Pokémon Go* EX Raid system at Columbus Circle in New York City. This was among the first wave of field tests and the first one on the east coast of the United States. The raid offered a small group of trainers an early opportunity to catch the highly coveted Pokémon Mewtwo. Participation was by invitation only: Trainers were preselected by Niantic according to their level of play and their geographic location. They were issued an exclusive Raid Pass usable only at the Columbus Circle gym during a prescribed hour-long window.

That same day, thousands of peaceful protesters gathered outside the Trump International Hotel, also located at Columbus Circle. President Trump had just announced the repeal of the Deferred Action for Childhood Arrivals (DACA) law; the protest called for reinstating provisions for the millions of undocumented immigrants in the United States. The New York Police Department (NYPD) deployed units to manage the protest and established barricades around Columbus Circle. This meant that the NYPD also inadvertently barricaded the gym location. It was impossible for trainers to get close enough to the gym (overlaid on a large statue of Christopher Columbus) to participate in the raid. Intrepid trainers pleaded with the NYPD for entrance to the gym, and officers relented by allowing entrance for those players who could display on their phones a valid EX Raid Pass for Columbus Circle. It was an extraordinary case of the gaming world's ability to influence not only the everyday lives of individuals, but also the actual, structural, state-supported apparatuses of power.

Important differences mark the two groups converging on Columbus Circle. The DACA protesters were anonymous. Theirs was a mass identity—supporters of DACA and the DREAM (Development, Relief, and Education for Alien Minors) Act—and this identity was contingent, tied to the particular time and space of their coming together to protest. This is the kind of identity that characterizes protest coalitions: The source of their rhetorical power is their massing as one group to make political claims as and on behalf of a community. The injustice to that community is defined by the protest as structural—as unfair at the level of group membership—and the redress to the injustice is similarly defined in terms of the group: This is what *the people* demand. This relatively spontaneous and short-lived group was denied access as part of the standard policing procedures for such a gathering—procedures that index state discomfort with mass protest and reveal the investments of the state in things like private property, commerce (the protest could not disrupt traffic or other movement in this highly commercial space), and individualized rights over group rights.

The other group, the Pokémon trainers, were specific individuals able to prove their singular identities via the exclusive Raid Pass. Although, as readers will see in more detail below, the trainers were loosely organized as high-level gamers, their identity was primarily that of individuals seeking private advancement or entertainment in a single-player game. In other words, their interests aligned perfectly with those the police barricades were set up to protect: individual consumers asking for the right to pursue their own bought-and-paid-for entertainment. Although these interests may have required a bit of work to communicate to the police, the police ultimately recognized these players as non-threatening and gave them access to the space, with one important proviso: that they be able to prove their identities and their right, as consumers, to be in that space. This is how the Raid Pass on trainers' phones became a kind of identification and access pass. It literally cosigned their identities as consumers, individuals with singular, non-political pursuits that would not threaten the interests the police were put in place to protect.

The accessibility of the space helps demonstrate how *Pokémon Go* in particular and augmented reality (AR) in general is always embedded in historical and material conditions. The EX Raid example demonstrated how in-game capital affords privilege that transcends into real life. The elite Pokémon trainer has had hours of time and considerable money to spend on attaining a high level in the game. He or she is unlikely to belong to a group with a grievance against the status quo, for such time and capital investment is unavailable to those living in poverty or those whose bodies are policed in the public space necessary for game play. Already then—and likely in sharp contrast to the group of DACA protesters—the Raid Pass holders were an elite group in the socio-political sense, as well as at the level of their game play. While this was probably not the conscious thought process of the police who let them through the barriers, it certainly tacitly informed the way the trainers approached police (that is, with a sense of safety and entitlement) and the way the police responded (as we will see below, largely with friendliness and respect).

The Raid Pass thus functioned to identify its holder not only as an accountable, legitimate person, but also crucially as an ally of capital. It carried the unspoken message that the NYPD had no need to protect the public space from them, for the EX Raid Pass itself functioned as a marker of the holder's consumerist success and public accountability. The threat therefore was not to public safety or to political stability but to capital. In this, the holders of the Raid Pass were seen not only as neutral, but as exceptional. They were high-level consumers who deserved special access.

Our analysis employs interviews of raid participants along with an interpretive analysis of discourse for the raid and the protests in the popular press as well as relevant Reddit forums. This method facilitates a look at the structures that shape game design alongside the agency of trainers to act in accordance with the privilege afforded by capital. The analysis complicates digital utopianism by demonstrating how AR may not only uphold but also create new forms of privilege in real life. Seen through an historical materialist lens, *Pokémon Go* and AR have consequences that come from the blurring of the line between virtual space and the built environment. Specifically, our analysis suggests that the real/virtual divide is less helpful in thinking about these dynamics, and that the most important trail to follow is the flow of capital.

We begin with a brief literature review of analysis of social power and AR gaming. We then introduce our interviews of the trainers involved in the September 9 raid at Columbus Circle along with a description of available discourse around the event from YouTube videos and Reddit discussions. We then conclude our analysis with a discussion of how this Ex Raid was in fact not a victory for the virtual world or for gaming, but rather reveals how capital, in this case the kind of platform capitalism that monetizes online spaces, is the proper location for analysis and critique. It is the offline world in which trainers, protesters, and police alike are living, and its rules are what govern access and identity.

Power and Pokémon Go

AR games such as *Pokémon Go* do not transcend social conditions present in virtual and physical spaces. Franks (2017) asserted that the inequalities are reproduced within game design, arguing that "when existing inequalities are unacknowledged and unaddressed in the 'real' world, they tend to be replicated and augmented in virtual realities" (p. 503). Inequality discourse for *Pokémon Go* primarily concerns race and geography: for example, assertions that rural areas, African-American neighborhoods, and Hispanic neighborhoods are underserved with fewer Pokémon spawns, Stops, and gyms (Juhász & Hochmair, 2017).

Poké Stops are physical places where trainers can acquire necessary game materials through the AR of the game. Their original locations were determined via a submission process using *Ingress*, an AR game created by Niantic, Inc., that preceded *Pokémon Go*. *Ingress* players submitted requests for portals, a location relevant in the physical world and also in the game world. These portals were later used as the locations for Poké Stops, presumably because the relevant coding was already in place. A study of Washington, D.C., conducted by the Urban Institute, found the following: "In neighborhoods that are majority white, there are 55 portals on average, compared with 19 portals in neighborhoods that are majority black" (Kooragayala & Srini, 2016). The unequal distribution of Poké Stops, following the *Ingress* portal submission, led to considerable outcry from the public, particularly in the weeks following the game's launch. Probably the harshest declaration came from the claim that *Pokémon Go* was guilty of redlining, defined as the denial of services based on race or ethnicity for particular geographic areas (Akhtar, 2016).

Other critics have called attention to the neoliberal logic of the game mechanics. Shum and Tranter (2017) argued that trainers playing *Pokémon Go* occupy the position of a neoliberal subject, untethered from any overarching narrative and free to travel the world with the sole purpose of accumulation. The lack of an end game or structured focus is often criticized in the game (Tassi, 2017). However, one could also assert that the addition of raids and raid bosses, while not a substitute for an end game, offers a practical focus for trainers and a narrative element where communication with fellow trainers is often necessary to accomplish a particular goal. Nevertheless, this goal is still accumulation, tied to reaping additional rewards such as added experience points, stardust, rare candy, and other perks more valuable in a raid than in normal encounters. One could say that EX Raids in particular reflect the neoliberal bent of the game insofar as there is a direct link to retail environments. While not the case for the Columbus Circle raid, subsequent EX Raids have been most prevalent in either public parks or sponsored locations (currently Sprint, Boost Mobile, and Starbucks retail spaces in the United States and McDonald's in Japan).

Game design thus appears to set the political agenda of game play, with baked-in assumptions about class and race via their "choices about which aspects of our lived history they want to replicate, enhance, or change" (Franks, 2017, p. 503). However, it's not just developers who determine game play. Games such as *Pokémon Go* are frequently updated in response to comments from players and other shifting dynamics of the physical world and the virtual world. Franks outlined how developers cope with social inequality in relation to the design of virtual and AR games by presenting a three-part typology: (1) Developers can build efforts to redress inequality into the design, (2) Developers can respond to claims of inequality by restructuring the design, or (3) Developers can largely ignore claims of inequality (p. 503). Arguably Niantic can be seen in the second category insofar as it has reopened portal submissions to help redress often-repeated claims that poor urban areas and rural areas comprised mostly of African-Americans and Hispanics are not given the same virtual opportunity as other areas.

In addition to the structural adjustments made by Niantic, it's important to note the agency of trainers to use the game as leverage against other existing power structures. A clear example of the reinscribed utopianism of the virtual side of digital dualism is found in claims that assert the ability of user-generated content to democratize production for the masses. Ritzer and Jurgenson (2010) asserted that "prosumers," a clever blend of "producer" and "consumer," exemplify a system with new abundance and new possibilities that exist untethered from material constraints (p. 22). *Pokémon Go*, as the leading example of mass-market AR, allows us to see clearly a major problem with the redemptive narrative for non-binary notions of virtual and physical interactions. *Pokémon Go* trainers function as prosumers in the way defined by Ritzer and Jurgenson (2010) in that they both produce and consume. Trainers consume digital mapping data, physical sites tied to the virtual world of the game, and of course Nintendo's intellectual property in the form of the Pokémon themselves. But how does their production work in turn to shape their own material circumstances in particular, let alone for capitalism in general?

Lures increase the number of Pokémon who spawn in a particular geographic location. An illustrative case is when community organizers used this game mechanic to bring a bigger crowd and more attention to a social protest. As part of the Black Lives Matter movement, for example, protestors chained themselves to the front doors of the office of the Oakland Police Officers Association (Kelly, 2016). Organizers put up *Pokémon Go* lures at the site and used social media to motivate sympathetic trainers to come to the location to support Black Lives Matter while also catching some Pokémon at the same time (Asians for Black Lives Matter, 2016). Trainers thus used the game's mechanics to lend support to a cause outside the scope of the game. Nevertheless, it should be obvious from this example that the Oakland organizers were deploying a prosumerist tactic to augment their organizing, one that appealed to individuals' desire to further their own gaming interests rather than a shared identity or political goal.

This is why we argue that to understand power in the context of AR requires a broader understanding of the vectors of influence. Specifically, critical work on algorithms and program design reveals the baked-in socio-cultural biases in the structure of online and AR spaces—biases that echo the structural inequalities of the real world. However, the crucial point here is to insist on the most powerful bias of all, which is that all of these platforms *must* be monetized. The endgame is always profit, and as such, the interests of those who are unlikely to generate profit are written out of the space. This isn't to say that the design has the final say—developers create a game architecture, which fans and critics in turn respond to and push against. Both sets of actors, however, function in the context of consumer capitalism and, more specifically, within the existing framework for monetizing AR gameplay. In the section that follows, we explore how these material circumstances shape *Pokémon Go* in general as revealed by the extraordinary events of the September 9 EX Raid.

An EX Raid Pass

A closer look at the circumstances of the EX Raid at Columbus Circle illuminates how capital plays a guiding role in the social process through which privilege is maintained and created via the virtual and physical interplay. On September 8, 2017, a select group of approximately 50 to 100 trainers found an EX Raid Pass in their *Pokémon Go* item inventory. The pass invited them to participate in an exclusive raiding opportunity to field-test the fledgling EX Raid system at a gym in New York City. The raid was scheduled for 4 to 5 p.m. the following day. In the days prior to the EX Raid invitations, online message boards such as those found on Reddit were clogged with excited speculation about these exclusive opportunities, as it was well known that this was a unique chance to catch the coveted Pokémon Mewtwo.

On September 5, 2017, U.S. Attorney General Jeff Sessions, under the direction of President Donald Trump, announced plans to repeal the DACA program. DACA was designed to provide work permits and protections against deportation for over 700,000 people, many of whom live in New York City, who illegally immigrated to the United States while children. In the days following the announcement by the attorney general, several protests occurred in New York City and across the United States, often located at real estate ventures that fell under the Trump brand (Whitford, 2017).

On September 9, 2017, Movimiento Cosecha, a volunteer organization that fights for the rights of undocumented immigrants in the United States, orchestrated a rally to support DACA. The rally followed a series of protests in New York City in places such as City Hall downtown and the National

Action Network's headquarters in Harlem (Slattery, 2017). There were upward of 3,000 protesters filling the sidewalks along Columbus Circle, a congested roundabout at one of the corners of Central Park in Manhattan. Their focus was the Trump International Hotel and Tower located at the northern end of Columbus Circle (Narizhnaya, 2017), where the rally began. Protesters then marched uptown via Central Park West to 72nd Street. The NYPD used several units, many of which were on scooters and bikes, while Community Response Team officers patrolled the area on foot (Lynch, 2017).

As the EX Raid start time neared, most of the protesters had moved on toward Central Park, but several police officers were stationed at entrances to Columbus Circle which was barricaded under police authority. Many trainers tried in vain to enter through the barricade to get ready to participate in the raid.

A representative of The Silph Road (TSR) eventually facilitated trainer access to the barricaded area. TSR refers to itself as the "largest grassroots network" for *Pokémon Go* (About the Silph Road, 2018). The organization was started when *Pokémon Go* was announced but not yet made available for play. The original function was to facilitate the trading of Pokémon, a foundational feature of the Pokémon games developed for Nintendo handheld devices that, as of February of 2018, had not yet been implemented in *Pokémon Go* (it has since been added). But the group expanded its function and grew in size and influence. TSR has three objectives: "constructing a real-world network of *Pokémon Go* enthusiasts, researching and discussing game mechanics and strategy, and helping newbies improve and learn" (About the Silph Road, 2018).

TSR administers large-scale data collection projects, analyzes the results, and presents them in reports shared via their subReddit and on thesilphroad. com. Commentators on the popular TSR subReddit (r/thesilphroad) called attention to the limits of gameplay such as the minimum number of trainers needed to defeat certain raid bosses using particular Pokémon or to identify the geographical boundaries for particular regional Pokémon. TSR is a testament to the continued popularity of the game as well as the depth of its possibilities when inspired trainers dig into the minutiae of the game. This grassroots organization ended up being instrumental to allowing trainer access to the restricted space for the EX Raid field test.

The trainer who orchestrated the penetration of the police barricade refers to herself as FireTheGoddess, and she is the U.S. Northeast Warden for TSR. She received an invitation to the Columbus Circle EX Raid for September 9, and she went to the event as a representative of TSR, clad in official Silph Road gear. There was no official or unofficial directive regarding TSR on the part of Niantic and in fact TSR explicitly stated on their website that they have no connection to the developers or to Nintendo. FireTheGoddess stated that her role at the raid was as a representative for TSR and to gather data and facilitate logistics. Since this was among the first EX Raids, and the first in New York City where TSR headquarters are located, she administered surveys for trainers with questions regarding the particulars of the raid such as feedback on the amount of time between the invitation being sent and the time of the raid. As FireTheGoddess explained via interview:

> I arrived 30 mins early and quickly realized that the entire area of Columbus Circle was barricaded off due to a DACA protest at Trump Towers. I found a section that I could cross safely and asked an officer how I could gain entry to the circle. There were other trainers nearby that had already requested entry but they were denied. I think that the only reason the police officers stationed there listened to me at all was because I arrived in my official TSR Warden shirt with official-looking questionnaires in hand and was able to show them my EX Raid Pass for the location at that exact time. After a bit of convincing I was able to get the officers to let the trainers with EX Passes into the area.

FireTheGoddess reported that interactions between trainers and the police were amiable. She said that, "At first, some of them were irritated with me speaking to them but a big smile and enthusiastic demeanor goes a long way to making people feel more comfortable with talking to you." She said that frustration on the part of the officers was more directed at Niantic, as one officer asked her to tell "Niantic to be more mindful about where they host these things." And clearly Niantic has worked to limit the disruption of EX Raids on public space by now limiting these events to public parks and sponsored gyms.

At the September 9 event, there was also interaction between officers and the trainers with the officers taking an interest in the game. One officer talked about one of his kids playing *Pokémon Go*. A YouTube video of the event, shot and posted by Alan Jourdan (2017), showed an officer taking a picture of a trainer's phone who has recently captured Mewtwo. The video showed a small group of 30 or so trainers standing around the Columbus statue with police standing at the barricaded entrances. It's clear to see that after seeing the EX Raid Pass on people's phones, the police officer stepped aside and allowed trainers entry into the protected space.

FireTheGoddess reported that, if anything, the police officers expressed a mild irritation at having to block off Columbus Circle in the first place. Yet there was also general discomfort expressed by an officer who heard a protestor express a desire to tear down the statue of Christopher Columbus in the center of the roundabout. The Columbus statue has been a subject of controversy with calls to remove the monument that some find an offensive symbol of settler colonialism. Shortly after the DACA protests, New York mayor Bill de Blasio stated that the Columbus statue would stay, and in appeasement the city would erect a monument to indigenous peoples somewhere else in the five boroughs (Gay, 2018). The controversy over the status may be the reason why the circle, within which the monument is centrally located, was barricaded.

Pokémon trainer and YouTuber Jourdan also reported positive interactions between police and trainers. He stated, "The police officers were very friendly and did not try to get rid of the trainers." He added that one officer "even asked to take a picture of the Mewtwo that one of the trainers caught." However, he noted that the dynamic was shaped by the fact that the protest had already moved on to Central Park and there was little to no overlap between the raid and the protestors. As he said, "If the demonstrators were there, it might've been a different story." And the friendly interactions stayed consistent throughout the raid.

Jourdan stated,

> Eventually the police asked us to leave the area, but not immediately. We had a good 30–40 minutes just to talk to each other, including with some of the officers. When we left, it was a mix of the police's request as well as our own gratefulness to the NYPD for letting us be there so we left.

The police's willingness to recognize the virtual Raid Pass led to the trainers' ability to take full advantage of it. FireTheGoddess reported that she didn't see any interaction between protestors and trainers, and the YouTube video of the event corroborates this assertion. The marchers had moved on by the start of the EX Raid, but the police barricade continued until later in the day.

Remember, the protesters and the trainers reflected differently structured identities: one collective and anti-government (if not explicitly anti-capitalist), and the other individual and prosumerist. Though The Silph Road is not associated with Niantic, FireTheGoddess' role there was to help facilitate feedback to the game architects and to get information from them when trainers had questions or issues. The two were working together, not for profit, but to share information and feedback. In this sense, the enterprise was highly successful, as Niantic did shift their future EX Raids to retail locations, thus minimizing the possibility of future conflicts like the ones the trainers navigated here.

Material Demands in an Augmented Reality

For a better understanding of how power is deployed through AR games, we must interrogate the very notion of AR. The EX Raid field test at Columbus Circle exemplified the way that capital flows across AR layers to provide and maintain privilege, but the overlay of code onto the built environment is not cleanly distinguished or universally regulated. Liberati (2018) asserted that AR games such as *Pokémon Go* "have objects everywhere, we cannot point a finger to a single place which is 'safe' from their contamination because space of the game is constituted of every spatial position in our paramount reality" (p. 224). In other words, there is no discrete boundary between virtual and material space when playing the game. The Columbus Circle gym is both in and out of the so-called real world, and AR afforded trainers privileges associated with the flows of capital when they were allowed to participate in the EX Raid field test.

A non-binary perspective on AR with no clear distinction between what is and is not the real world illustrates the capital flows that regulated access to the exact same space—in our example the monument at Columbus Circle. Jurgenson (2012) argued against what he termed "digital dualism" (p. 85) which he claimed is the reigning conceptual framework through which people understand material and virtual worlds. The so-called real world and the virtual world are viewed as largely separate, therefore allowing for both virtual utopianists and dystopianists to assert either that technology will lead to social progress or doomsday with equal rigor when their potentials are seen as distinct. AR offers an alternative to these claims only so far as it acknowledges that there is no distinctive power for networked modes of communication since "our augmented reality is one where the politics, structures and inequalities of the physical world are part of the very essence of the digital domain; a domain built by human beings with histories, standpoints, interests, morals and biases" (pp. 85–86). Clearly, the behavior of the police at Columbus Circle supports this claim, but *only* if one understands, as the NYPD officers came to do, that the EX Raid Pass holders are privileged individual and identifiable consumers.

To identify AR as having two layers, one of code and one of the physically built environment, doesn't capture the feel of user experience: "Because we collectively cling to the online/offline binary, the online aspects both of ourselves and our being in the world are consequently diminished and discounted" (Rey & Boesel, 2014, p. 173). But in addition to the lived experience of play, the material circumstances of virtual gaming call into question clear distinctions between virtual and physical space. Citing the logic of private property central to capitalism, game scholars have disputed the clean separation of the physical world and multiplayer online gaming worlds. A classic example relates to massively multiplayer online games such as *World of Warcraft*, where items that exist as code are sold via eBay for exorbitant prices. As Taylor (2009) argued, the selling of these items for "real money" confronts us "with the notion that sometimes our 'virtual' spaces leak over into our 'real' worlds, and the nature of concepts like ownership in shared multiuser space are not a given" (p. 151). Who has the right to things in the world, whether they consist of code or concrete, is determined by capital. Although the trainers may not be able to sell or trade their EX Raid Passes, they certainly own them in the sense that they paid for them.

Poké Stops and gyms are central assets to *Pokémon Go* because they penetrate the virtual layer of the game and take root in the material world. The large quantity of data compiled by users through their *Ingress* portal submission undergirds the Poké Stops and gyms. Niantic faced a threat to their market share when software developer Elyland developed a similar "Go" game called *Draconius Go* in 2017 that shared many similarities with *Pokémon Go*. In *Draconius Go*, players caught cute monsters, leveled up, participated in gym battles, and had incentives to walk around in physical space. Yet the in-game locations had no connection to real-world places unlike the Poké Stops and gyms in *Pokémon Go*. Thus, *Pokémon Go* offers a close connection between known physical sites and vital locations within the virtual game space. Soon after the game debuted, Niantic monetized their Poké Stops by making Starbucks, Boost Mobile, McDonald's (in Japan) and Sprint retail locations into Poké Stops. Capital flows through these monetized sites, and this blurring of virtual and physical space affords an opportunity to complicate a reinscribed utopianism of AR. In these physical sites, accessibility issues are precisely those of the real world, and if gameplay is centered around such sites, they are already exclusionary. Thus, a space like Columbus Circle, as seen above, may be meaningful to a group of protesters because of its proximity to Trump Tower, or because of its monument to Columbus and by extension to the genocide of native peoples. However, those rights to the space were carefully policed, while the EX Raid Pass holders were allowed full access to the site as a space of consumption.

As we have suggested above, the EX Raid Pass itself as a material object was crucial to the success of The Silph Road gaining access to the raid site. We argued that this is because the EX Raid Pass itself functioned as an identity card, proving that the holder was an individual with no interest in harming the interests of capital. The reason for this is because *Pokémon Go*, like other networked online systems, is monetized via the individual consumption of players, who can be traced back to a single identity that itself becomes a commodity, sold as an audience for ad content and so forth. To understand the EX Raid Pass as an identity card and all-access pass in the offline world, therefore, we need to understand how platform capitalism relies on user identity in much the same way the state uses ID cards, passports, and social security numbers as tools of regulation and surveillance.

The term "platform capitalism" refers to the monetization scheme typical of online networked systems (Langley & Leyshon, 2016; Srnicek, 2017). As user-generated data moves across networks and social contexts, it is made legible thanks to big data aggregation tools. This data, however, is only worth something if it can be correlated with a consumer identity. This is what Cho (2018) called "default publicness" (p. 3183)—the design architecture of these platforms privileges a discoverable, singular, stable user identity so as to facilitate the monetization of the platform via ad revenue. In the context of social media (where, as Cho argued, some users, particularly queer youth of color, may have urgent reasons to occupy multiple and mutually exclusive identities) posts and comments may be searchable and visible outside one's network, or may collapse contexts and appear across platforms or networks without the user's knowledge or consent.

In the case of *Pokémon Go*, which does not operate primarily as a social network, default publicness functions as a tether anchoring a user to a consumer identity. This happens either via in-app purchases or via the corporate sponsorship relationships. Thus, while *Pokémon Go* players might not be identifiable in the game interface with their offline identities (i.e., a player's avatar appearance and name may bear no resemblance to their offline self), they are legible to capital as consumers via a linked credit card account and GPS. Thus, even though one's avatar is a virtual invention, the account to which it must be linked is not. The avatars and *Pokémon Go* accounts may be multiple—indeed, many players have multiple accounts and play through multiple avatars. However, each of these accounts is public by default because each one is traceable to the same real-world person who pays the real-world bills. A player may have multiple accounts, but all of them lead to a credit card linked through iTunes or Google or PayPal, which again in turn maps to their email address or Pokémon Trainer Club account.

Trainers produce tremendous amounts of data about their consumer habits and geolocation patterns available for Niantic to package and sell as they see fit. The sponsored Poké Stops are just the tip of the iceberg. Trainers can be tracked at corporate sponsored Poké Stops, but it is equally possible to identify where trainers reside, work, shop, go to school, and more. Niantic, along with the majority of geolocation-based developers, have been cagey about how they use collected data in response to calls for more transparency given the lack of regulatory frameworks for AR games (It's Not a Game, 2016). This refusal of transparency marks the data aggregation as the site of the game's monetization, and thus a sort of "trade secret" Niantic is unwilling to reveal.

As we described above, elite *Pokémon Go* trainers rely on their socioeconomic privilege to attain that level of play. The game is almost totally inaccessible to wheelchair users and Blind and Deaf people; certainly, those disabilities would make elite trainer status all but impossible. Queer, trans, and gender-non-conforming bodies, as well as people of color, experience more difficulty in freely navigating the public spaces where *Pokémon Go* is played. In addition to these structural barriers, elite trainers need access to an enormous investment of capital to get to that level. Although the game is free to play, tools that make leveling up faster and more efficient such as egg incubators, lures, and larger storage boxes for items and Pokémon are all available for sale within the game (as Murnane explores in his essay in this volume). If a trainer doesn't buy these time-saving measures, he or she will need to dedicate enormous amounts of time to playing the game, such that other employment would be untenable. Each purchase is charged to the user's account via the public identity that will, in the end, render even AR multiple accounts vulnerable to data aggregation in the further monetization of the game, which happens through the key overlay of gameplay and offline geographical locations.

Therefore, the assumption built into the game architecture is that a player would have no reason to hide her movements or identity and that there would be no negative consequence for the kind of surveillance implied in this default publicness other than either success in the game or an enhanced consumer experience (via more targeted ads on other online platforms, corporate special offers from Sprint or others, etc.). As the critical scholarship has shown, those for whom this surveillance does have a negative consequence are the most vulnerable to state power and to structural inequality: people of color, queer and transgender people, and the economically disadvantaged (Noble, 2013; Cho, 2017; Nakamura, 2008).

Thus, when FireTheGoddess walked up to the police barricade to ask for access, it was more than just her Silph Road t-shirt and official-looking clipboard that convinced them. She carried herself with the entitlement of her status as a game player who had dedicated time and money to the pursuit. This isn't to say she didn't earn this status, and indeed, she may have done so despite significant challenges. However, we argue that it was this status—and not her friendliness or her "enthusiastic demeanor" so much as the confidence that comes with knowing that one has a *right to occupy a space*. She didn't need to demand this right, and indeed if she had, she might well have been denied. She simply needed to explain it in terms that the officers could understand.

Thus, insofar as the design architecture of the game privileges a default notion of public compatible with late capitalist state identity (Stanfill, 2015), EX Raid Pass holders were able to enter a (temporarily) state-controlled public space essentially by proving that they were privileged consumers. What we need is a finer understanding of how a non-binary perspective on AR doesn't fall prey to a repackaged digital utopianism and instead recognizes how power and privilege shape gameplay. The case study of the EX Raid in Columbus Circle offers a way of understanding how capital flows determine the interaction between material and virtual worlds.

The Columbus Circle EX Raid case study exemplified the way power works to protect spaces and, by extension, uphold privilege for AR. This case study is not unique to *Pokémon Go* and is not even unique within the game itself. Niantic scheduled an EX Raid in October 2017 in a cemetery in Oshawa,

Canada. The local police became aware that the raid was to occur; because five funerals were scheduled for the day of the raid, out of respect for the mourners, the police contacted Niantic asking them to move the event (AtakuHydra, 2017). The company responded by rescinding the Raid Passes and canceling the event altogether. These situations remind us of the need to look more closely at the way power shapes the ability to act and to inhabit particular spaces, whether those spaces exist in physical or augmented reality.

Conclusion

The term "augmented reality" is a bit of a misnomer, covering the dynamics of money and power that link the virtual and physical world. Rather, we see *Pokémon Go* working within what Taylor (2009) termed "nondichotomous models" (p. 153), which reframe gaming worlds outside of the real/virtual binary. But with so-called augmented reality, it's a bit trickier because the mode of interaction differs slightly from clearly virtual or clearly physical games. An AR signals that the game is best understood as a layer of code over the built environment to enhance the game experience while navigating a location. And certainly, the action of trainers in catching, hatching, and raiding depends upon the interplay of complex code and the geography of one's immediate surroundings. However, the case study of the Columbus Circle EX Raid allows us to see more clearly the ways in which game space is determined by the flow of capital. Navigating spaces, and by extension the ability to act in the game, is established by privileges that transcend common categories of virtual or physical worlds. In this case the privilege to access Columbus Circle was given to Raid Pass holders, not to protestors who were fighting for the rights of the undocumented. We can see how power works to identify worthy objectives, grant access to achieve that objective, and make value judgments about what matters in the material circumstances for those bodies living in and around Columbus Circle on that September day. This all goes to show that AR needs historical materialism more than ever.

The EX Raid case thus intervenes between the real world/virtual world binary with the result that these two worlds are linked by a single flow, that of capital. Famously, capital itself breaches the distinction between the real and the material—"all that is solid melts into air" (Marx & Engels, 2013) under a system where value mediates goods, services, and identities. This extraordinary EX Raid illustrates the power of online capital flows. What got the players through the police barricades was neither their real-world status nor their player status, but instead a privileged relationship to capital that only the interaction of real-world and game status could materially demonstrate.

REFERENCES

About the Silph Road (2018). Retrieved from https://www.reddit.com/r/TheSilphRoad/comments/4tll96/welcome_to_the_silph_road_heres_what_you_need_to/.

Akhtar, A. (2016, August 9). Is *Pokémon Go* racist? How the app may be redlining communities of color. *USA Today*. Retrieved from https://www.usatoday.com/story/tech/news/2016/08/09/pokemon-go-racist-app-redlining-communities-color-racist-pokestops-gyms/87732734/.

Asians for Black Lives Matter [Asians4BlkLives]. (2016, July 20). 8 hours down, 2 #PokemonGo lures up! [Tweet]. Retrieved from https://twitter.com/Asians4BlkLives/status/755993517025992704.

AtakuHydra. (2017, September 29). Durham regional police ex-raid response [Reddit post]. Reddit.com. Retrieved from https://www.reddit.com/r/pokemongo/comments/734via/durham_regional_police_exraid_response/.

Cho, A. (2018). Default publicness: Queer youth of color, social media, and being outed by the machine. *New Media & Society, 20*(9), 3183–3200.

Franks, M.A. (2017). The desert of the unreal: Inequality in virtual and augmented reality. *UC Davis Law Review, 51*, 499–538.

Gay, M. (2018, January 12). Christopher Columbus statue will stay in Columbus Circle. *The Wall Street Journal*. Retrieved from https://www.wsj.com/articles/christopher-columbus-statue-will-stay-in-columbus-circle-1515777407.

It's Not a Game. (2016, August 8). *Broadcasting & Cable, 146*(27), 28.

Jourdan, A. [Alan Jourdan]. (2017, September 13). First Mewtwo EX Raid in New York City–What happened (4K) [Video file]. Retrieved from https://www.youtube.com/watch?v=ZXyfyKNZIrU.

Juhász, L., & Hochmair, H.H. (2017). Where to catch 'em all? A geographic analysis of *Pokémon Go* locations. *Geo-Spatial Information Science, 20*(3), 241–251.

Jurgenson, N. (2012). When atoms meet bits: Social media, the mobile web and augmented revolution. *Future Internet, 4*, 83–91.

Kelly, G. (2016, July 20). Protestors chained to Oakland Police Officers Association's office. *East Bay Times*. Retrieved from https://www.eastbaytimes.com/2016/07/20/protesters-chained-to-oakland-police-officers-associations-office/.

Kooragayala, S., & Srini, T. (2016, August 5). *Pokémon GO* is changing how cities use public space, but could it be more inclusive? *Urban Institute*. Retrieved from https://www.urban.org/urban-wire/pokemon-go-changing-how-cities-use-public-space-could-it-be-more-inclusive.

Langley, P., & Leyshon, A. (2016). Platform capitalism: The intermediation and capitalisation of digital economic circulation. *Finance and Society, 3*(1), 11–31.

Liberati, N. (2018). Phenomenology, *Pokémon Go*, and other augmented reality games: A study of a life among digital objects. *Human Studies: A Journal for Philosophy and the Social Sciences, 41*(2), 211–232.

Lynch, S. (2017, September 10). Crowds protest in Central Park against Trump's DACA repeal [Photos]. *Gothamist*. Retrieved from http://gothamist.com/2017/09/10/photos_hundreds_protest_in_central.php.

Marx, K., & Engels, F. (2013). *The communist manifesto* (2nd ed.). (F.L. Bender, Ed.). New York, NY: W.W. Norton.

Nakamura, L. (2008). *Digitizing race: Visual cultures of the Internet*. Minneapolis: University of Minnesota Press.

Narizhnaya, K. (2017, September 9). Thousands gather in Midtown to protest Trump's DACA decision. *New York Post*. Retrieved from https://nypost.com/2017/09/09/thousands-gather-in-midtown-to-protest-trumps-daca-decision/.

Noble, S.U. (2013, October 29). Google search: Hyper-visibility as a means of rendering black women and girls invisible. *InVisible Culture: An Electronic Journal for Visual Culture, 19*. Retrieved from https://ivc.lib.rochester.edu/google-search-hyper-visibility-as-a-means-of-rendering-black-women-and-girls-invisible/.

Rey, P.J., & Boesel, W.E. (2014). The web, digital prostheses, and augmented subjectivity. In

D.L. Kleinman & K. Moore (Eds.), *Routledge handbook of science, technology, and society* (pp. 173–188). London, England: Routledge.

Ritzer, G., & Jurgenson, N. (2010). Production, consumption, prosumption: The nature of capitalism in the age of the digital "prosumer." *Journal of Consumer Culture, 10*(1), 13–36.

Shum, A., & Tranter, K. (2017). Seeing, moving, catching, accumulating: *Pokémon GO*, and the legal subject. *International Journal for the Semiotics of Law, 30*(3), 477–493.

Slattery, D. (2017, September 9). New Yorkers protest "sociopath" Trump's move to end DACA and deport young immigrants. *New York Daily News*. Retrieved from http://www.nydailynews.com/new-york/new-yorkers-protest-sociopath-trump-move-daca-article-1.3483466.

Srnicek, N. (2017). *Platform capitalism*. Malden, MA: Polity Press.

Stanfill, M. (2015). The interface as discourse: The production of norms through web design. *New Media & Society, 17*(7), 1059–1074.

Tassi, P. (2017, January 22). "*Pokémon GO*" has had the same problem for six months: No endgame. *Forbes*. Retrieved from https://www.forbes.com/sites/insertcoin/2017/01/22/pokemon-go-has-had-the-same-problem-for-six-months-no-endgame/.

Taylor, T.L. (2009). *Play between worlds: Exploring online game culture*. Cambridge, MA: MIT Press.

Whitford, E. (2017, September 5). [UPDATES] Arrests outside Trump Tower as protestors rally to defend DACA [Photos]. *Gothamist*. Retrieved from http://gothamist.com/2017/09/05/daca_protest_trump_tower.php#photo-1.

For Anatopistic Places

Pokémon Go *vs. Milwaukee County*

KRISTOPHER PURZYCKI

The first weeks of July 2016 had been harsh to Milwaukee, Wisconsin. Negative attention toward the unrest that had erupted in the city's inner core following the death of Sylville Smith was beginning to subside and people were beginning to venture forth from their dwellings. One of several major green spaces in the city, Milwaukee's Lake Park is an especially popular destination to take in the fleeting summer days. Instead of the typical spattering of strollers, cyclists, and joggers, however, the park was engorged by visitors. Spurred by the release of *Pokémon Go,* a mass of people had taken to the length of parkway in search of digital creatures. What made this particular park so attractive to would-be Pokémon trainers was the volume of Poké Stops couched along one section of the trail that snakes along the park. Seemingly overnight, the normally docile area was transformed into a burgeoning green space teeming with activity, its ravines and hollows blanketed in players seeking out Pidgeys, Charmanders, and other charming creatures associated with the popular Pokémon franchise.

As was the case with many cities impacted by the release of *Pokémon Go*, the sudden explosion of activity was met with a mix of curiosity and consternation by residents. Neighbors to Lake Park seemed to display a mostly positive response, with some even joining the bustle of players. Barkers peddled wares and quartets practicing their concertos set up for a distracted but appreciative audience. Others set up chairs and picnicked among the crowd, eager to participate in the cajoling of several hundred strangers chasing after Pokémon. Other area residents, however, were not so welcoming and complained to local legislators about the public disruption as well as the destruction to the park area. The Lake Park Friends, a civic volunteer group dedicated to the park's maintenance and development, were among the most vocal. This group soon enlisted a local legislator to spearhead a campaign to curb activity within Lake Park that would culminate in a litigious debate over regulation of augmented reality (AR) game developers and licensing fees to use public space as virtual arenas for play.

Using the above scenario as a backdrop, this essay touches upon the impact of *Pokémon Go* on public space to reflect on the player as she is embodied within remediated, virtually augmented space. First, I examine the conflict that ensued between the communities that convened in an already politicized public space. More specifically, I first describe in greater detail the friction between Niantic, Inc., and Milwaukee County. Although this burdens the essay somewhat with stodgy bureaucracy, the portrait provided illustrates several issues at stake for the parties involved. Turning my attention to the group of players that coalesced that summer and continue to play the game, I focus on the *Pokémon Go* player's sense of place. Unlike the vast majority of game studies which focus on spatial theory, I argue that place is a concept crucial to recognizing the phenomenon of play. Rather than describing the conflict between *Pokémon Go* and Lake Park as overlapping space, I argue that considering this debate in terms of overlapping *senses of place* articulates the phenomenon of the anatopistic place, or place-out-of-place.

Reviewing the discourse in this way hints at why so many players came to play *Pokémon Go* at Lake Park despite there being other areas to play in Milwaukee. More importantly to this essay, looking at this case in terms of place and the *genius loci* of the park provides games scholars with a player model that originates from outside the spatially oriented discipline. Because a thorough survey of space and place is well beyond the scope of this essay, in it I primarily dwell on those aspects that contribute to the more critical consideration of the player as one who is self-emplaced within places that are resistant to occupation. This theory, which positions the player as a self-emplacing figure, opens up new perspectives about games and anticipates how AR games might potentially work to intervene in prevailing powers as embodied in designed spaces.

Places of Play: Milwaukee County versus Niantic, Inc.

During summer 2016, the release of Niantic's AR juggernaut *Pokémon Go* enabled fans of the pop-culture phenomenon to visualize their favorite Pokémon in the off-screen world. Using their mobile devices, players located various real-world landmarks that had been transformed through the game's interface into Pokémon-attracting Poké Stops. (For the sake of this essay, I am precariously using the term "real" to indicate the physical world that exists with or without the aid of virtual augmentation.) Social media and other communications networks enabled players to convene in groups and take on more challenging battles at *Pokémon Go* gyms. More savvy players utilized browser-based applications to locate additional, perhaps more unfamiliar areas where sought-after Pokémon could be found. One of the more popular of these applications is the "Pokémon Go Map," a project unaffiliated with Niantic (PokemonGoMap.info, 2018). Built on OpenStreetMap, an open-source set of global mapping data, this overlays a map of the selected area with icons designating Poké Stops and gyms in real time.

Lake Park

In Milwaukee, Wisconsin, a mid-size city located on the western shore of Lake Michigan, one of the more popular areas to play *Pokémon Go* during that summer was Lake Park, a mile-and-a-half long parcel of public space. Covering over 138 square acres of land, Lake Park is revered by Milwaukee residents as a place to escape the city. On the northern end, the park is capped by the intersection of Lake Drive and Kenwood Boulevard which continues west before arcing south along Lake Michigan as Lincoln Memorial Drive. This eastern border continues below a steep bluff until reaching St. Mary's Hill, a popular sledding spot that is traced by the winding Water Tower Road that serves as the foot of Lake Park. Just north of the point where this road breaches the hill is the beginning of Wahl Avenue where some of the more valuable real estate marks the western border of the park. Bartolotta's Lake Park Bistro, a fine dining restaurant that occupies what once was a fieldhouse, sits securely in the middle of the park, which is accessed by Lake Park's main entrance located on the prestigious Newberry Boulevard.

Nestled between two of the more affluent neighborhoods in Milwaukee, Lake Park is regarded as the flagship of the city's renowned fleet of green spaces. Its aesthetics, which suggest that the carefully crafted space had been carved from the pristine, virgin wilderness of a bygone era, actually consist of a carefully engineered chain of parcels. Several landmarks—including a Native American burial mound and commemorative Civil War statuary—punctuate the park along the Oak Leaf Trail, an accessible, paved path that winds through the length of the park. Despite containing a large playground, courts for tennis and lawn bowling, a small stage, and a small par-three golf course, there is still plenty of space for more open activities throughout. Overseen by revered landscape artist Frederick Law Olmsted, Lake Park is remarkable for its capacity to emplace visitors in an environment seemingly removed from the city. Manufactured waterfalls and winding ravine paths, signatures of Olmstead's designs, simulate the natural world. Large swaths of open grassland, circumvented by groves of towering oak, displace the city lurking the next block over. Other spaces, such as a playground and tennis court, are more explicitly designated for structured activity. Creeks and paths that lead down to the road below course through more densely wooded areas to mimic nature's meander.

The Release of *Pokémon Go*

This amount of open space, combined with the number of landmarks that had been transformed into Poké Stops, contributed in no small measure to the popularity of Lake Park with the release of *Pokémon Go* on July 6, 2016. Although the release of the game was highly anticipated by fans, its enormous popularity was evidenced to others by the crowds that immediately descended upon public spaces across the city. Few places were more popular with Milwaukee players than Lake Park. Just south of the Bartolotta's parking lot, a once-cloistered ravine suddenly became host to a crowd of idling players; its stone cut steps were quickly lined with an overflow of foot traffic from the path above. The usually serene Oak Leaf Trail itself was swiftly overwhelmed with the highest concentration of mobile players, most of whom stood staring intently at their phones (see Eanes and van den Broek's essay in this collection for further discussion of the zombie-like stance many players took during this time period). For hours, the river of players roiled back and forth along a Pokémon-packed half-mile stretch that runs between a parking lot located at the end of Newberry Boulevard and the intersection of Belleview Place and Wahl Avenue. Skateboards, bicycles, and rollerblades were deployed by those hoping to migrate between Poké Stops with greater expediency. Occasionally, someone would cry out "*CHARIZARD!*" or similar, instigating a sprinting exodus towards a spot where a rare Pokémon had been spotted.

This frenzy of activity would frequently spill out into an open grassy area that exposes a large stretch of the path's southern end to the residents that live along Wahl Avenue, a two-lane street that borders the western edge of this stretch of Lake Park. From the vantage point of those living across the street from the park, the scene must have seemed extraordinary, if not disconcerting. Neighbors and residents of the area were quick to point out the impacts. Within days, steps were taken to reduce the perceived chaos and deter after-hours visitors. Subtle measures were taken and makeshift ashtrays were placed near Poké Stops as well as signs asking players to kindly watch out for the wildflowers.

Despite these gestures, the city of Milwaukee was urged to respond. In addition to the increase in foot and vehicular traffic, complaints about litter and the seemingly wanton destruction to the foliage began trickling into the offices of local legislators. Minimum- and medium-security prisoners were brought in to help clean up, exacerbating concerns by neighbors (Henry, 2016). Meanwhile, police on horseback lorded over the crowd as chaperones, surveilling the crowd from within. Lights along the path remained off long after dusk in an attempt to make it difficult for those that would have remained into the night to play to do so. All of this did little to dissuade occupancy during the evening hours when the park is closed to the public and several hundred players who had made the mistake of lingering received citations (Behm, 2016). This confusing situation within the park was echoed by proceedings in the legislature.

On August 16th, John Dargle, Jr., Milwaukee's Director of Parks, Recreation and Culture, sent a letter to John V. Hanke, CEO of Niantic, requesting restitution for the costs incurred by accommodating *Pokémon Go* players (Dargle & Foley, 2016; Wild, 2016). Although admitting that the AR game promoted "many new positive recreation experiences," Dargle pointed out that impacts on Lake Park had been severe (Wild, 2016, para. 4). More to the point, Dargle demanded that Niantic disable all *Pokémon Go* sites in Milwaukee County parks until they complied with the geocaching guidelines established by the county. These reportedly included regular monitoring and maintenance of the physical grounds on which those sites were located. Although there is a link to a page on Milwaukee County's website that once detailed the permit process, at the time of this writing this link is inactive. Many misinterpreted Dargle, believing that these new regulations required players to purchase a permit to play *Pokémon Go.* Attempting to clarify the confusion, an announcement entitled "We WANT You to Pika-choose Milwaukee County Parks" was released on behalf of County Executive Chris Abele on August 25, 2016, but this only complicated matters: In this statement, "Exeggutor" Abele declared (awkwardly deploying the parlance of the game) that the county was thrilled about the increase in park activity (such as having a "Poke-nic") and that it would be "Tentacruel" to require permits of players (Abele, 2016).

This affable (yet cringeworthy) response contrasted sharply with that of County Supervisor Dr. Sheldon Wasserman, who spoke on behalf of Lake Park and its neighbors. During a phone conversation with me in July 2017, Wasserman's exasperation was evident in his description of how the game had "changed the neighborhood overnight" (S. Wasserman, personal communication, July 2017). One source of this frustration, he told me, was how the media had painted the permit as a form of "class warfare" pitting the affluent residents of Milwaukee's Lake Park neighborhood against those from the inner core of the city. Offering an alternative culprit, Wasserman described Niantic as "taking advantage" of both the public park system and the players themselves, using the "atmosphere of wealthy versus poor" described by the media to turn a profit (S. Wasserman, personal communication, July 2017). Although not discussed in our conversation, another source of concern must surely have been the lawsuit initiated by another AR game developer, Candy Lab, over the permit requirement. In a lawsuit filed that same month (*Candy Lab v. Milwaukee County, Milwaukee County Board of Supervisors, and Milwaukee County Department of Parks, Recreation, and Culture*), the developer sued the county and the departments involved in the implementation of the permit and the restrictions imposed on their game *Texas Rope 'Em* (Candy Lab Inc. v. Milwaukee County, 2017). The case was settled later in 2017 with the county, who had since removed the permits; the county ended up covering Candy Lab's legal fees in the amount of $83,000 (Moreno, 2017, para. 2).

Aftermath

Since that time, the player base of *Pokémon Go* has subsided. Crowds the size of those seen during the game's initial release are today relegated to highly controlled events such as *"Pokémon Go* Day" which was held in Chicago over two days in July 2018. During the time since releasing the game, Niantic has quietly removed many Poké Stops. In Lake Park, the small cluster of stops most visible to residents along Wahl Avenue have been removed. Not so coincidentally, they have been replaced by a formation of saplings that were planted in fall 2016. However, if they were planted to obscure neighbors' views of players, there are no longer any crowds to obscure. Although the game no longer compels the majority of players to convene en masse on Pokémon-rich public places, a strong player base was still established. In a 2018 survey I conducted of one hundred active players, over 60 percent claimed to play several times a day. The vast majority of these respondents have been playing since release (Purzycki, 2018). The other significant change shared by respondents is that gameplay occurs during everyday moments as a way to fill idle time.

Wasserman's frustration with the accusation of a class war underscores the concerns that city residents have had about issues of space and boundary. Milwaukee's long and tortured history of racial injustice is retold in the streets of the city. As seen in a map of Milwaukee drafted in 1939 by the Home Owners Loan Corporation (HOLC), the "redlining" of Milwaukee has had a disastrous effect on the city (University of Virginia Digital Scholarship Lab, n.d., n.p.). The map recalled many of the common attitudes expressed nearly one hundred years later: neighborhoods along the northern shore are celebrated as "best" while those within the city's core are deemed to be "definitely declining" or even "hazardous" (n.p.). Although the red lines that once striated the city map may have shifted over time, they still impose the same prejudices in the way Milwaukee's citizens regard certain streets as borders designating neighborhood quality. Viewing the city on "The Racial Dot Map" (Cable, 2013, n.p.), a color-coded presentation of 2010 Census data, clearly illustrates the demarcation between communities that are drawn. In a city such as Milwaukee, where racial and class biases were instituted by early architects and urban planners, public places become smoldering fault lines between the privileged and discarded citizenries.

Despite the intentions of Olmstead (who as a journalist railed against slavery and racial injustice), Lake Park embodies Milwaukee's legacy and the means by which the city privileges the wealthy. The forms of leisure that are warranted in Lake Park, in other words, are not those typically enjoyed by those of little means. This bias is mirrored in *Pokémon Go* but is embodied in the disparity in distribution of Poké Stops and gyms throughout the city. *Pokémon Go*'s crowdsourced predecessor *Ingress* (also produced by Niantic, Inc.), which was built from player-contributed data, reflects the technocratic essence of its player base. In the transfer of geolocational data from the niche *Ingress* to its vastly more popular spawn, *Pokémon Go*, the resulting map of Poké Stops in Milwaukee is almost identical to the Redline map.

Comparing Lake Park to Olmstead's other projects, Washington Park and Riverside Park, illustrates this reality. In Lake Park, there are currently twenty-three Poké Stops and five gyms (not including the two that were removed) within its 138 acres. Riverside Park, a small 15-acre parcel nestled between Riverside High School and the Milwaukee River, is a small wilderness area containing nine Poké Stops and three gyms. Washington Park, which is most comparable to Lake Park in size at 128 acres, has four Poké Stops and two gyms within its borders. Reasons for this include a comparable lack of landmarks and thresholds approved by Niantic. Riverside Park, which has seen improvements and increased use after adoption by local non-profits, houses statuary, bridges, and structures that have been incorporated into *Pokémon Go*. Displaying a dearth of in-game representation, Lake Park's inner-city sister Washington Park is located in an area with one of the highest crime rates in Milwaukee. The scarcity of Poké Stops and gyms in this space, which are limited to a few major built structures, a small plaque, and the sign at the park's entrance, presents in stark contrast to the number found in Lake Park.

This resplendent entrance and well-maintained landscaping makes for an inviting space that certainly contributed to the crowd of players that beset Lake Park in summer 2016. Despite a lack of convenient parking and nearby public transit, people travelled to this space specifically to play *Pokémon Go*—not to refine their golf game or admire the landscaping. This disparity of intentions is an undercurrent of the arguments attempting to justify actions taken by the city to curtail playing the game. Some have maintained the position that Lake Park simply isn't designed to handle such enormous amounts of activity concentrated in a single area. While I don't disagree with this position, it raises the following question: What activity is the park then designed for? It is clear the park privileges those activities that aren't likely to draw crowds. More critical to this essay, how did *Pokémon Go* overcome the rhetorics embedded within this space to attract players in such large numbers? In other words, how did this simple, buggy, and somewhat crude game displace the sociocultural expectation of this venerable park, disrupting the conventions of such a thoroughly engineered space? To answer this, I suggest that we must prioritize the player's sense of place and consider how this can subvert even the most stalwart of spaces.

Given that there are so few opportunities to play *Pokémon Go* in Milwaukee's inner city, it's unsurprising that people from those regions with a dearth of in-game representation would travel to those areas that had far more opportunities to join the world in an event so extraordinarily significant within pop culture. Niantic was not only successful in tapping into the collective nostalgia and appeal of the Pokémon franchise, they did so in such a way that those who had been historically disenfranchised by public spaces were compelled to subvert the structures that had inhibited occupation. All this to play a simple game?

Players and the Place-Out-of-Place

Games and play enable us to escape the everyday but we typically do so in spaces that are approved for these activities: playgrounds, arenas, massively multiplayer online role-playing games, etc. In the case of *Pokémon Go* and AR games, the space of the game usurps that of the world of flesh and blood. Phenomenologically speaking, players and player groups create places that are anatopistic, or out of place. These anatopistic places of play are disruptive to space and the activities and behaviors that are allowed within them. This has historically been the case. When play is motivated by a subjective or intersubjective sense of place, it generates a meaningful place that can threaten, intervene with, and even overturn dominant senses of place. As seen in the playing of *Pokémon Go* within Lake Park, power reclaims place through the manipulation of the space in contention.

Geek subcultures have been particularly keen at subverting place. Pop-culture conventions have not only thrived but have been vital components to the experience of communities interested in gaming, science fiction, and other "geek" activities. Contemporary anthropological and sociological research has increasingly considered journeys to non-religious destinations as conveying a sense of meaning similar to that bestowed by their more traditional kin. Badone (2004), for example, focused on *Star Trek* convention attendees when considering how pop-culture destinations offer the same significant meaning for pilgrims (p. 161). Elvis Presley's estate Graceland is likewise considered a mecca for fans whose faith and devotion is displayed through ritualistic visitation to the musician's grave (King, 1993, p. 101). For game enthusiasts, gaming conventions have become annual events for devoted players as well as a lucrative business model.

For table-top game players, there are numerous gatherings dedicated to those interested in finding new titles as well as the chance to play industry stalwarts like *Dungeons & Dragons* with others. Since its inception over fifty years ago, Gen Con has become the culminating event of the year for players of board and pencil-and-paper role-playing games, drawing crowds to Indianapolis, Indiana, for the four-day event. Drawing from this rich history, computer games are also inherently social places. Converging with a well-tracked tradition of wargames and table-top role-playing games, these works channeled the imaginations of early hackers. In the tradition of playful intervention, the earliest computer game designers disregarded the austere purposes of early mainframe computers. With limited access and shared resources, the designer-player community that developed around games did so imbued with the sense of place that comes from a community in the throes of nurturing an emergent culture.

In other words, play and place are closely related, folding over one another constantly as the player—particularly one beholden to a strong imagination—constantly tears down and rebuilds the place in which she plays. For the purposes of this essay, I focus on those that are significant to the players and the relationship they have to the places they create, as well as the effect this has upon the space that anatopistic places subvert. Discovery through exploration and experimentation is fundamental to not only many games but particularly to the development of three-dimensional digital spaces. Focusing on the perspective of the player rather than the game or the space in which it's played provides the luxury of sidestepping the distinctions between the virtual and the real. From the vantage point of the player, claimed Malaby (2007), meaningful experiences procured from both of these spaces are equally viable (p. 97). This is especially true for places of play and for players who seek meaningful, even transcendent, experiences from play.

Places of Play

A proper discussion of spatial theory is beyond the scope of this essay (see Andrade's contribution to this collection for a respectable treatment) but an overview of spatial theory as it pertains to play is crucial. Play historian Chudacoff (2008) described how the setting and the site of play is one of the "most basic factors in children's abilities to assert their own culture" (p. 4). This assertion of place became more pronounced as the places in which children play began to disintegrate while the population densities of urban areas exploded. Beginning in the 19th century, the playground replaced the open field to become the designated zone for play. "A playground is a pure play context," described Sicart (2014), "a separated space devoid of any other functionality than being a context for playing" (p. 7). For children who were running out of places to play, this entailed the invention of new places.

If one's sense of place emanates from a feeling of engagement with a location and the community therein, this took the form of emergent play in locations around the city. Green (2013) ascribed this to the child's sense of place arising out of a sense of stewardship to places (p. 9). Alleyways, streets, and sidewalks were canvases upon which a dizzying array of games were invented, many of which survive to this day. The struggle to maintain colonization of these parcels of asphalt became increasingly dangerous, however, as the world drew closer to war on a global scale and anxious parents corralled their children indoors or into yards and other sanctioned play spaces. While Green noted that these "over structured environments … may interfere with children developing their own initiative and relationship with place" (p. 27), we must also trust play to act as an agent of intervention with any given order. Just as the play of children often imitates the activity of the adults in their lives, so too would their struggle for a sense of place echo the emergence of the postmodern in Western society.

Playground alternatives that foster these impulses are everywhere in the city. Further expanding on the works of Huizinga and other early thinkers about play, Sicart (2014) reflected on a fresh attention to the spaces in which play takes place, and described how play is not limited to the intentions of toys and playgrounds: "Play is creative when it is taking over, or occupying, a context" (p. 71). "Appropriation leads to a carnivalesque creativity," he continued, "which might lead to a critical approach of the context … or the activity that is being playfully occupied" (p. 72). Even without AR games (to which we will return briefly), the concrete jungle teemed with opportunities to play with the diversity and density that defines the urban condition. As play became more of an indoor activity, toys and literature became increasingly popular. As a point of convergence between the two, the board game—a commercialized form of war games that had been popular for centuries—became a family activity.

Born out of living rooms and garages of the mid–20th century, the computer game was the progeny of this tradition of interior play and the reclamation of place. As many histories of computer games account for, the first games *Tennis for Two* (1958) and *Spacewar!* (1962) were simulations of physical space. Crowther's *Colossal Cave Adventure* (1976), however, took a narrative path to creating space. The version of Kentucky's Mammoth Cave that Crowther created, however, was born out of a place of affinity for spelunking as well as wanting to be closer to his daughters. A few years later, Garriott released the first title in his *Ultima* (1980) series. Throughout these games, Garriott recreated the places he had experienced in playing *Dungeons & Dragons* and live-action role-playing with the Society for Creative Anachronism. The inspiration drawn from Garriott's passion for creating a place within the computers is demonstrated in the legacy of open-world games that have followed. What hasn't been preserved throughout this lineage is the privileging of place and the player's relationship to those places that produce digital space.

Game studies as a field has thus far not focused much on place and its phenomenological primacy. Theorizing computer games as primarily a spatialized medium, much of game studies canon has extended the rhetoric of the engineering and computer science departments. Aarseth (1997) evoked the labyrinth of Crowther's *Adventure* in *Cybertext*, Wolf (2001) discussed diegetic and non-diegetic spaces in computer games, and Murray (1998) deployed theatrical metaphors in *Hamlet on the Holodeck*; since then, the academic discourse surrounding computer games has been spatially oriented. Wolf's comparison to cinematic spaces would be later echoed by Manovich (2001) who, in *The Language of New Media,* focused mainly on the player orientation in "navigable space" (p. 213), reifying space's stubborn hold on game studies. As the discipline continues to mature, however, it is worth investigating the subjective and intersubjective potentials of the player's *sense of place* within these digital worlds. The importance of place has not been lost to games scholarship and has emerged as an undercurrent of study.

Nitsche's (2008) thorough and explicitly spatial focus on computer games also traipsed along theories of place. In his book *Video Game Spaces*, in which a solitary chapter is devoted to discussion of place, the author relied upon an architectural examination of space as an influence on behavior. While Nitsche's work is important for any discussion of space and place in digital media, it suffers from an exaggerated focus on the individual in pursuit of discrete goals. Nitsche's three criteria for place-making within space, for example, are "identity, self-motivated and self-organized action, and traces of memory" (p. 191). Nitsche's argument is one of the more succinct yet robust approaches to place seen in game studies thus far. The missing component of this discussion, however, is that of the social and the intersubjective quality vital to place and our own sense of place.

Nitsche is not the only theorist to tease out place within computer games. In *Designing Virtual Worlds*, Bartle (2004) extolled on the placemaking capacity of games and their significance as meaning-making machines. Using his vantage point from behind the developer's curtain as the co-creator of the first multi-user game space, *MUD1* (1978), reflected upon the history of game development and how shifts in self-branding between "simulation" and "service" diminished the importance of games (p. 473). It was the creation of virtual worlds, Bartle argued, that helped audiences and developers alike recognize that digital spaces were more than electronic architecture and algorithms. "Virtual worlds are places," he declared. "They may simulate abstractions of reality; they may be operated as a service; creating them may be an art; people may visit them to play games. Ultimately, though, they're just a set of locations. Places" (p. 475). Bartles' impassioned advocacy for virtual worlds' importance fell short in distinguishing place from space and maintained the Cartesian formulae commonplace to game studies.

To better understand place and how a sense of place works within computer games, we must look outside of game studies. While many approaches consider place as derivative of space, geographer Tuan (1977) reversed this, arguing instead that space is constituted from networks and layers of places. For Tuan, place is the home, the community, and a sense of security around which the walls and borders are constructed. The Tuanian view is that one's sense of place comes from a state of being attentive to the everyday. Phenomenologically speaking, this state is comparable to Heidegger's (1962) notion of *Being-in-the-world* (p. 82) from which a sense of place is derived. Focusing on place as the phenomenon of "throwntogetherness," Massey (2005) argued for place as multifaceted with layers of overlapping significance (p. 130). Agency was a much more prominent component of Massey's formulation of experience, however; she noted that, because places are so dynamic, the act of place-making demands one be "open to the challenge of negotiating a here-and-now" (p. 140). This mindful, conscious openness to place has a hard time taking root in the simulations of digital space, however.

In the case of *Pokémon Go* and Lake Park, this is complicated by the overlapping of mediated spaces and the places from which they have sprung. With respect to Lake Park, the space that we see today is the product of over a century's worth of landscaping and design which, in turn, was developed to approximate the woodland bluffs that had existed prior to being destroyed by the area's settlers. Unlike these previous states, the current iteration has one distinction: it was created with intent. For anthropologist Augé (1995), the "non-place" is embodied through those spaces that are constructed in anticipation of a certain end state (p. 76). Lake Park, for example, was created specifically to sequester visitors from the rest of the city and the concerns therein. But the non-place also includes the relationships that occupants have with these spaces. For Augé, these relationships are mediated through the representations of spaces which fuel our imagination. For those who seek to preserve Lake Park, these representations include the park's status as the crown jewel of Milwaukee's park system and the park's connections to the celebrity of Olmstead and New York City's cosmopolitanism that his legacy provides. Visitors to Lake Park are there to reap the affordances of leisure as well but in a space that is ostensibly distinct from those of the city. But the park also conjures up the wilderness that it simulates. Although the gulley looks as though it had carved its way through the rock over eons, it has actually been hardly a century since human hands steered water along its current course. A single burial mound of an ancient indigenous people is a solitary testimonial to the innumerable mounds that were decimated over time. Atop these myriad interfaces with non-place, we add yet another.

In light of all the strata of significance found in Lake Park, *Pokémon Go*'s handheld window into yet another place seems inconsequential. AR, much like cyberspace itself, also constitutes a non-place. As I've discussed, players of *Pokémon Go* were initially compelled to travel to Lake Park due to a lack of places to play in areas that, while being more proximate, harbored few places to play the game. As a primary form of entertainment, games are one of our first methods for escaping the everyday. When the spaces of a game so closely reflect those of the everyday, a game is stripped of its capacity to transport players in a satisfactory way. "It is not a place of escape from contemporary society, or indeed from the physical world," argued Bolter and Grusin (1999) in describing cybernetic non-places (p. 179). This window into a world occupied by digital creatures does not also serve as a portal where we can hide from our responsibilities. Especially for those who received tickets for playing after dark, the world has a way of catching up.

But for fans of the franchise (such as my children) as well as newcomers (such as myself), *Pokémon Go* invokes nostalgia, community, and a playful form of labor. In a survey of players I conducted in August 2018, the majority of the nearly one hundred respondents attributed a myriad of reasons for playing (Purzycki, 2018). Many cited the collection of Pokémon and the competition that occurs at gyms. The vast majority of them cited socialization, either with family members or with a larger community of those familiar and strange, as the primary reason for playing. These are all qualities that have been incorporated into the franchise since its inception, and might be considered the tradition of Pokémon. Anti-structures such as pilgrimage are traditions that can enable participants to emplace themselves, renegotiating the demands of time and space—at least temporarily (Turner, 1969). As distinct from the everyday, these forms of tradition have the potential to emplace the practitioner beyond those spaces designated by those in power.

In the case of the playing of *Pokémon Go* within Lake Park, the game supplants existing, traditional uses of Lake Park with those ascribed by Niantic and acted upon by players. To use the park, tradition states, one should be participating in those activities for which the space has been designed. These designations are reinforced by the spatial configurations of open areas, buildings, paths, and landmarks as well as the practices of those that, over generations, have accommodated those designs through activities deemed appropriate. *Pokémon Go* players discarded these traditions by accepting the new meanings and intentions of these structures. The statue of Brigadier General Erastus B. Wolcott, erected in 1920, no longer commemorated his service during the Civil War. New battles between *Pokémon Go* teams were being lived out at the gym erected at his feet. Ritualized dog-walking had become impossible due to the sheer volume of pedestrians wandering the pathway ignoring public decorum while in pursuit of Pokémon. New traditions threatened to uproot the old.

Conclusion: New Traditions of Play

Local and national media had barely removed their cameras from Milwaukee's Sherman Park area when *Pokémon Go* was released. Although the racial borders, cemented in the streets of Milwaukee, had once again seen to everyone's "proper place," this new phenomenon was unscathed by neither histories nor geographies of prejudice. It wasn't that a class war had been instigated by *Pokémon Go*, but that the game had revealed a class war that had existed for almost as long as the city itself. The structures and means by which power is enacted through space, in other words, were simply being exhumed through foreign means. In the case of Milwaukee, these powers are very much about class and even more so about race. Even though Olmstead and his collaborators may not have designed Lake Park to inhibit use by those who are not white and middle class, the park has nonetheless been shaped over time to reflect the demands of those most interested in seeing it thrive. The activities that are privileged by the space of Lake Park, and those who are implicitly permitted to *make place* within it through their leisurely participation in these activities, were and continue to be of white, middle-class backgrounds.

In their introduction to *Sacred Sites, Sacred Places,* Carmichael, Hubert, and Reeves (1994) described the sacred site as a location that is designed to orchestrate behavior. These places often present a representational claim to the metaphysical plane that lies beyond the humdrum of the everyday (p. 3). Neighbors to Lake Park, a simulation of nature designed to provide escape from the grit of city life, are likely to view the park as sacred. When contested by outsiders, these "owners" of the Park not only see it as an infringement but as a "spiritual deprivation" of their sacred place (p. 5). But *Pokémon Go* players are acting through their own sense of place, one that is significant in that it is neither familiar nor strange but a liminal, place-out-of-place. Looking at *Pokémon Go* from this perspective, the player resembles a pilgrim engaged in pursuit—not of digital creatures—but of a sense of place.

Like most games, *Pokémon Go* isn't significant because of any ground-breaking mechanical or aesthetic quality. Even the game's nostalgic appeal, along with the game's overall popularity, has diminished since July 2016. So, it's not that residents near Lake Park were in danger of losing their place— let alone a class war. Even more resonant is the recognition of other antopistic places that are equally vibrant and powerful. The real threat of *Pokémon Go*, however, comes from the way it illuminates the fragility of space and our sense of place. We may dismiss a children's game, but as a socio-cultural phenomenon, AR has demonstrated a capacity for mobilization. If places can be inspired by a children's game, we have to wonder what other movements could be inspired by such things.

Just who *is* out of place?

References

Aarseth, E.J. (1997). *Cybertext: Perspectives on ergodic literature.* Baltimore: Johns Hopkins University Press.

Abele, C. (2016, August 25). We WANT you to Pika-choose Milwaukee County Parks [Press release]. Milwaukee County Executive. Retrieved from https://county.milwaukee.gov/EN/County-Executive/News/Press-Releases/We-WANT-You-to-Pika-choose-Milwaukee-County-Parks.

Augé, M. (1995). *Non-places: An introduction to supermodernity* (J. Howe, Trans.). New York, NY: Verso.

Badone, E. (2004). Pilgrimage and the IDIC ethic: Exploring Star Trek convention attendance as pilgrimage. In E. Badone & S.R. Roseman (Eds.), *Intersecting journeys: The anthropology of pilgrimage and tourism* (pp. 160–179). Champaign: University of Illinois Press.

Bartle, R.A. (2004). *Designing virtual worlds.* Indianapolis: New Riders Publishing.

Behm, D. (2016, September 13). No common ground on *Pokémon Go. Milwaukee Journal Sentinel.* Retrieved from https://www.jsonline.com/story/news/local/milwaukee/2016/09/13/no-common-ground-pokemon-go/90322362/.

Bolter, J.D., & Grusin, R. (1999). *Remediation: Understanding new media.* Cambridge, MA: MIT Press.

Cable, D. (2013). *Racial dot map* [Image]. Weldon Cooper Center for Public Service, Rector and Visitors of the University of Virginia (Dustin A. Cable, creator). Retrieved from https://demographics.coopercenter.org/racial-dot-map.

Candy Lab Inc. v. Milwaukee County, Milwaukee County Board of Supervisors, and Milwaukee County Department of Parks, Recreation, and Culture (2017). Case no. 17-CV-569-JPS. Retrieved from https://cdn.arstechnica.net/wpcontent/uploads/2017/06/wilwaukeedefense.pdf.

Carmichael, D., Hubert, J., & Reeves, B. (1994). Introduction. In D.L. Carmichael, J. Hubert, B. Reeves, & A. Schanche (Eds.), *Sacred sites, sacred places* (pp. 1–8). New York, NY: Routledge.

Chudacoff, H.P. (2008). *Children at play: An American history.* New York, NY: New York University Press.

Dargle, J., Jr., & Foley, C. (2016, August 16). Re: *Pokemon Go* in Lake Park, Milwaukee, Wisconsin. Milwaukee County Parks. Retrieved from https://milwaukeecounty.legistar.com/View.ashx?M=F&ID=4655727&GUID=35D95AC9-9EAC-43C9-B416-06E13B56A8AC.

Green, C. (2013). A sense of autonomy in young children's special places. *International Journal for Early Childhood Environmental Education, 1*(1), 8–28.

Haas, J. (2016, September 8). *Pokémon Go* sites within Milwaukee County Parks (INFO).

Milwaukee County Parks. Retrieved from https://milwaukeecounty.legistar.com/View.ashx?M=F&ID=4667558&GUID=09818612–46BA-4E77-A2C8-B1FA64C222C9.

Heidegger, M. (1962). *Being and time* (J. Macquarrie & E. Robinson, Trans.). Cornwall, England: Blackwell.

Henry, C. (2016, August 25). *"Pokémon Go"* players leave condoms, heroin needles in Lake Park, neighbor says. *WISN 12 News.* Retrieved from https://www.wisn.com/article/pokemon-go-players-leave-condoms-heroin-needles-in-lake-park-neighbor-says/6334391.

Huizinga, J. (1949). *Homo ludens: A study of the play-element in culture.* Boston: Routledge.

King, C. (1993). His truth goes marching on: Elvis Presley and the pilgrimage to Graceland. In I. Reader & T. Walter (Eds.), *Pilgrimage in popular culture* (pp. 92–104). London, England: Palgrave Macmillan.

Malaby, T.M. (2007). Beyond play: A new approach to games. *Games and Culture, 2*(2), 95–113.

Manovich, L. (2001). *The language of new media.* Cambridge, MA: MIT Press.

Massey, D. (2005). *For space.* Thousand Oaks, CA: Sage.

Moreno, I. (2017, November 30). Wisconsin county settles suit over augmented-reality games. Phys.org. Retrieved from https://phys.org/news/2017–11-wisconsin-county-augmented-reality-games.html.

Murray, J.H. (1998). *Hamlet on the holodeck: The future of narrative in cyberspace.* Cambridge, MA: MIT Press.

Nitsche, M. (2008). *Video game spaces: Image, play, and structure in 3D worlds.* Cambridge, MA: MIT Press.

PokemonGoMap.info. (2018). *Pokémon Go* map. Retrieved from https://www.pokemongomap.info.

Purzycki, K. (2018). [*Pokémon Go* survey]. Unpublished raw data.

Sicart, M. (2014). *Play matters.* Cambridge, MA: MIT Press.

Tuan, Y.-F. (1977). *Place and space: The perspective of experience.* Minneapolis: University of Minnesota Press.

Turner, V.W. (1969). *The ritual process: Structure and anti-structure.* New York, NY: Routledge.

University of Virginia Digital Scholarship Lab. (n.d.). Mapping inequality: Redlining in New Deal America [Interactive map of Milwaukee Co., WI, October 22, 2018]. Retrieved from https://dsl.richmond.edu/panorama/redlining/#loc=15/43.0730/-87.8750&opacity=0.8&sort=201&city=milwaukee-co.-wi.

Wild, M. (2016). Milwaukee County Parks are trying to remove *Pokémon Go* from Lake Park. *Milwaukee Record.* Retrieved from http://milwaukeerecord.com/city-life/milwaukee-county-parks-is-trying-to-remove-pokemon-go-from-lake-park/.

Wolf, M.J.P. (Ed.) (2001). *The medium of the video game.* Austin: University of Texas Press.

A Tale of Two Screens

Space, Ubiquitous Computing and Locative Gaming

LUIZ ADOLFO ANDRADE

When Dickens wrote the classic book *A Tale of Two Cities,* perhaps his intention was to refer to the two main cities related to the events in his novel (Paris and London). Many years later, Picón appropriated Dickens's title in an attempt to portray his concept regarding smart cities. For Picón (2015), the quest for the smart city is as though two distinct projects, such as in *A Tale of Two Cities*, emerged simultaneously in the name of a single ideal and within a single movement of city transformation through information and communications technology. One is related to cybernetic thought in the 1950s and 1960s, while the other is linked to the notion of a city that set out to reinvest its citizens with the capacity to invent community living spontaneously.

The idea of a smart city may have been shaped by the rise of the ubiquitous computing (ubicomp) paradigms that have developed since the early 1980s (Weiser, 1995). Likewise, the spread of ubicomp fed the idea of a smart city; technologies such as smartphones, wireless networks, and wearable computers created the foundation for an emerging phenomenon: locative gaming. Locative games use physical space as the basis for a player's action. Flanagan (2009) "understands that locative games offer an ambiguous ambient game experience because the players explore both participation and space," particularly the space of the city, "by combining physical and technological play" (as cited in Andrade, 2018, p. 54). However, the mandatory use of locative media in its settings can distinguish a locative game from other genres like pervasive games, alternate reality games, transmedia games, and other terms that don't describe different and disconnected traditions but are all attempts to grasp this emergent phenomenon.

This essay discusses the role of space and ubiquitous computing technologies in locative games, particularly *Pokémon Go*. It hypothesizes that *Pokémon Go* introduces a kind of playful use of wearable computing (a wristband or watch) connected to locative media (a smartphone), both important ubiquitous computing technologies. At the same time, they appropriate space as support for a place-based communication process among the players, the game, and everyday life. Thus, *Pokémon Go* may create an important legacy regarding game design for further experiences in locative gaming, showing how designers can divide a game platform between two devices or two screens.

I used actor-network theory (ANT) as my methodological approach in this work. ANT asserts that social connections are not established only among human beings; they include both humans and non-human entities, such as devices, objects, rules, laws and so on. ANT could be useful to analyze locative games like *Pokémon Go* because its gameplay connects players to several non-human entities like smartphones, wristbands, everyday objects, and urban space. Some scholars believe that ANT is more a method than a theory (Fragoso, 2018; Law, 2004) because it provides a useful toolkit to document an emergent phenomenon such as locative gaming; this toolkit includes expressions like actant, mediator, intermediary, translation, delegation, inscription, black box, and controversy.

The game sessions I describe in this essay took place in the urban space of Copenhagen, Denmark, in summer 2017. To play *Pokémon Go*, I used two devices—or two screens, as the essay's title suggests—an Apple Watch and an iPhone 7. They could be respectively labeled as a wearable computer and locative media because the first one is a machine that a user wears like clothing and the second device operates according to the positioning of antennas and users. I show that the use of a wrist device connected to a smartphone can modify the game session, making some interactions easier and faster on *Pokémon Go*; this situation introduces new agencies in the locative gaming network.

Ubiquitous Computing: The Birth of Locative Gaming

The term ubiquitous computing was coined in the late 1980s by Weiser to label an emergent paradigm in computer science. According to Weiser (1995), ubiquitous computing highlights an environment where many embedded computers and wireless networks would support the user's everyday interactions:

Hundreds of computers in a room could seem intimidating at first, just as hundreds of volts coursing through wires in the walls did at one time. But like the wires in the walls, these hundreds of computers will come to be invisible to common awareness. People will simply use them unconsciously to accomplish everyday tasks [p. 933].

Weiser's paradigm is related to two core concepts respectively called calm technology (Weiser, 1995; Weiser & Brown, 1997) and embodied virtuality (Weiser, 1995). The first concept defines technologies that easily move from the periphery to the center of the user's attention (e.g., writing, electricity, and now computing). The second describes the opposite of virtual reality (VR): embodied virtuality defines the spread of computer systems, functions, and networks in the environment and everyday things, while VR relates to digital representation that appears on computer screens, glasses, and headsets such as Gear VR, HTC Vive, and PlayStation VR. Supported by these definitions, Weiser presented in the 1990s three ubicomp technologies called *tab*, *pad*, and *board*.

Roughly a decade later, Rosen published a post on *Low End Mac*, a specialized website on Apple devices, pointing out the connections among the tab, pad, and Apple's smartphone and tablet. According to Rosen (2010),

The Tab has evolved via the convergence of the PDA, the cell phone, the RFID badge, and other discreet devices into today's small handheld computers—more commonly called smartphones. The smartphone is personal, portable, stores data, interacts with "the cloud," reports on locations, etc. … The iPhone (and smartphones in general) are at an exciting point in their development; we're past the initial "isn't this cool" stage and are developing new unforeseen applications upon which we rely daily. … The Apple iPad marks the clearest emergence yet of the Pad as a component of ubiquitous computing—a cross between a full computer and a handheld smartphone, with a user interface already familiar to users of both devices [para. 13–14, 18].

Thus, Weiser's 1990s tab has evolved into today's smartphones, used today to play locative games like *Pokémon Go*, which could also be defined as locative media. Paterson, Smite, Smits, & Tuters (2017) originally proposed this terminology as a label for location-based technologies (e.g., GPS, wireless networks, smartphones, tablets, and antennas) and location-based services (e.g., maps, geotags, augmented reality browsers, social networks that add geospatial information to users' messages like Facebook, Twitter, or Foursquare).

Smartphone users can wear wristbands or an Apple Watch to play *Pokémon Go*, thus participating in wearable computing. The concept of wearable computing was formally proposed in the 1990s to refer to computers that were developed to wear as headsets, glasses, watches, bracelets, and so on (Randell, 2005). According to Mann (1997), a wearable computer is worn like clothing, not carried like smartphones, notebooks, and tablets. This synergy between ubiquitous computing, locative media, and wearable computing sets up the platform for locative games like *Pokémon Go*.

The rise of locative gaming could be pinpointed at the beginning of the 21st century. One of the first locative games was geocaching, launched in May 2000; its core mechanic forces the player to seek hidden caches around the world using GPS coordinates. Since geocaching, other locative gaming projects have been launched. Looking at the time span between 2000 and 2018, it's possible to distinguish three different waves in the history of locative gaming.

The first wave started with geocaching and others in early 2000s. There were no smartphones or mobile operating systems with enough technological resources to support these games. Thus, game designers considered two ways to build a platform for their projects:

• appropriation of devices such as a personal digital assistant (PDA), handheld computers, GPS receivers, antennas, and networks, or use of technologies specifically crafted for gameplay use, such as the games *Pervasive Clues* (2001), *Pirates!* (2001), *Can You See Me Now?* (2001), *Pac-Manhattan* (2004), and *Epidemic Menace* (2005).

• Use of available services such as websites (hidden content), GPS coordinates, phone calls, and short message service (SMS), among others, which directed a player to specific locations in geographical space; such games included *The Beast* (2001) and *I Love Bees* (2004).

The second wave of locative gaming started around 2005 with the rise of the so-called Web 2.0 alongside the popularization of location-based technologies such as GPS, wireless networks, and smartphones such as Nokia's NSeries as well as location-based services which included QR codes, digital maps, social networks, Wireless Application Protocol (WAP) tools, and so on. Some web-based social networking services such as YouTube, Facebook, WordPress, and others often played an important role in spreading game content online. In this wave, some of the more exemplary works included *The Lost Experience* (2006), *Year Zero* (2007), *The Lost Ring* (2008), and *Why So Serious?* (2009).

It's important to highlight that between the first and second waves, there occurred a kind of genre distinction in locative gaming, which optimized the identification and consumption of locative games. Thus, some projects launched using labels such as pervasive game, alternate reality game (ARG), mixed-reality game, and others, with each label referring to a special feature in the gameplay. For instance, pervasive games focus on the mechanics of live action role-play (LARP), which is augmented with computing and communication technology in a way that combines physical and digital space, integrating the game to everyday environments (Montola, Stenros, & Waern, 2009; Schneider & Kortuem, 2001). On the other hand, the alternate reality game (ARG) genre presents a story running alongside the game mechanics and puzzles, which uses media content to blur the boundaries between the gameworld and everyday life (Andrade, 2015; McGonigal, 2007; Szulborski, 2005).

The third wave in locative gaming started at the end of the first decade of the 2000s alongside the improvement of smartphones and mobile operating systems. The launch of Android (2008) and iOS (2008) gave rise to a kind of service that provided mobile application sales and distribution, such as the App Store and Android Market (which was replaced by Google Play Store in 2012). These locative games were released as mobile operating system applications, creating an "app ecology and economy" as proposed by Leorke (2019, p. 93). Alongside the creation of a new distribution model, the app settings allowed the game to connect with some smartphones features such as the accelerometer, the GPS receiver, and the camera. Some examples of games with these features include *CodeRunner* (2012), *Ingress* (2012), and *Pokémon Go* (2016).

The Communication Process in Locative Gaming

Given this brief history regarding locative gaming waves, we can see how the communications processes used in these platforms have paralleled those that make up ubiquitous computing technologies such as wearable computing and locative media; here, as a rule, transmission and reception of information should take place at the local level, providing services according to the user's position (Andrade, 2016) and promoting new uses of space (Lemos 2011). Locative gaming has the same communicative features provided by ubicomp technologies; thus, locative media and wearable computers highlight new roles for space and place in the mediation.

As some geographers, philosophers, and sociologists have argued, people and things always operate in connection to issues regarding space and place. For Tuan (1977), "the meaning of space often merges with that of place. 'Space' is more abstract than 'place.' What begins as undifferentiated space becomes place as we get to know it better and endow it with value" (p. 6). According to de Certeau (1984), places are products of an instantaneous setting of positions, in which the elements are distributed according to coexistence relationships, each one occupying a specific location in geographical space. Cresswell (2004) went even further by arguing that every place has three basic components: (1) location, related to the intersection of latitude and longitude coordinates that matches the place's position in the geographical space; (2) locale, which refers to the place's physical form and appearance, including issues of infrastructure and structure; and (3) sense of place, tied to the symbolisms, emotions, and the sense of belonging that could be evoked by a place. Thus, locative games such *Pokémon Go* use locations over space as support for players's interaction; these agencies occur at the local level, and they temporally change the meaning that people often associate with everyday places, producing a new sense of place.

According to Kitchin and Dodge (2011), "spaces are subtly evolving layers of context and practices that fold together people and things and actively shape social relations" (p. 13). Thus, social interactions could be considered as a tool to tie people and things to a space, creating a kind of place-setting process. In attempt to understand the root of these forces, Lefebvre (1991) presented some initial clues in his classic book *The Production of Space*. Lefebvre built the idea of social space based on a conceptual triad he called perceived, conceived and lived realms—or in spatial terms, spatial practice, representations of space, and representational spaces:

1. *Spatial practice*, which embraces production and reproduction, and the particular locations and spatial sets characteristic of each social formation. Spatial practice ensures continuity and some degree of cohesion. In terms of social space, and of each member of a given society's relationship to that space, this cohesion implies a guaranteed level of *competence* and a specific level of *performance*.

2. *Representations of space*, which are tied to the relations of production and to the "order" which those relations impose, and hence to knowledge, to signs, to codes, and to "frontal" relations.

3. *Representational spaces*, embodying complex symbolisms, sometimes coded, sometimes not, linked to the clandestine or underground side of social life, as also to art (which may come eventually to be defined less as a code of space than as a code of representational spaces) [p. 33, emphasis in original].

The Lefebvrean idea of space is connected to issues of social life. For instance, in spatial practices, the reproduction of social relations is predominant; in contrast, the representation of space is based in both knowledge and power among people. This leaves only the narrowest leeway to representational spaces, which are limited to works, images, and memories whose content relates to the sensory or clandestine side of social life. From this perspective, space is often seen as a set of unfolding social practices—or agencies—between humans and non-humans (i.e., things, rules, and objects) rather than as a container for them.

Inspired by Lefebvre's thoughts, Shields (1991) argued that the agencies people often perform in social space context set up a kind of social process called "spatialization" (p. 31). Looking back to the platform for locative games, Falcão, Andrade, Ferreira, and Bruni (2011) claimed that, due the ludic use and appropriation of locative media, these games produce spatialization to create a special place, which game scholars often call the magic circle.

The idea of the magic circle appeared for the first time in the work of the historian and foundational play theorist Huizinga (1980). Years later, the term was appropriated by Salen and Zimmerman (2004) to refer to the special place commonly associated with the location where play activity happens:

> Although the magic circle is merely one of the examples in Huizinga's list of "play-grounds," the term is used here as shorthand for the idea of a special place in time and space created by a game. The fact that the magic circle is just that—a circle—is an important feature of this concept. As a closed circle, the space it circumscribes is enclosed and separate from the real world. As a marker of time, the magic circle is like a clock: it simultaneously represents a path with a beginning and end, but one without beginning and end. The magic circle inscribes a space that is repeatable, a space both limited and limitless. In short, a finite space with infinite possibility [p. 95].

Regarding the idea of magic circle and the space it inscribes, Juul (2008) pointed out that "the space of game-playing is but one type of space governed by special rules, and as with other types of space, the space of game-playing is social in origin" (p. 57). Here it is possible to realize an important connection to Lefevbre's conceptual triad, considering that the game space enabled by the magic circle metaphor is essentially social, such as the perceived-conceived-lived triad, because it demands interaction between people and game systems. The magic circle concept highlights a kind of temporary place—or social space, according to Lefebvre—in which play activity happens. It could be tied to all sorts of games, from analog formats like board games and card games to digital media and ubiquitous computing technologies (or video games and locative games, respectively) such as *Pokémon Go*.

Following this line of thought, Heili, Xu, and Crane in their essay in this collection highlighted that *Pokémon Go* mobilizes social energy (i.e., the agencies among humans—the players—and non-humans—the game app, the rules, the space, urban planning, locative media, wearable computing, and so on) toward the creation and reproduction of places that are meaningful to players both in terms of gameplay as well as in the physical world beyond the game. Thus, I suggest that the magic circle of *Pokémon Go* is a place that operates as a mediator between the players, the game, and everyday life; it serves as a way to both inform players of its rules and make players aware of the actions that surround them.

Drawing on the magic circle concept, Nitsche (2008) proposed five main conceptual levels of game spaces:

1. *rule-based space* as defined by the mathematical rules that set, for example, physics, sounds, AI, and game-level architecture;

2. *mediated space* as defined by the presentation, which is the space of the image plane and the use of this image including the cinematic form of presentation;

3. *fictional space* that lives in the imagination, in other words, the space "imagined" by players from their comprehension of the available images;

4. *play space*, meaning space of the play, which includes the player and the video game hardware; and

5. *social space* defined by interaction with others, meaning the game space of other players affected [pp. 15–16, emphasis in original].

It is possible to realize in *Pokémon Go* the same conceptual spaces presented by Nitsche. The rule-based space corresponds to the code of the game present in the app. Mediated space could be related to the visible content in the user interface, such as the city map, a player's avatar, Pokémon, Poké Stops, gyms, and so forth. The fictional space corresponds to the imagery and content evoked by the fantasy universe of Pokémon, released by Nintendo and The Pokémon Company in the 1990s. The play space includes some physical components, such as the player's body and the hardware that supports the game, like the smartphone and the watch. The social space is impacted by the players' agencies as they play *Pokémon Go*. However, Nitsche's model of game space is tied to the idea of a videogame, not to a locative game. In this case, it is important to consider the importance of geographical space to at least two of those levels. First, geographical space plays another role in play space considering that it supports the agencies between the players, the game systems, and the platform. As a result, the rule-based space also has a different kind of connection with the geographical space based on the idea of code/space.

Kitchin and Dodge (2011) proposed the concept of code/space as a way to consider how "software ... alternatively modulates how space comes into being through a process of transduction," i.e., "the constant making anew of a domain in reiterative and transformative practices" (p. 16). According to the authors, "space from this perspective is an event or a doing—a set of unfolding practices that lack a secure ontology—rather than a container" (p. 16), corroborating Lefebvre's thoughts. They argue that "society consists of collectives that are hybrid assemblages of many kinds of non-humans (Latour 1993), wherein the relationship between people, material technology, time, and space is contingent, relational, productive, and dynamic" (p. 16); this claim corroborates the core of actor-network theory I describe in the next section of this essay.

Thus, Kitchin and Dodge showed that code/space occur "when software and the spatiality of everyday life become mutually constituted" (p. 16); here, they argued, "spatiality is the product of code, and the code exists primarily in order to produce a particular spatiality" (p. 16). In other words, the concept of code/space refers to the impact of the software on the space and its consequences for everyday life. The authors presented an airport's check-in area as an example of code/space; in this setting,

> if the [check-in] software crashes, the area reverts from a space in which to check in to a fairly chaotic waiting room. There is no other way of checking a person onto a flight because manual procedures have been phased out due to security concerns, so the production of space is dependent on code [Kitchin & Dodge, 2011, pp. 16–17].

Similarly, we can use Copenhagen as an example of how code/space works in *Pokémon Go*. The game content spreads across the outside area of the Royal Library in Copenhagen. As in most of the city, this space has a flattened relief with a cozy garden, closed in by nearby walls and buildings. There is a Poké Stop and a *Pokémon Go* gym available there, which attract many players to join raid battles and defeat the players currently holding the gym, or just to get game tokens such as potions, Poké Balls, and so forth.

In late 2016, members of the Danish press reported that these players were disturbing the library users by crowding the space, making too much noise, and increasing the production of garbage. According to some news reports, this situation led to several complaints from the library's administrators regarding the game and the shifts it caused in that space. Here, we have a situation that is the opposite of the airport check-in area example. If the *Pokémon Go* software crashes, people will simply walk by and not interact with the space. To promote shifts in the space, *Pokémon Go's* software had to work, and not crash (as with the check-in system). There are other examples of code/space in Copenhagen's urban space, such as the Fisketorvet–Copenhagen Mall and the city center, which revealed other features of locative gaming, which I will describe after presenting the methods adopted in this work.

On Actor-Network Theory

Actor-network theory is a subset of social theory coined by Callon in the late 1970s and developed by scholars such as Law (2007) and Latour (2005) to describe approaches to scientific and technical innovation. Latour argued that social relations are the result of constant and renewed associations between humans and non-humans; this action always takes place in networks in which the actors influence each other in momentary agencies. Actor-network theory offers a specific vocabulary that can provide useful insights to other scholars such as those in game studies, especially scholars who focus on locative games research (Andrade, 2018).

"Actant" is perhaps the core concept in ANT because it is linked to the idea of the "actor" in the network (Latour, 2005, p. 46); to Latour, *actant* makes more sense than *actor* when it is used to describe both human and non-human roles in the network, while some people commonly agree that *actor* could refer only to human beings. Following this idea, *mediator* is the term that makes reference to the actant's role in the network (p. 39); mediators are entities that do things and make others do things in the network. On the opposite side of mediators, Latour situated the intermediaries: entities that transport information without changing. In other words, with intermediaries, the input meaning "is enough to define its outputs" (p. 39), while with mediators, the outgoing information is different from the incoming information. In short, the social is association, every action is mediation, and the agents are actants or intermediaries (Lemos & Rodrigues, 2014, p. 1018)

Agency is the expression that matches the issue of action in actor-network theory. There are at least three important agencies that could support locative gaming analyses. First, there is translation; this consists of the processes operated by mediators to transform and send information to another actant; it could be realized when an actant simply chooses to activate the network or if another mediator starts to become stronger than the first one; also, there is translation even if a force becomes indispensable to make another movement in the network (i.e., it's obligatorily to buy a ticket to take a bus). The second agency is delegation; it often happens after a translation process. Delegation occurs when a mediator transfers the agency from another network to make another actant do something (Callon, 1986; Latour, 1987, 2005). Finally, the agency of inscription corresponds to the process by which a designer embeds a special way for the users to interact with a designed object, sometimes supported by a script that was previously created (such as laws, maps, codes, rules, etc.). J. D. Jessen and C. Jessen (2014) argued that every "game can be studied as a designed object with inscriptions that has agency and does something with the [player], because the user invokes a network of actors and agency when he or she starts playing a game" (e.g., "following the rules of the game world inscribed in the code's software") (p. 224).

For the purposes of this essay, it is important to highlight the expression "cartography of controversies," which Latour introduced in the 1990s as a methodological approach in the ANT context; Latour said that the task is to "just look at controversies and tell what you see" (as cited in Venturini, 2010, p. 259). Venturini (2010) added, it "is nothing more than 'observing and describing'" (p. 259). To Brazilian theorist Lemos (2013), a controversy is the perfect situation to reveal agencies, mediations, and the formation of intermediaries. Controversy has a meaningful function in ANT because it highlights a situation where the actors disagree, which is a productive moment for the researcher to start his work. In a broader sense, the label "locative" attached to game could be controversial because the activity of "playing a game" is always connected to issues of location and place, expressed in the idea of the magic circle presented in this essay.

In game studies, some scholars have used actor-network theory in their research (see Bienia, 2016; Chen, 2010; Cypher & Richardson, 2006; Giddings, 2006; Hung, 2017; J. D. Jessen & C. Jessen, 2014; Silva & Tomimatsu, 2013). For instance, Bienia (2016) used ANT as a method in order to analyze role-playing games. For Bienia, "actor-network theory is a mixed method that adds to the repertoire of methods available to game studies, because it focuses not solely on people, but encourages attention to all of the actors of the networks that constitute games" (p. 163).

Because it provides useful concepts for understanding the role of each actor in the network created by *Pokémon Go*, and because it considers humans and non-humans equally, ANT appears a fruitful methodology for locative game research. In *Pokémon Go*, the player interacts with other actants beyond the game app, such as smartphones and wristbands (e.g., Nintendo *Pokémon Go* Plus; Codejunkies' Go-tcha); also, he or she must deal with everyday objects, vehicles, pedestrians, and traffic rules, among other things, in the urban space.

Open the Black Box: Describing the Network in Pokémon Go

Through the ANT lens, it is possible to see the emergence of a broader controversy between the first generation of Pokémon videogames and *Pokémon Go*. Both were designed for mobile devices (the Nintendo Game Boy and smartphones, respectively) but *Pokémon Go* improves the players' mobility more than the classic game does; for the classic game, to play with more than one person, the players must first locate each other physically and then connect two Game Boy devices using a cable. However, sometimes the Game Boy mobile devices become immobile during a shared game session. On the other hand, *Pokémon Go* players are far more mobile in the city, able to play with more than one person in gym or raid battles without the need for cables.

The game platform (i.e., the technological support that people can use to play) is an actant in the network created by *Pokémon Go*. The platform could be divided into two main devices. The first is the smartphone, which supports all the interactions allowed in *Pokémon Go*; the second is the wristband, if used. I used an Apple Watch to play in these game sessions, but the player can choose other wrist devices, such as the wristbands from Nintendo (*Pokémon Go* Plus) and Codejunkies (Go-tcha for *Pokémon Go*).

The use of a wristband or watch in connection with the smartphone can transform the game network because they simplify interactions like hatching eggs, spinning Poké Stops, and capturing nearby Pokémon; they also notify the player about nearby Pokémon and Poké Stops. In this network, the wristband becomes a mediator that modifies the game session to make many inter-actions easier and faster.

The smartphone and the wristband delegate agency. The smartphone can make the wristband perform the procedures listed above; on the other hand, the wristband can send information to the smartphone that forces the player to make choices, such as to decide which direction to go in order to reach a specific Poké Stop or whether or not to catch a nearby Pokémon. The delegation between both mediators relies on the support of two intermediaries: the Bluetooth network, which connects the smartphone to the Apple Watch or wristband, and wireless networks such as 3G/4G, which connect the game to the Internet.

Pokémon Go is a mediator that works alongside this platform; it uses the agency of inscription to transform the game code into the content the player interacts with in these two screens. As with every kind of game, *Pokémon Go* has rules, like the need to interact with the smartphone in certain ways to catch a Pokémon or the need to go to a gym location to join raid battles. Initially, the rules probably appear like intermediaries if we consider the mere function of transporting the information from the game to the player. However, in this game network the rules could be alternatively conceived as non-human mediators because they make the player do things that can be considered as game mechanics, such as "walking," which is also considered by Murnane (in this collection) as one of the three key inputs for the player in *Pokémon Go*, or "first person shooting," as in the case of catching Pokémon.

The *Pokémon Go* app is connected by inscription to other background networks as well, such as the urban space of Copenhagen and the game design process; this network includes several actors like urban planners, pedestrians, architects, vehicles, streets, buildings, and houses, while the second has human actants such as game designers, interface designers, programmers, executive producers, and beta testers, and also non-humans as in the case of the game design document, scripts, rules, and the game code. There is another agency of inscription that links the game design process of *Pokémon Go* and *Ingress*: Many Poké Stop locations and *Ingress* portals are the same. In late 2017, Niantic reopened the Ingress portal submission system; thus, every Ingress Agent who is level 10 or higher can create an Ingress portal and submit it for evaluation; if Ingress approves this portal, by inscription it will become a Poké Stop in *Pokémon Go* as well. Here, the agency of inscription connects *Pokémon Go* to *Ingress* and connects both games to the geo-information database that supports Google Maps, thus highlighting how these two different games overlap through shared geographical references.

The idea of code/space links intrinsically the code of *Pokémon Go* app to geographical space, such as in my experience in Copenhagen's urban space.

Likewise, the earlier example of the Royal Library's outside area in 2016 is a similar example of code/space when compared to the Fisketorvet–Copenhagen Mall in 2017. There are some sponsored Poké Stops in the mall's location, which often attracts a lot of players. The gathered players share space with customers, sellers, and others, creating temporary places that make these spaces crowded. Using Lefebvre's (1991) work, here we have an example of how spatial practice, such as gameplay supporting a locative game, overlaps with a previously conceived space, such as the shopping mall. Through this lens, *Pokémon Go* could temporally change the sense of place as proposed by Cresswell (2004) and the mall becomes an example of Lefebvrean perceived space.

Space and place are mediators connected to the game app in the game network. When a player starts a *Pokémon Go* game session, spatial features can modify the game session; for example, if the player has to walk over a rugged area or has to cross a crowded space, the game session could become harder. Likewise, some actions initially tied to a place can modify the game session as well, such as being required to be quiet inside a library. If somebody starts playing *Pokémon Go* there, the player should respect these rules; otherwise, perhaps we have a situation close to the Royal Library situation.

This synergy between space, place, the game app, and the player often happens through translation agencies, which may be realized every time a player starts a *Pokémon Go* game session by activating a network and shifting the focus to himself or herself, or when a player has to climb a hill to reach a Poké Stop or a gym. At first glance, the game app and the player could appear as strong mediators in the game network; however, space takes the forefront when the player is climbing a hill to reach a Poké Stop. The same situation happened in the case of the Royal Library of Copenhagen; originally, the library was a quiet place, but a player shifted the focus to himself or herself when he or she starts to make noise while playing *Pokémon Go*. If the player changes the space that is used for gameplay, like changing a hill to a flattened surface or substituting the library for a park, the game session will be affected.

Finally, there is also translation every time the player uses a means of transportation to reach different places in an urban space in a short time. Bicycles are very common in Copenhagen and a player could use a bike to easily reach more game locations. For instance, the player can access the website gomaps.dk to monitor Pokémon locations in all of Denmark. By clicking the link to Copenhagen, the player is able to find locations and go there using the app navigation tools in an attempt to locate Pokémon and join raid battles. However, if the player's original location and the intended location are far apart, a bike or other means of transportation become an indispensable force; alongside the translation agency of the transportation device, the website becomes a mediator that transforms the game network and modifies how the game session works by directing the player to the Pokémon's current location.

Final Thoughts

I want to point out some thoughts regarding the use of "two screens"—those screens being the Apple Watch and the smartphone in the game network connected to *Pokémon Go*. This game introduced a kind of playful use of a distributing platform in the "third wave" of locative gaming history, splitting its content through wearable computers (watches and wristbands) and locative media (the smartphone). While a player may use these two screens to play *Pokémon Go*, only the smartphone can modify the game session; its modification makes some procedures easier and faster, such as hatching eggs or catching nearby Pokémon. Thus, I argue that *Pokémon Go* provides a useful resource for locative game design by introducing the use of a distributing platform in locative gaming, which connects wearable computing and locative media to the game network.

As I argue in this essay, this configuration appears as a fruitful framework for analysis using ANT because ANT considers humans (the players and the pedestrians) and non-humans (smartphones, wearable computers, wireless networks, physical space, everyday objects, software, rules, and so on) equally. In the same way, ANT provides useful concepts for understanding the roles of agents in a locative game network, such as mediators, intermediaries, agencies of inscription, delegation, and translation. Actor-network theory offers a new perspective for examining *Pokémon Go* and is a fruitful tool for analyzing location-based and AR applications. Along with describing networks, agencies, and mediators, ANT could provide profitable information to game designers they can use to improve their locative gaming projects. For instance, the agency of delegation supports connections among players and the distributing platform; in the same way, I show that *Pokémon Go* is connected by inscription to Ingress, another locative game developed by Niantic, Inc.; this agency highlights a way to share the same georeferenced database as support for two different locative gaming projects. Also by inscription, *Pokémon Go* is connected to other background networks as well, such as the game design process and urban space.

It is important to highlight that game designers can find a mechanism to promote shifts in the space where a locative game session takes place by considering the five levels of space proposed by Nitsche (2008) and the concept of code/space provided by Kitchin and Dodge (2011). I presented in this essay some examples that reveal how *Pokémon Go* can modify physical spaces by attracting players to engage in raid battles or to catch Pokémon, as in the examples of the Copenhagen Royal Library and the Fisketorvet shopping mall. Thus, I understand that *Pokémon Go* provides an important legacy regarding gameplay for further experiences in locative gaming, showing how the designers can distribute the locative game platform across two devices or two screens. Finally, space works as a mediator in the game network connected to *Pokémon Go*. Following along the same lines proposed by Heili, Xu, and Crane (in this collection) and others, we can conclude that *Pokémon Go* mobilizes social energy produced by agencies between humans and non-humans during the game session toward the creation of meaningful and temporary places or "magic circles" atop physical space; it highlights a place-based communication process among the players, the game, and everyday life that uses the space as support for the agencies in the locative game network.

Acknowledgments

Thanks to Professor Espen Aarseth and other researchers from the Center for Computer Games Research (IT-University of Copenhagen/Denmark) for hosting this work; to Coordination for the Improvement of Higher Education Personnel (CAPES/Brazil) and The State University of Bahia (UNEB/Brazil) for the financial support. This work was supported by CAPES Postdoctoral Stage Scholarship, process number 88881.119487/2016–01.

References

Andrade, L.A. (2015). *Jogos digitais, cidade e (trans)mídia: A próxima fase*. Curitiba: Appris, 2015.

Andrade, L.A. (2016). *Jogos locativos (Locative Games)*. Salvador: Editora da Universidade Federal da Bahia.

Andrade, L.A. (2018). Research method for locative games. *MedieKultur: Journal of Media and Communication Research*, 64, 52–70.

Bienia, R. (2016). *Role playing materials*. Braunschweig, Germany: Zauberfeder Verlag.

Callon, M. (1986). The sociology of an actor-network: The case of the electric vehicle. In M. Callon, J. Law, & A. Rip (Eds.), *Mapping the dynamics of science and technology: Sociology of science in the real world* (pp. 19–34). Basingstoke, England: Macmillan.

Chen, M. (2010). *Leet noobs: Expertise and collaboration in a* World of Warcraft *player group as distributed sociomaterial practice* (Doctoral dissertation, University of Washington). Retrieved from https://digital.lib.washington.edu/researchworks/handle/1773/16275?show=full.

Cresswell, T. (2004). *Place: A short introduction*. Oxford, England: Blackwell.

Cypher, M., & Richardson, I. (2006). An actor-network approach to games and virtual environments. *Proceedings of the 2006 International Conference on Game Research and Development, CyberGames '06, USA*, 254–259.

da Silva, S.T., & Tomimatsu, K. (2013). Game prototyping with community-driven narrative: Actor-network theory applied for massively multiplayer online games development. *Proceedings of the 2013 IEEE 2nd Global Conference on Consumer Electronics, GCCE 2013, USA*, 376–378.

de Certeau, M. (1984). *A invenção do cotidiano* [*The practice of everyday life*]. Petrópolis, Brazil: Editora Vozes.

Falcão, T., Andrade, L.A., Ferreira, E., & Bruni, P. (2011). Locative media and playful appropriations, or how electronic games help to redefine the meaning of space. In R.J. Firmino, F. Duarte, & C. Ultramari (Eds.), *ICTs for mobile and ubiquitous urban infrastructures: Surveillance, locative media and global networks* (pp. 186–204). Hershey, PA: IGI Global.

Fragoso, S. (2018). Os modos de existência do gameplay: Um exercício de aplicação com *Cities: Skylines* [The modes of existence of gameplay: An applied exercise with *Cities: Skylines*]. *MATRIZes, 12*(2), 33–51.

Giddings, S. (2006). *Walkthrough: Videogames and technocultural form* (Doctoral dissertation, University of the West of England). Retrieved from http://citeseerx.ist.psu.edu/viewdoc/summary?doi=10.1.1.108.324.

Heili, W., Xu, C., & Crane, N.J. (2019). *Pokémon Go*, cyborgs, and placemaking: Challenging the digital-physical divide. In J. Henthorn, A. Kulak, K. Purzycki & S. Vie (Eds.), in this volume.

Huizinga, J. (1980). *Homo ludens: A study of the play-element in culture*. London, England: Routledge.

Hung, A.C.Y. (2017). Beyond the player: A user-centered approach to analyzing digital games and players using actor-network theory. *E-Learning and Digital Media, 13*(5–6), 227–243.

Jessen, J.D., & Jessen, C. (2014). Games as actors—Interaction, play, design, and actor-network theory. *International Journal on Advances in Intelligent Systems, 7*(3–4), 412–422.

Juul, J. (2008). The magic circle and the puzzle piece. In S. Gunzel, M. Liebe, & D. Mersch (Eds.), *Conference Proceedings of the Philosophy of Computer Games 2008* (pp. 56–67). Potsdam, Germany: University Press.

Kitchin, R., & Dodge, M. (2011). *Code/space: Software and everyday life*. Cambridge, MA: MIT Press.

Latour, B. (1987). *Science in action: How to follow scientists and engineers through society*. Cambridge, MA: Harvard University Press.

Latour, B. (1993). *We have never been modern*. New York: Harvester Wheatsheaf.

Latour, B. (2005). *Reassembling the social: An introduction to actor-network theory*. Oxford, England: Oxford University Press.

Law, J. (2004). *After method: Mess in social science research*. London, England: Routledge.

Law, J. (2007). *Actor network theory and material semiotics, version of 25th April 2007*. Retrieved January 19, 2018, from http://www.heterogeneities.net/publications/Law2007ANTandMaterialSemiotics.pdf.

Lefebvre, H. (1991). *The production of space* (D. Nicholson-Smith, Trans.). Oxford, England: Blackwell Publishers.

Lemos, A. (2011). Locative media and surveillance at the boundaries of informational territories. In R.J. Firmino, F. Duarte, & C. Ultramari (Eds.), *ICTs for mobile and ubiquitous urban infrastructures: Surveillance, locative media and global networks* (pp. 129–149). Hershey, PA: IGI Global.

Lemos, A. (2013). *A comunicação das coisas: Teoria ator-rede e cibercultura* [The communication of things: Actor-network theory and cyberculture]. São Paulo, Brazil: Annablume.

Lemos, A.L.M., & Rodrigues, L.P.B. (2014). Internet das coisas, automatismo e fotografia: Uma análise pela Teoria Ator-Rede [Internet of things, automatism and photography: An analysis by actor-network theory]. *Revista FAMECOS: Mídia, Cultura e Tecnologia, 21*(3), 1016–1040. doi:10.15448/1980-3729.2014.3.18114.

Leorke, D. (2019). *Location-based gaming: Play in public space*. Singapore: Palgrave Macmillan.

Mann, S. (1997, February). Wearable computing: A first step toward personal imaging. *Computer, 30*(2), 25–32. doi:10.1109/2.566147.

McGonigal, J. (2007). The puppet master problem: Design for real-world, mission-based gaming. In P. Harrigan, & N. Wardrip-Fruin (Eds.), *Second person: Role-playing and story in games and playable media* (pp. 251–264). Cambridge, MA: MIT Press.

Montola, M., Stenros, J., & Waern, A. (2009). *Pervasive games: Theory and design*. Burlington, MA: Morgan Kaufmann.

Murnane, E. (2019). To be the very best … you gotta pay: Motivation, resources and monetizing frustration. In J. Henthorn, A. Kulak, K. Purzycki & S. Vie (Eds.), in this volume.

Nitsche, M. (2008). *Video game spaces: Image, play, and structure in 3D worlds*. Cambridge, MA: MIT Press.

Paterson, A.G., Smite, R., Smits, R., & Tuters, M. (2017, March 28). [2003] Locative media workshop images, Liepaja-Karosta. Retrieved September 11, 2018, from https://archive.org/details/agryfp-2003-locative-media-workshop-images.

Picon, A. (2015). *Smart cities: A spatialised intelligence.* West Sussex, England: Wiley & Sons.

Randell, C. (2005). *Wearable computing: A review* [Technical report]. Retrieved January 19, 2018, from http://citeseerx.ist.psu.edu/viewdoc/summary?doi=10.1.1.60.7898.

Rosen, A. (2010, March 16). Ubiquitous computing: Tabs, pads, books, and clouds [blog post]. *Low End Mac.* Retrieved January 19, 2018, from http://lowendmac.com/ed/rosen/10ar/ubiquitous-computing.html.

Salen, K., & Zimmermman, E. (2004). *Rules of play: Game design fundamentals.* Cambridge, MA: MIT Press.

Schneider, J., & Kortuem, G. (2001). *How to host a pervasive game–Supporting face-to-face interactions in live-action roleplaying.* Position paper for UbiComp 2001 Workshop on designing ubiquitous computing games. Retrieved January 19, 2018, from http://citeseerx.ist.psu.edu/viewdoc/summary?doi=10.1.1.29.3258.

Shields, R. (1991). *Places on the margin: Alternative geographies of modernity.* Abingdon, England: Routledge.

Szulborski, D. (2005). *This is not a game: A guide to alternate reality gaming.* Santa Barbara, CA: New-Fiction Publishing.

Tuan, Y.-F. (1977). *Space and place: The perspective of experience.* Minneapolis: University of Minnesota Press.

Venturini, T. (2010). Diving in magma: How to explore controversies with actor-network theory. *Public Understanding of Science, 19*(3), 258–273. Retrieved January 19, 2018, from http://pus.sagepub.com/content/19/3/258.

Weiser, M. (1995). The computer for the 21st century. In R.M. Baecker, J. Grudin, W.A.S. Buxton, & S. Greenberg (Eds.), *Human-computer interaction: Toward the year 2000* (2nd ed.) (pp. 933–940). San Francisco: Morgan Kaufmann.

Weiser, M., & Brown, J.S. (1997). The coming age of calm technology. In P.J. Denning & R.M. Metcalfe (Eds.), *Beyond calculation: The next fifty years of computing* (pp. 75–85). New York, NY: Springer Science+Business Media.

Placemaking Across the Digital-Physical Divide

Location-Based Mobile Gameplay as a Relay in the Emergence of Singularities

WILLIAM HEILI, CHEN XU *and*
NICHOLAS JON CRANE

More than many other video games, *Pokémon Go* mobilizes social energy toward the creation and reproduction of places that are meaningful to players both in gameplay and in the physical world beyond the game. In doing so, *Pokémon Go* challenges the physical-digital dualism that runs through much of the popular and scholarly commentary on cyberspace. Contrary to extant literature that maintains a strong distinction between the digital and offline worlds, this essay suggests that *Pokémon Go* should be understood as a mode of computation by which physical reality is produced. Basing our analysis upon post-humanist currents in the humanities and social sciences that approach representations in terms of their capacity to affect and effect, and not simply to signify (see Anderson, 2018; Barad, 2003), we argue that *Pokémon Go* should be conceived as a *relay* in placemaking. This conceptualization draws from but exceeds Deleuze and Guattari's writing on linguistics and communication (Deleuze & Guattari, 1987, pp. 75–110), as we discuss in greater depth below. We accordingly characterize *Pokémon Go* as a technology that effectuates the emergence of singular places by eliciting gameplay that establishes coordinates for behavior in a given location and, in that sense, realizes a collective sense of place. We reflect upon the experience of playing *Pokémon Go* and examine its role in the creation of places, both in terms of their materiality and also their representation through the *Pokémon Go* platform, to show how player behavior in the physical world is affected by messages received through interactions in cyberspace. We show that the game creates a unity such that Pokémon exist in a digital-physical reality from which places are shaped, and we consider how a relational and distributed form of agency is facilitating the emergence of singular places through acts that always and necessarily introduce physical space into cyberspace and vice versa.

The essay is organized in two sections. The first section stages a conversation between literatures on place and cybernetics. This prepares the ground for an analysis of *Pokémon Go*'s effects on players' perceptions of place and behavior in place, and of how the game elicits play that creates and reflects a collective sense of place. We argue that cybernetics requires us to rethink how places may be constituted, demanding that we open place beyond the "introverted, inward-looking history" through which the uniqueness of a place is traditionally thought to be constructed (Massey, 1994, p. 152) to instead recognize the emergence of singular places from the convergence of the "bits and atoms" that constitute our modern world (Mitchell, 2004, p. 3). We suggest that places must be understood as "articulated moments in networks of social relations and understandings" (Massey, 1994, p. 152) for which technologies like *Pokémon Go* perform the function of a relay, allowing places to emerge and take shape through a transition from immateriality to materiality. The second section draws on experiences of gameplay to reflect on *Pokémon Go* as a relay in placemaking and complements that reflection with an interpretation of place representation in the user interface (UI) and from the wider discourse on places of possible gameplay. We suggest that gameplay works to transform players' sense of place, away from a sense of place grounded in assumptions of a digital-physical dichotomy toward one informed by experiences of digital-physical convergence. Here, *Pokémon Go* is a relay in the production of explorable spaces that are both digitally and physically constituted.

Placemaking and Cybernetics

Two worlds, physical and virtual, are gradually but steadily synthesizing and unifying. Scholars have recently drawn attention to how video game development creates virtual environments in ways that "parallel" the design of built environments by engaging users through the construction of shared meanings and perceptions, or a shared sense of place (Álvarez & Duarte, 2018, p. 209). Examining the relay function of location-based mobile gameplay as we do will challenge an understanding of these two configurations of the world as parallel but nonetheless separate (Tække, 2002). It appears that activities in both spaces are better understood as intersecting with each other at particular locations to the effect of articulating particular places. Following Massey (2006), we conceive of places as events of intersection with greater or lesser degrees of durability, or as geographical singularity points (p. 46).

Singularity, a concept borrowed from mathematics (Hawking & Penrose, 1970), has recently been circulating through the popular discourse on artificial intelligence. This is evident, for example, in the futuristic vision offered by the February 2011 *Time Magazine* cover story "2045: The Year Man Becomes Immortal," where technological singularities represent a state in which human and machine are merged (Kurzweil, 2014). In this essay, the term singularity describes the point where cyberspace and physical space merge. A transcendence happens at these singular points where certain restrictions of geographical space are broken down (e.g., space-time compression) and immaterial information materializes in physical space (e.g., in location-based GPS games in general and *Pokémon Go* in particular). Cyberspace created through platforms such as Twitter regularly plays a crucial role in establishing virtual togetherness through technologies such as spoofing, which lets users at physically separate locations converge digitally to a single geographic location on a map. Immaterial messages like tweets accordingly exert sensible force by facilitating interactions and relations in the offline world. Readers need only recall the anecdotal stories of social media use in the Arab Spring to get a glimpse of such dynamics (see Gregory, 2013).

While the notion of singularity resonates with the work of human geographers like Massey, who, without explicit reference to information communication, theorized the uniqueness of place as a singular effect of relations that converge at a specific locus in physical space (see also Shields, 2013), these singular places also express activity in cyberspace (Kitchin & Dodge, 2011). Singular places emerge through acts that always and necessarily introduce physical space into cyberspace and vice versa. Singularity therefore denotes a material location in the physical world that emerges through the convergence of at least two simultaneous processes of inseparable spatialization (digital and physical). There is a possibility of misalignment, and the *Pokémon Go* Death Tracker, a website that tracks gameplayer accidents, gives tragic examples of misalignment. More important, singularity implies the necessity of two agencies, one in physical space and the other in cyberspace, that facilitate the emergence of novelty. The term cyborg describes this collaborative unity.

The cyborg, or cybernetic organism, is a unity of technology and biology that challenges liberal humanist assumptions about individual free will (Haraway, 1991/1999). Conventionally conceived, the cyborg is realized by implanting digital technologies into the bodies of human or non-human organisms. But we are arguably "joined in a dynamic coevolutionary spiral with intelligent machines [and] other biological species" which exceeds this conventional conception of the cyborg form (Hayles, 2006, p. 164; see also Rosen, 2012). We use the concept to summarize the relations through which singularities emerge as well as to make sense of the role of individuals who are using various digital information technologies. Rather than relying on implants that translate outside stimuli directly into the organism's neural network, the agency at issue here relies on human sensory organs as sensors, which through informational extension provided by digital devices amplify their cognitive capacities, resituating otherwise individuated bodies in what Hayles (2006, p. 161) called the "cognisphere." By participating in "distributed cultural cognitions" that are "embodied both in people and their technologies" (Hayles, 2006, p. 160), individuals act into a dynamic information flow between two processes of spatialization out of which singularities emerge. To dissect these dynamics, and to the effect of revealing the spatiality of the cyborg in ways that Donna Haraway did not in her pathbreaking essay (see Thrift, 2006, pp. 193–194), we use the framework offered by cybernetics; we also demonstrate that the framework is of enduring relevance (see Thrift, 2006, p. 191).

Cybernetics is a science of communication, information, and control. Cybernetics studies how self-regulating organisms and machines control goal-seeking behaviors through information communication. The fundamental mechanism that sustains the functionality of cybernetic systems is the production-consumption of information, or, what Deleuze and Guattari (1987) characterized as the deployment of order-words or statements that impose "semiotic coordinates" for action to come (pp. 75–79). This process demands *relays*—that is, the various technologies that facilitate this production-consumption of information, so that statements can "intervene directly" in assemblages of bodies (Deleuze and Guattari, 1987, p. 89). As a relay, *Pokémon Go* transmits order-words and elicits practices of gameplay that always and necessarily introduce physical space into cyberspace and vice versa. The relay function facilitates what Tham and Smiles, in this collection, described as transduction.

Information, following Claude Shannon (1959) and Norbert Wiener's definition (1950), is patternized code that is able to trigger actions; these actions demand at least two participants, a sender and a receiver. The sender encodes intention in order-words and, through a communication mechanism, the receiver receives, decodes, and reacts. Humans bring subjectivity into the process, to the effect that the action of the receiver might deviate from the intention of the sender, entangling the actions of both the sender and the receiver in a constellation of social relations. The entanglement demands that we learn to recognize the effect of participants' subjectivities through two simultaneous processes of spatialization that are situated in an ecosystem consisting of cyberspace builders and cyborgs. We accordingly propose cybernetics as a framework for examining the collaborations between the self-regulating gameplay system and players, as information feedback loops manifest in the behavior of players.

Human behavior in contexts like those of *Pokémon Go* gameplay reflects an apparent digital-physical divide, which reconfigures our worlds as posthuman realities where a message encoded as information by the play of human subjectivity can be detached from and may betray the human's bodily presence (Hayles, 1999). Material presence in physical space is sometimes represented as antagonistically opposed to the patternized code of cyberspace. Attempts to cheat personal health tracking gadgets (Wieczner, 2016) are humorous yet profound examples of this sense of detachment. Our attempts to affect the relay between two modes of ordering creates complex possibilities at the intersection of the two spatializations. Behind the informational curtain lies the body of infinite material possibility, which suggests the depth of our challenge to understand human experience in posthuman conditions.

When humans create such intimate bonds with information communication technologies, information becomes life-sustaining. We echo Hayles' (1999) assessment that "the emphasis on information technologies" in our everyday lives "foregrounds pattern/randomness" (pp. 48–49); the material world has been figured as secondary to the virtual world in many domains of life, and that this affects how we live in the material world. We are witnessing an accelerating digitization of our physical world, which, through coding, forms patterns out of randomness and facilitates the emergence of relatively durable singularities. Current information communication technologies are grounded on the conception of information as an entity that externally exists as a pattern of signals that can be faithfully received by information receivers. For example, Shannon and Weaver (1998) tactically but problematically excluded the contextualized meaning invested in such patterns in order to facilitate information communication for engineering solutions. Encoded messages can be transmitted through the Internet as a stream of binaries, but the description of the message demands the encoding context. Thus, to exclude practices of meaning-making from the model is to leave information decontextualized and raises a series of questions that analyses like ours would suggest. When information communication technology is promoted by technology optimists as a corrective for ecological and social crises, can cyborgs be expected to act amidst tension if they are situated only in a cyberspace of decontextualized pure forms? Has physical space been reshaped through information in ways that are locally meaningful? Or differently, is the physical process of spatialization being made meaningful to cyborgs, including those that we see being drawn into new relations with the physical world by technologies like *Pokémon Go*?

The technologies of what Hayles (2006) called the "cognisphere" (p. 161) now facilitate information storage and collective cognition in cyberspace that, through relays like *Pokémon Go*, mediate human relationships. Cognisphere-mediated human relationships appear to be different from human relationships built on direct bodily interactions and can certainly disrupt intimacies among humans. Modes of computation that shape our physical world are designed, and even if their effects exceed the intentions of their designers, their capacities are restricted by what is allowed in code. In *Pokémon Go*, Niantic programmers and game players (in their role as co-designers) create a game space where the physical world is a playground. However, beyond eliciting a frenzy to chase Pokémon, how is the game facilitating transformations of our physical world?

Technology optimists would have us believe that the development of information technologies will lead to a better world, but this would demand a transformation of the relation between information and materiality at places where tensions exist. Following the cybernetic understanding of information, this transformation will not be neutral. Instead, the transformation from material to information and back, and the creation of singular places that results, will be mediated by a process of filtering that is shaped by the cyberspace builders' subjectivity and their use of place. Similar to placemaking traditionally conceived, this process of filtering will create meaningful vortexes, but in the form of patternized code. But again, not just in parallel but as a relay, the activity in virtual space will intersect with activity in physical space and thereby articulate particular events of "meeting" (see Massey, 1994, p. 154). When collective effort to create meaningful places has become a fundamental mechanism to entice participants, can digital technologies facilitate re-presentation of the physical world so that both cyberspace and physical space are altered?

Pokémon Go *and Places as Singular Effects*

Recent characterizations of video game development as "parallel" to spatial design (e.g., Álvarez & Duarte, 2018, p. 209) suggest an enduring need to correct analyses based on a layered model of the relationship between the physical world and cyberspace. A cybernetic lens allows us to recognize the role of information communication in catalyzing a transformation of the relation between these two configurations of the world. This raises the question of *how* information flows introduce physical space into cyberspace and vice versa. Services like Foursquare, a user-driven location-based search platform, facilitate a unidirectional flow between the physical world and cyberspace, which reinforce "global patterns of visibility, representation and voice that we are used to in the offline world" (Graham, 2013, p. 181), thus giving activity in cyberspace a highly constrained capacity to shape physical space. *Pokémon Go*, however, suggests a more thorough disruption of the digital-physical divide because it facilitates bidirectional flows.

Information communication in the user interface (UI) is realized in a physical place, and players build reputations among peers by capturing otherwise purely digital creatures. Further, *Pokémon Go* transforms users' perceptions of and behavior in the physical world by enabling a designed cyborg agency that facilitates users' navigation in physically anchored cyberspace. *Pokémon Go* is in that sense a manifestation of the synthesis of bits and atoms (Mitchell, 2004). The immaterial nature of bits (i.e., Pokémon), while invisible to the naked eye, exist not only in the informational realm but in the physical realm. The two entities, Pokémon and our physical surroundings, are mashed up and revealed to the player only through a specialized apparatus: the game UI. As such, placemaking at singularities begs to be understood through a relational conception of space that takes into account flows of bits and atoms mobilized for the same effect. The result of this synchrony is that, while the embodied experiences of individual players (as cyborgs) are restricted by physical laws, the world-making capacity of their cognition or imagination is significantly augmented and thus can be virtually everywhere, as in the case of location spoofing (Zhao & Sui, 2017). Thus, as the player walks the streets of their neighborhood or pretends to be thousands of miles away from home in pursuit of Pokémon, their cyborg agency is continuously engaged in processes of meaning-making that stitch together digital and physical spaces into singular experiences. The effectuation of singularities through gameplay is made possible by the imaging agent, the UI. Cyborgs act simultaneously in physical space and cyberspace, introducing the one to the other so that their visible behavior in the physical world is affected by messages received from and returning to reshape cyberspace. The following analysis presents this dynamic as a cybernetic loop of geographic information and gameplay that facilitates the emergence of singularities.

Our analysis is informed by field research with a convenience sample of players on the University of Wyoming (UW) campus in April 2017 as well as by an examination of representations of place from both the UI and a wider discourse on places of possible gameplay. The field research involved a focus group discussion with five university students. The primary site of the gameplay experiences is the university campus in the town of Laramie, Wyoming. UW draws students from local, national, and international backgrounds. The campus itself is largely traversed on foot by students and faculty, particularly the central green space on campus known as Prexy's Pasture (or "Prexy's"; see Figure 12.1). These conditions combine to give the campus a pedestrian character, which allows the campus to facilitate interactions that are more akin to those of the ideal-typical urban-built environment with which *Pokémon Go* gameplay is popularly associated.

Rather than simply presenting a map of campus with a layer of objectives, the game's representation of campus transforms space for player-cyborgs. Instead of a ground-level view, the player is given a third-person aerial view of their avatar and its location in space, which is void of other players but littered with interactive elements. Some of these elements can be several blocks away from the player, invisible to one's line of sight but prominent in the UI. Natural environments are flattened in favor of a grass-colored plain; the built environment is reduced to base footprints. Pokémon sprites likewise appear within and outside of buildings, having little regard for barriers that the physical world might impose on the intrepid Pokémon trainer. Clearly, the UI re-orders the landscape to elevate digital-physical landmarks over physical obstructions. Consequently, the player-cyborg perceives spaces of gameplay differently, leading them to change the ways in which they interact with space. The game mobilizes a synthetic and collective agency and allows the player-cyborg to do considerable work in creating or revising flows of meaning-making and material that constitute places.

It is important to consider not only the social ramifications of this prioritization (Eanes & van den Broek, in this collection) but to analyze the new characterizations of places that emerge as well. Places that take shape through *Pokémon Go* gameplay are manifestly explorable. Game

Figure 12.1. A screenshot photograph of the *Pokémon Go* UI (March 24, 2017). The screenshot captures a view of Prexy's Pasture.

mechanics dictate that this message of explorability is routinely repeated and integrated into the everyday spatiality of users, shifting their hermeneutic for place toward a game utility orientation by encouraging players to routinely encounter physical space "as-if" it was game terrain (Hjorth & Richardson, 2017, p. 5). Evidence for game-based explorability can be found in stories of adventures shared by players at UW. A focus group discussion among five UW students, including one of the authors of this paper (Heili), revealed how players act in ways that introduce the configuration of the world offered by the UI into the configuration of the world evident to pedestrian non-players on campus and, in that way, participate in the functioning of *Pokémon Go* as a relay in placemaking.

Several players suggested that the university campus was so favorable that it stood out in their experience as *the* place to play. One focus group participant went so far as to say that "it's not even worth it to play other places." This statement reveals how the game elicits a change in perception so that players come to see familiar spaces through the lens of game utility, and how physical places come to be evaluated through game logic. *Pokémon Go* allows and encourages players to create new ideas about what constitutes a meaningful place and what, in a given place, is of value for daily routines. A majority of the players who sat for the focus group discussion noted that they had used the proximity of game elements (Poké Stops in particular) to select the buildings in which they would routinely study. Clearly, the introduction of cyberspace into physical space has come to influence the behavior of player-cyborgs in ways that relate to but also exceed their performance in the game. Singularities emerge from actions in such a way as to ensure that player-cyborgs realize value in both game utility and non-game value.

The functioning of *Pokémon Go* as a relay, so that the game elicits behavior that synthesizes game logic and real-world logic, is not limited to phenomena at such a relatively small scale. At a larger scale, for example, players mobilize the logic of Pokémon types and environments in the physical world in an attempt to account for the appearance of certain types of Pokémon sprites over others (for example, the presence of a Water-type Pokémon near ponds and rivers). One of the focus group participants, having come to UW from outside the state, observed differences between her experience of gameplay in Laramie and at home that "in the Midwest there's a lot of Grass Pokémon [while] here in Wyoming you find a lot more Rock Pokémon and Fire Pokémon," and she attributed the differences to differences in natural environment. The significance of this statement is not necessarily that the player correctly identified a biome pattern that amateur empirical studies confirm (Silph Road, 2017), but that the player applied the logic of Pokémon types and environments to understand their physical surroundings in relation to the spatial distribution of Pokémon types. This move suggests that the player-cyborg sees little real distinction between the physical and the digital and assumes that the digital world makes sense in terms of the physical world and vice versa.

Interactions between digital and physical processes of spatialization through *Pokémon Go* result in the synthesis of discrete digital and physical agencies into a relational, distributed, cyborg agency to shape and be shaped by the emergence of singular places and corresponding senses of place. This new agency is not neutral, however, and it facilitates certain effects. In the context of *Pokémon Go*, a ubiquitous effect of cyborg agency is its representation of physical space as readily explorable and navigable. Even when one is not looking for Pokémon explicitly, the game interface serves as a basic wayfinding application that highlights local points of interest to the player-cyborg. Two of the focus group participants shared that *Pokémon Go* adventures beyond campus had led them to discover a "weird statue on the other side of the mini-mall because it was a Poké Stop." *Pokémon Go*, then, appears distinctly able to channel players' attention toward discoveries and place relationships that may not have otherwise been realized. In another story, one of the authors (Heili) and his sisters used *Pokémon Go* and a limited understanding of local street names to explore the neighborhoods and shoreline of an unfamiliar Wisconsin town, successfully navigating hours away from home and returning unassisted. He even offered directions to a lost driver based only on what he had learned from his time playing the game. By reducing the world into simple, legible maps, *Pokémon Go* turns even relatively unknown areas of physical space into explorable landscapes that are more accessible to the player-cyborg than to those traveling without any assistance from the UI. The creation of this explorable space is the basis for creating meaningful place-based relationships.

How does this production of explorable space matter for the everyday life of players as cyborgs? The focus group with UW students again revealed how singularities are integrated into practices of everyday life. The earlier example of the "weird statue by the mini-mall" is particularly revealing of how *Pokémon Go* facilitates the reconfiguration of players' perception and thereby creates opportunities for players to interact with previously unknown sites in the cultural landscape of the university. Digital information is materialized in the players' interactions with a site in the physical world and transforms how the physical and digital are experienced at a given location. This contextually specific meaning-making flies in the face of Shannon and Weaver's (1998) aforementioned de-contextualization of information communication for engineering solutions. Indeed, *Pokémon Go*'s work to enhance the explorability of the physical world challenges our thinking in cybernetics, and re-contextualizes the previously de-contextualized digital information in physical space so as to facilitate the emergence of a collectively held sense of place.

This is not to say that unfamiliar locales are the only places subject to this dynamic. As revealed earlier, players tend to spend most of their time playing the game in the regularly traversed spaces of their everyday lives. For example, the third focus group participant shared that she sometimes opens *Pokémon Go* on her phone just to "see what's around" as she walks her daily route. In this context, the perception of explorability constructs singularities alongside other existing understandings of a given place. The same student further commented, "I love how Rex is a gym," referring to a statue of a T. Rex outside of the geological museum (see Figure 12.2).

This statue, the existence of which predates the arrival of *Pokémon Go* by many years, is a prominent site in student life recognized by university

Figure 12.2. A cell phone image by William Heili of the T. Rex statue (January 9, 2018).

administration, alumni, and campus visitors. Superstition holds that if a student can throw a pinecone into the statue's open mouth, they will succeed on their final exams that semester. Accordingly, the ground near the statue is littered with pinecones, and the full mouth of the T. Rex showcases the dedication of generations of students. At this location, already embedded within UW's network of meaningful places, *Pokémon Go* adds another meaning through a new agency, making the site notable and attractive to a population at UW who may otherwise never have discovered the statue or valued its lore. For players who have already learned to perceive Rex as a meaningful site on campus, rediscovering the site through the UI grants the satisfaction of seeing a familiar place re-invented and made accessible in a new way. With the arrival of *Pokémon Go*, a flow of digital information was introduced into the existing spatiality of campus life, which allowed the place to be re-articulated as an information-material singularity. *Pokémon Go* has elicited gameplay that renovates constellations of meaning around sites in the cultural landscape, and has created new places on campus for the player-cyborg to experience.

Our analysis reveals a theme of explorability that is integrated into the spatiality of everyday life through routine engagement with *Pokémon Go*. It also suggests that gameplay elicits a shift in players' sense of place, integrating an awareness of game utility with existing understandings such that new networks of meaning coalesce and, in effect, create the emergence of new places at the "meeting up" of two processes of spatialization (see Massey, 1994, p. 154). The player-as-cyborg simultaneously enacts singularities and is shaped by them; one enacts the singularity by applying the logic and pattern of cyberspace to the physical world, thus materializing it, and is at the same time shaped by the singularity because gameplay re-invents one's relationships to previously known and heretofore unknown locations. *Pokémon Go* allows for information communication that ultimately imposes semiotic coordinates on the physical world and facilitates the extension of a new horizon for players in which the known is supplemented and the unknown is playfully made available. The cyborg's ability to act in the physical world is thus facilitated by the articulation of singularities. Whether or not these singularities are perceived to exist across local or at larger scales, the actualization of digital information in a physical context requires the construction of new relationships between cyborgs and places of gameplay.

Conclusion

The cybernetic framework allows us to understand interactions between the *Pokémon Go* platform and game players, and between physical space and cyberspace, as modes of purposeful communication and control that shape processes of placemaking. If, as Poole (2000) suggested at the turn of the century, "the inner life of video games … is bound up with the inner life of the player" (p. 11), contemporary location-based mobile gameplay realizes a more radical vision of intimate "couplings between organism and machine" (Haraway, 1991/1999, p. 272), or cyborgs.

The concept of the cyborg overcomes the inadequacy of a traditional representational framework for understanding the relationship between cyberspace and the physical world. Writing near the turn of the millennium, Hayles (1999) noted that, in virtual reality systems, "the user learns, kinesthetically and proprioceptively, that the relevant boundaries for interaction are defined less by the skin than by the feedback loops connecting body and simulation in a technobio-integrated circuit" (p. 27). *Pokémon Go's* augmented reality may be seen as a more sophisticated version of such a system. The result of this sophistication and its location-responsive component is that the boundaries of the virtual are made to be (selectively) synonymous with the boundaries of the real, rendering physical presence and digital information even more intertwined than previously conceived. In fact, the necessity of embodiment that *Pokémon Go* creates is well aligned with the epistemology Hayles (1999) sought to realize; insisting that presence/embodiment (and thus spatiality) cannot be ignored in the information era, she called for a new epistemology of the human that "opens up the possibilities of seeing pattern and presence as complementary rather than antagonistic" (p. 49). By allowing for such a creative tension to exist, the cyborg becomes a useful concept for analysis and sheds light on how both physical and digital processes of spatialization can be synthesized in a way that transforms space around us.

Cybernetics requires us to rethink the ways in which place may be constituted, paying attention to the hybridity of places at the convergence of the bits and atoms that constitute our modern world. If, as relational thinking and the concept of the cyborg might suggest, we are "inhabitants of globally interconnected networks … joined in a dynamic co-evolutionary spiral with intelligent machines" (Hayles, 2006, p. 164), then changes in digital technologies will undoubtedly shape how individuals interact with the spaces of their everyday lives and routines. *Pokémon Go* presents a unique opportunity to explore how the digital and the physical worlds have been co-constructed, with the access codes necessary to be placed digitally now intimately tied to one's physical location. This marks an evolution of a cybernetic epistemology because it makes place a part of the pattern used to distinguish between those who do and do not have the right to act in a space (Hayles, 1999, p. 40). The entanglement of presence and informational access through the cyborg user of *Pokémon Go* therefore forces the existence of a new space accessible to the cyborg alone that, like the cyborg, is simultaneously emergent from the bi-directional exchanges of existing digital and physical processes of spatialization. In our analysis, the singularity is the place in which the cyborg acts as well as what it enacts; the cyborg and the singularity are engaged in a co-evolutionary dance in which both physical space and cyberspace shape one another in new ways, driven by new technologies that alter human perception. The result of this cybernetic interaction is that *Pokémon Go* is uniquely able to mobilize the social energy of many actors toward the creation and maintenance of places that are meaningful to players in both physical and digital ways.

REFERENCES

Álvarez, R., & Duarte, F. (2018). Spatial design and placemaking: Learning from video games. *Space and Culture, 21*(3), 208–232. doi: 10.1177/1206331217736746.

Anderson, B. (2018). Cultural geography II: The force of representations. *Progress in Human Geography.* Advance online publication. doi: 10.1177/0309132518761431.

Barad, K. (2003). Posthumanist performativity: Toward an understanding of how matter comes to matter. *Signs: Journal of Women in Culture and Society, 28*(3), 801–831.

Deleuze, G., & Guattari, F. (1987). *A thousand plateaus: Capitalism and schizophrenia* (B. Masumi, Trans.). Minneapolis: University of Minnesota Press.

Eanes, R.S., & van den Broek, C.Y. (2019). Playing alone, together: *Pokémon Go,* public mobility, and locational privacy. In J. Henthorn, A. Kulak, K. Purzycki & S. Vie (Eds.), in this volume.

Graham, M. (2013). Geography/Internet: Ethereal alternate dimensions of cyberspace or grounded augmented realities? *The Geographical Journal, 179*(2), 177–182.

Gregory, D. (2013). Tahrir: Politics, publics and performances of space. *Middle East Critique, 22*(3), 235–246.

Haraway, D. (1991/1999). A cyborg manifesto. In S. During (Ed.), *The cultural studies reader* (2nd ed.) (pp. 271–291). New York: Routledge.

Hawking, S.W., & Penrose, R. (1970). The singularities of gravitational collapse and cosmology. In *Proceedings of the Royal Society A,* Great Britain, 529–548. Retrieved from http://rspa.royalsocietypublishing.org/content/royprsa/314/1519/529.full.pdf.

Hayles, N.K. (1999). *How we became posthuman: Virtual bodies in cybernetics, literature, and informatics.* Chicago: University of Chicago Press.

Hayles, N.K. (2006). Unfinished work: From cyborg to cognisphere. *Theory, Culture & Society 23*(7–8), 159–166.

Hjorth, L., & Richardson, I. (2017). *Pokémon GO*: Mobile media play, place-making, and the digital wayfarer. *Mobile Media & Communication, 5*(1), 3–14.

Kennon, T. (2017, February 28). 5 new brain disorders that were born out of the digital age. *The Week.* Retrieved from http://theweek.com/articles/677922/5-new-brain-disorders-that-born-digital-age.

Kitchin, R., & Dodge, M. (2011). *Code/Space: Software and everyday life.* Cambridge, MA: MIT Press.

Kurzweil, R. (2014). The singularity is near. In R.L. Sandler (Ed.), *Ethics and emerging technologies* (pp. 393–406). London, England: Palgrave Macmillan.

Massey, D. (1994). *Space, place, and gender.* Minneapolis: University of Minnesota Press.

Massey, D. (2006). Landscape as a provocation: Reflections on moving mountains. *Journal of Material Culture, 11*(1/2), 33–48.

Mitchell, W.J. (2004). *Me++: The cyborg self and the networked city.* Cambridge, MA: MIT Press.

Poole, S. (2000). *Trigger happy: Videogames and the entertainment revolution.* New York, NY: Arcade.

Rosen, L.D. (2012). *iDisorder: Understanding our obsession with technology and overcoming its hold on us.* New York, NY: Palgrave Macmillan.

Shannon, C.E. (1959). Coding theorems for a discrete source with a fidelity criterion. *Queen's University at Kingston Department of Mathematics and Statistics.* Retrieved from https://mast.queensu.ca/~math474/shannon59.pdf.

Shannon, C.E., & Weaver, W. (1998). *The mathematical theory of communication.* Champaign: University of Illinois Press.

Shields, R. (2013). *Spatial questions: Cultural topologies and social spatialisations.* Thousand Oaks, CA: Sage Publications.

The Silph Road. (2017). A very detailed report on how spawns work in *Pokémon Go.* Digg.com. Retrieved from http://digg.com/video/how-spawns-work-in-pokemon-go.

Tække, J. (2002). Cyberspace as a space parallel to geographical space. In L. Qvortrup, J.F. Jensen, E. Kjems, N. Lehmann & C. Madsen (Eds.), *Virtual space: Spatiality in virtual inhabited 3D worlds* (pp. 25–46). London, England: Springer.

Tham, J., & Smiles, D. (2019). Rhetorical augmentation: Public play, place, and persuasion in *Pokémon Go.* In J. Henthorn, A. Kulak, K. Purzycki & S. Vie (Eds.), in this volume.

Thrift, N. (2006). Donna Haraway's dreams. *Theory, Culture & Society, 23*(7–8), 189–195.

Wieczner, J. (2016, June 10). Fitbit users are finding creative ways to cheat. *Fortune.* Retrieved from http://fortune.com/2016/06/10/fitbit-hack-cheat/.

Wiener, N. (1950). *The human use of human beings.* London, England: Houghton Mifflin.

Zhao, B., & Sui, D.Z. (2017). True lies in geospatial big data: Detecting location spoofing in social media. *Annals of GIS, 23*(1), 1–14.

About the Contributors

Luiz Adolfo **Andrade** is a game designer and researcher working on locative gaming. He holds a PhD in contemporary communication and culture (cyberculture) from the Federal University of Bahia, Brazil, and is an adjunct professor at the State University of Bahia (UNEB) in Brazil. Between 2017 and 2018, he worked as a postdoctoral visiting scholar (postdoctoral researcher) at the Center for Computer Games Research, IT—University of Copenhagen (2017–2018), supported by a CAPES Postdoctoral Stage Scholarship.

Ginger **Burgoon** graduated with a BA in linguistics from the University of Oklahoma in Norman. Her senior thesis studied how classic Americana was translated and adapted for Russian-language audiences. She has worked as a freelance copy editor and is an avid gamer.

Kristen L. **Cole** is an assistant professor in communication studies at Indiana University–Purdue University Columbus (IUPUC) in Columbus, where she teaches courses in rhetoric, political communication, and health communication. She received her PhD from the University of New Mexico in 2013 and her MA from Colorado State University in 2009. Her research investigates representations of identity, agency, and pathology, particularly as they intersect with discourses of gender, race, sexuality, and disability.

Nicholas Jon **Crane** (PhD, Ohio State, 2014) is an assistant professor of geography at the University of Wyoming, where he teaches courses in human geography. His ongoing projects examine social movements and political organizing in Mexico and the United States. He is also the section editor for political geography in *Geography Compass*.

Ryan S. **Eanes**, PhD, PRC, is an assistant professor of business management at Washington College in Chestertown, Maryland, where he teaches courses in digital marketing, consumer behavior, and advertising. His research focuses on consumer knowledge and awareness, information diffusion, and "opinion marketing," particularly as these pertain to food, drink, bars, restaurants, and hotels. His work has appeared in *Digest*, *Gastronomica*, and *Mobile Media & Communication* as well as in several edited volumes.

William **Heili** is a senior at the University of Wyoming, where he is pursuing a bachelor's degree in secondary education with a concentration in geography. He was inducted into the geography honor society Gamma Theta Upsilon in spring 2017. This is his first published work.

Jamie **Henthorn** is an assistant professor of English and director of the writing center at Catawba College. She teaches courses in composition, visual rhetoric, writing for the web, and professional writing. Her research analyzes everyday uses of technology, particularly when playing video games. She regularly conferences at Computers & Writing, the Southwest Popular/American Culture Association (SWPACA), and the Conference on College Composition and Communication (CCCC).

Andrew **Kulak** is a doctoral candidate in the Department of English at Virginia Tech, where he studies digital rhetoric and human-centered design. His research interests include video game criticism, Internet culture, online learning environments, and the design of sociotechnical systems. He is working on a dissertation exploring the dichotomy between digital and physical objects and the rhetorical negotiation of digital and physical hybridity in social, legal, and pedagogical contexts.

Cody **Mejeur** is a PhD candidate in English at Michigan State University, specializing in new media, narrative theory, queer studies, cognitive humanities, and digital humanities. He has published on games pedagogy, representations of gender and queerness in games, and narrative in popular culture. He works with the LGBTQ Video Game Archive on preserving LGBTQ representation in video games. He is a graduate lab lead in MSU's Digital Humanities and Literary Cognition Lab and adjunct faculty at Ivy Tech Community College.

Jill Anne **Morris** is an associate professor of English and foreign languages at Frostburg State University in Frostburg, Maryland, where she studies historical rhetoric and communication in American amusement parks. She is the author of *The Internet as a Game* and is an editorial board member of the journal *Kairos: Rhetoric, Technology, and Pedagogy*.

Eric **Murnane** is an assistant professor of digital media at the University of Central Florida, where he obtained a PhD in text, and technology. He studies games at the intersection of player and system and has presented at several national and international conferences, including the Foundation for Digital Games, Computers and Writing, the Popular Culture Association, and the Society for Cinema and Media Studies, among others.

Alexis **Pulos** is an assistant professor at Northern Kentucky University, where he teaches courses in game design, communication theory, and media studies. He received his MA from Colorado State University in 2009 and his PhD from the University of New Mexico in 2013. His research focuses on the ways agency and meaning are structured and produced through the design and social regulation of games and systems.

Kristopher **Purzycki** is a doctoral student at the University of Wisconsin–Milwaukee, focusing on digital media studies. His research interests include broadcasting and publication, open access in the digital humanities, and media philosophy. He is at work on his dissertation which considers the player's sense of place within computer game play as a phenomenon that simulates sacred experience.

Peter **Schaefer** is an associate professor of communication and media arts at Marymount Manhattan College. His research focuses on critical and historiographic approaches to understanding media. He has published in journals such as *Critical Studies in Media Communication*, *New Media & Society*, and *Amodern*, as well as in several anthologies.

Margaret **Schwartz** is an associate professor of communication and media studies at Fordham University. She is a feminist materialist media theorist with a particular interest in the role of embodiment in communicative praxis. She is the author of *Dead Matter* (2015) and is at work on a project that concerns feminist ontology in the digital age.

Wendi **Sierra** is an assistant professor at St. John Fisher College in Rochester, New York, where she teaches classes on game design, history, and analysis. Her work has appeared in *Kairos* and *Syllabus Journal*, and she is working on a book about the design of evocative narratives in gaming environments.

Deondre **Smiles** is a PhD student in the department of geography at Ohio State University. His primary research interests lie at the intersection of indigenous, political, and critical geographies, especially surrounding indigenous ontologies of death. His secondary research interest lies in cultural geographies and its intersections with rhetoric. He has been published in *Geoforum* and is active in other research and publishing endeavors.

Jason Chew Kit **Tham** is a PhD candidate and emerging technologies researcher in the Department of Writing Studies at the University of Minnesota, Twin Cities. He has a broad interest in the sociotechnological aspects of technical and professional communication and the pedagogy of critical, rhetorical, and ethical communication. Some of his projects can be found in *Technical Communication*, *Computers and Composition*, *Journal of Technical Writing and Communication*, and *IEEE Transactions on Professional Communication*.

Claire Y. **van den Broek**, PhD, is an adjunct professor of literature at Southern New Hampshire University in Manchester, where she teaches courses in literary theory, American literature, and world literature. Her research focuses on the nineteenth century in Europe, trauma studies, and the history of psychiatry. She has previously coauthored a translation of East-German author Franz Fühmann's book *Science Fiktion* and her work has appeared in *Monatshefte*, *Absinthe*, and *No Man's Land*.

Stephanie **Vie** is a professor and the chair of the Department of Writing and Rhetoric at the University of Central Florida in Orlando. She is a coeditor of the collection *Social Writing/Social Media* and has been interviewed by national and international media outlets regarding social media, privacy, and the use of hashtags for digital activist efforts. Her work has been published in numerous edited collections and journals, including *Computers and Composition*, *Kairos*, and *First Monday*.

Chen **Xu** (PhD, Texas A&M University, 2010) is an assistant professor of geography at the University of Wyoming. His research interests include geocomputation, geospatial big data, and volunteered geographic information technology and science. His studies focus on using cybernetics for examining geographic relationships between people and spatialized information technologies.

Index